THE COLUMBUS CENTRE SERIES

LICENSED MASS MURDER

THE COLUMBUS CENTRE SERIES

STUDIES IN THE DYNAMICS OF PERSECUTION AND EXTERMINATION

General Editor: Norman Cohn

ANTHONY STORR
Human Destructiveness

HENRY V. DICKS
Licensed Mass Murder

DONALD KENRICK & GRATTAN PUXON
The Destiny of Europe's Gypsies

Forthcoming

LEON POLIAKOV
The Aryan Myth

Licensed Mass Murder

A Socio-psychological study
of some SS killers

by

HENRY V. DICKS

BASIC BOOKS, INC., *Publishers*

NEW YORK

© 1972 by Henry V. Dicks
Library of Congress Catalog Card Number: 72-76924
SBN: 465-03934-0
Printed in the United States of America
72 73 74 75 10 9 8 7 6 5 4 3 2 1

Contents

PART ONE

PART TWO

CONTENTS

EDITORIAL FOREWORD

Following a proposal originally advanced by the Hon. David Astor, a research centre was set up in the University of Sussex in 1966 to investigate how persecutions and exterminations come about; how the impulse to persecute or exterminate is generated, how it spreads, and under what conditions it is likely to express itself in action. The Centre was originally called the Centre for Research in Collective Psychopathology, but later adopted the more neutral name of the Columbus Centre, after the Trust which finances it.

The Centre's work has now resulted in a series of books and monographs on subjects ranging from the roots of European nationalism and racism to the fate of the Gypsies as a minority, from the causes of the persecution of "witches" to the causes of the exterminations carried out under the Third Reich, and from the biological to the psychological roots of the very urge to persecute or to exterminate.

From the beginning, the Centre's work was designed on a multidisciplinary basis. The disciplines represented in the present series include history, sociology, anthropology, dynamic psychology and ethology. Moreover, while the research was being done and the books written, the various authors constantly exchanged ideas and information with one another. As a result, while each book in the series belongs to a single discipline and is the work of a single author, who alone carries responsibility for it, the series as a whole is coloured by the experience of inter-disciplinary discussion and debate.

The enterprise was also designed on an international scale. Although this has been a British project in the sense that it was sponsored by a British university and that 95 per cent of its finance was also British, the people who did the research and wrote the books came from several different countries. Indeed, one of them was a Frenchman who worked in Paris throughout, another a German who worked in Berlin. Everything possible was done to exclude national bias from a study which might all too easily have been distorted by it.

The work was financed throughout by the Columbus Trust. It was originally made possible by massive donations to the Trust from the Hon. David Astor, the late Lord Sieff of Brimpton and Sir Marcus Sieff, and the Wolfson Foundation, promptly followed by further most generous contributions from Mr Raymond Burton, the Rt Hon. Harold Lever, Mr I. J. Lyons, Mr Hyam Morrison, Mr Jack Morrison, Sir Harold

EDITORIAL FOREWORD

Samuel, the American Jewish Committee, the J. M. Kaplan Fund, Inc., and the William Waldorf Astor Foundation. His Grace the Archbishop of Canterbury, Sir Leon Bagrit, Lord Evans of Hungershall, and Messrs Myers & Company, also showed their goodwill to the enterprise by giving it financial assistance.

Since the Centre came into existence many people have devoted a great deal of time and energy to one or other of the various financial and advisory committees associated with it. They include the chairman of the Columbus Trust, the Rt. Hon. the Lord Butler of Saffron Walden; two successive Vice-Chancellors of the University of Sussex, Lord Fulton of Falmer and Professor Asa Briggs; the Hon. David Astor, Professor Max Beloff, Professor Sir Robert Birley, Professor Patrick Corbett, Professor Meyer Fortes, Dr Robert Gosling, Mr Ronald Grierson, Professor Marie Jahoda, Dr Martin James, Professor James Joll, the Rt Hon. Harold Lever, Professor Barry Supple, Dr John D. Sutherland, Professor Eric Trist, Professor A. T. M. Wilson, Mr Leonard Wolfson, and the Registrar and Secretary of the University, Mr A. E. Shields, who has acted as the secretary of the Centre's Management Committee. It is a pleasure to acknowledge the support and counsel they have so willingly given.

The series also owes a great deal to the devoted service of the late Miss Ursula Boehm, who was the administrative secretary to the Centre from its inception until her death in 1970.

NORMAN COHN

AUTHOR'S PREFACE

As Professor Norman Cohn's Preface has indicated, the study on which this volume is based was made possible by the invitation which the Columbus Centre extended to me to join its first research team on a part-time basis. I wish here to record my thanks for such an opportunity to collaborate with excellent colleagues on a project of great moment.

My inability to devote my full time to this work owing to other commitments has limited its originally conceived scope. There were also hopes that I would be able to make the group of persons to be studied a larger and better balanced sample of the Nazi extermination teams. On my list of 32 names were not only those of the lower echelons who did much of the actual killing. There were also two SS generals—one from Himmler's head office and another who was formerly a senior police chief in occupied countries. There were to be more law-yers and administrative or bureaucratic personnel of senior rank. How-ever, their availability depended on who among them would give his consent to be interviewed. "The luck of the draw" has resulted in a preponderance—among a very tiny total number of volunteers prepared to see me at all—of NCO "manual" killer types. The resulting book is thus slanted towards this low echelon and does not present enough of a picture of the psychology, motivations and attitudes of the higher, "armchair" murderers. I did not regard it as feasible or adequate by way of complementing this picture to include second-hand biographical analyses. Some brief references to several such biographies were re-quired as background to the men I actually interviewed but these are not intended to be read as equivalents to the case studies. The book, as a result, has turned out somewhat differently from the original blue-print. I think it was remarkable that I was able to see any of these condemned men at all as a foreigner from a former "enemy" country. I attribute this good fortune to the very kind intervention on behalf of the Centre of H. E. the German Ambassador in London, Herr Herbert Blankenhorn, and to two gentlemen of his staff who were most interestedly and courteously helpful: Herr Ziefer in 1967 and Herr Dr J. Wilmanns in 1969. My gratitude also extends to the unknown gentlemen at the relevant Ministries of Justice, at Federal and at Länder levels, who sponsored my entry into a number of high security prisons by very accurate and informed communications in advance. Warm personal thanks are an inadequate discharge of my feelings at the friendly

xi

and extremely helpful reception by the Heads of the several institutions. Every facility and comfort was offered—in some instances the Director's own study—for these interviews. The following are the gentlemen whom I wish to thank again: Herr Regierungsdirektor Ihle, of Werl, and his aide, Herr Inspektor Aust; Herr Regierungsdirektor Ballensiefer, Herr Assessor Berg and Pastor Knipper, of Rheinbach; Herr Oberregierungsrat Dr Meyer-Velde and Herr Kruppa, of Ziegenhain; Herr Regierungsdirektor Schroeder, of Straubing, in whose absence Herren Giegerich and Kronzucker very kindly received me; and lastly, Herr Oberregierungsrat Frenz, of Tegel, Berlin.

For my work in preparation for these visits I used the excellent material of personality files and microfilms at the Wiener Library, London, whose staff went to great trouble to search out what I required. I wish to express my very sincere thanks to them all, but perhaps most particularly to Mrs Johnson.

I owe much to all my colleagues of the Columbus Centre, for their helpful criticism during many team meetings. I must, however, single out our project director, Professor Norman Cohn, for his encouraging kindness as well as painstaking editorial scrutiny of this MS, which as the result is less obscure and more readable. On the plane of historical accuracy Dr Wolfgang Scheffler has been a tower of strength and my stern mentor, greatly adding to my grasp of Nazi and SS affairs, and in M Léon Poliakov's expertise in our field I could always find clarification and support.

I should like here also to pay a grateful tribute to our Centre's first secretary, Miss Ursula Boehm whose untimely death we all felt as a personal grievous loss of a valued friend and collaborator. To Mrs Mollie Tupholme who has had the onerous task of typing and preparing the manuscript I owe sincere thanks for making order out of chaos. During the greater part of the interviewing I had the utmost support and secretarial assistance from my wife who recorded all the raw material, and also made our sombre tour of German prisons humanly bearable.

Finally, it is my pleasant duty to record here my gratitude to the authors concerned for kindly allowing me to cite portions of their published work for my purposes, as acknowledged in references at the relevant points of the text.

Included here are: Dr Martin Wangh of New York; Prof. Nathan Leites, Chicago University; Mr D. A. Black of Broadmoor Hospital

AUTHOR'S PREFACE

and Mr R. Blackburn, now of Rampton Hospital; Dr Arthur Hyatt Williams of H. M. Prison Wormwood Scrubbs. A special sense of obligation is gladly acknowledged to Prof. Stanley Milgram of the City University of New York, for his personal permission to quote from a paper he himself plans to incorporate in a forthcoming book.

I also wish to thank Dr Joseph Sandler, Editor of the *International Journal of Psychoanalysis*, for his permission to quote Wangh and Hyatt Williams as well as an old paper by W. Bromberg; the Editors of the *British Journal of Criminology* for allowing me to cite Blackburn; and Messrs. Weidenfeld & Nicolson for permission to quote from *The Commandant of Auschwitz* by R. Hoess.

London, N.W.1.   November 1971

PART ONE

CHAPTER ONE

THE CONCEPTUAL APPROACH

The study of mass destructiveness is the task which the Columbus Trust entrusted to a multi-disciplinary group. Our team of historians, social and political scientists, psychiatrists and ethologists worked on the basic assumption that collective behaviour cannot be fully understood except by reference to its social matrix in space and time; but that the great currents of group and mass action remain enigmatic if we exclude from their study the influence of the strivings and roles of individual actors—leaders and led. Our inspiration came in no small measure from a solemn gathering in memory of the victims of Nazi atrocities. It was thus to be expected that the "German case" was chosen by us as a paradigm of a planned, highly organized mass-murder operation. In this case the psychological factor was so blatant that it could not be ignored even by those who prefer to see history as determined by impersonal forces, ignoring the insights that modern psychological science can contribute. Hence my role became that of examining the evidence for and against the "popular", lay view that the Nazi movement, especially as expressed in their mass extermination of helpless, unarmed citizens of their own and other countries, was a "collective madness" led by insane individuals and carried out by fiends as inhuman as Nazi propaganda pictured its own enemies. While my fellow psychiatrist on the team, Anthony Storr, has marshalled the general concepts used to explain human aggressivity,[1] I have tried to apply relevant parts of this socio-psychiatric theory to the face-to-face study of the personalities and life stories of a small sample of men who actually, manually or executively, perpetrated these organized, official persecutions, tortures and murders.

Though aware that such personal studies, 25 years after the events, had limitations, the team decided that we needed to get a first-hand professional "feel" of at least some of these "fiends" who had in their time and place so willingly—even eagerly—planned and carried out some of the vilest acts of human history. Our own armchair ideas about Hitler's hangmen would be tested by actual psychiatric data, and answers suggested to such urgent questions as (a) "Were they insane?" (b) How do human beings descend to the degradation of serving in murder squads, manning concentration camps, and so on? (c) What individual and group pressures and sanctions made such actions seem both possible and even laudable to them? (d) What happened to these attitudes when the collapse of Hitler's power removed the official sanctions and pressures, and how did these men view their past murderous activities 25 years later? (e) Could indirect light be shed on the mentality of their companions, not interviewed by us, and of their higher leadership, not a topic of this book, but relevant to our project as a whole?

It may justifiably be asked why we chose the Germans, when there was and is mass torture and extermination going on in other parts of the globe that could be studied, as it were, *in flagrante*? The answer is that the Nazi period is very fully documented from many sources. Legal process of the German Federal Republic has placed the records of each of the men I interviewed (as of countless others) on as reliable a foundation of attested facts as possible. Its governmental authorities, moreover, most helpfully gave us access to these records and to the men who were serving sentences in German prisons for the crimes we were studying. I have elsewhere acknowledged our great indebtedness for this exceptional courtesy and co-operation towards a foreign investigator. Early in our planning we had considered the desirability of a "flying team" of qualified observers ready to go out to a massacre—but who would let them near the scene, and who would pay the bill? Moreover, one of the aims of the Columbus Centre was to alert responsible opinion to the potentialities for murderous destructiveness in members of so-called "advanced" societies close to our own ethnically and historically. The Nazi murders by their scale, no less than by their cold-blooded and technological "efficiency", had aroused the fears and consciences of millions and left their imprint on current social climates and tensions, precisely because Germans are our cousins. If, what I have found out about these SS men turns out to have wider validity, then the German paradigm will perhaps throw light also on the SS's accursed confrères of other times and climes: the inquisitors of the Holy Office; the Tsar's Ochrana and its descendants the OGPU and MVD; the Turkish units who massacred Armenians—and many others.

Before I can hope to make the interview findings contained in Part II of this volume intelligible beyond a circle of specialists, I must briefly outline the psychological and historical framework I use. Though it overlaps with the already cited monograph by Storr I cannot assume my readers' familiarity with it. Nor does Storr quite cover the specific fields from which I draw the working hypotheses on which my interview schedules were constructed. These have necessarily to include a modicum of general and developmental psychology (very close to Storr's), and also a good deal of special background relating to my previous "clinical" work in studying German (Nazi period) military morale, regularities of personality traits; ideology; culture patterns; values and consequential authority structure.[2] The content and aims of my present interviews, the "variables" I sought, require a change of focus from the generally accepted elements of modern dynamic psychology and psychiatry on to what seems especially "German", thence to what, within the German, is National Socialist, and within the latter to the distinct elements of its most radical and extreme manifestation— the SS. The first part of this book, then, contains these necessary introductory matters which also form some conceptual links between medico-biological approaches and sociological and historical studies in a complex inter-disciplinary no-man's land.

I. THE SOURCES OF SOCIAL ADAPTATION

The usual explanations advanced for the Nazi atrocities include: insanity, personal or collective; psychopathy; sex perversion; fanaticism; xenophobia, especially that focused on Jews. These all require psychiatric expertise to assess, even though inexpert observers frequently bandy these terms about freely, while objecting to psychoanalytic excursions into historians' or political scientists' terrain. Let us then no longer falsely separate the intrapersonal and the group aspects if we aim to construct realistic models of social behaviour and process. Psychoanalytic and psychiatric contribution to history begins with the proposition that the child is father to the man. The potential for making positive, responsible social relations is developed or stunted in the earliest relationships of children to the figures in their primary world (clumsily called "objects" after Freud). It is a cornerstone of modern psychiatry that, in contrast to lower animals, human infants' slow maturation as biological organisms imposes a disproportionate weight on adult care as essential for their survival. While ethology has shown us that animals, too, "learn" to adapt to environmental threats and to living in herds, the human infant's expression of its elemental inborn needs is to a much greater extent modified by the constant impact of its human environment which alone can satisfy the hunger and thirst and the need for contact and warmth of a helpless, almost totally dependent being.

Freud's original discoveries in the consulting-room were largely focused on the inner, unconscious workings of the individual's need systems (which were then still called instincts) during successive phases of neural and mental maturation. They also opened up the field of study of the effects of nurtural, parental and other external influences on the course of this development. We could now see the human personality as the product of a conflict or parallelogram of forces: the inborn drives towards satisfying its needs for love, attachment, mastery of opposition, procreation or security meeting the weight of the given parents' or educators' prescriptions and norms for shaping the expression or inhibition of these needs in the "right" way. A full assessment of an individual, be he ill or well, can never ignore the multiple determinants of personality, but must ask what are: (i) the genetically given endowments and drives; (ii) the internalized socially derived components, in his thinking, feeling and action; and (iii) what syntheses, compromise or failure to weld them into a functioning whole has he been able to achieve in order to deal with present reality?

Personality becomes socially defined as the characteristic way in which an individual relates to others, meets his own needs, deals with frustration and stress and perceives himself. It is the psychiatrist's business to be able to assess, indeed (techniques permitting) to measure the capacities and degrees of success or failure in personalities in given life situations and to ascertain the interplay of forces that accounts for the variances. Before the coming of psychoanalysis, psychiatry was limited to a descriptive level in which the labelling of a patient's condition in terms of the recognized types of "disorders" exhausted the possibilities. Psychoanalysis has helped us to identify the said "interplay of forces" in people, to "decipher" and make meaningful the hitherto incomprehensible, bizarre verbal and behavioural phenomena that have constituted "madness", hysteria, obsessions, sexual perversions and the like. It is this second level of diagnosis or insight which links our encounter with our patients in the Here and Now with that profile of a "geological" record of the outcomes of the moulding pushes and pulls between outer forces and inner impulsions we call a life history. Every society tends to mould its new generation into dealing with its biological drives and needs in the ways that constitute its cultural "wisdom" and values. The biological maturational potential from within receives constant and highly sanctioned interference from outside. The educative or "socializing" process opposes the child's "I want" with the elders' "Not this way—*our* way", or outright "You shall *not*".

From the generalizations derived from recurring observations in many people of the same outcomes for personality of these histories in depth we can make hypotheses about human development and about breakdowns of the ability to cope with problems. These hypotheses can become the starting-points of empirical investigation. In clinical practice the psychiatrist of this way of thinking will be chiefly concerned with the individual patient's unique combination of personal and social factors. But it is permissible and fruitful for research to change the focus on what is recurrent and typical for a given human category, be they delinquents, backward children or schizophrenics— or indeed political voters or "consumers" in market research. For the purposes of this book my focus is (as it was in my war-time studies) on the effects of the interaction between certain German males of military age and their cultural environment. The description of the environment which had shaped the personalities of the men I interviewed will be taken up in the following chapters. Here I want to deal with the concepts which make intelligible the process by which a cultural influence—good or bad—becomes, so to speak, part of an individual.

The hypotheses which attempt to answer the question of how culture and personality reciprocally influence each other are crucial to our understanding of the essentially mysterious processes by which so much history is made and which are too often taken for granted. I refer to such basic phenomena as group cohesion, obedience, loyalty; and also to the dissolution of these into apathy, rebellion or treason towards the purposes of the same in-group and its leaders. Before presenting the concepts by which we try to explain "how the culture got inside the child"—and stayed there—it is relevant to refer briefly to some aspects of culture itself. Contrary to the trite saying that "human nature is always the same", anthropology has demonstrated how great a variety of human culture patterns (Ruth Benedict)[3] the different "mixes" of encouragement, prohibition, emphasis and taboo on this or that natural trend have produced. Not only invention of tools and implements but also of "*styles*" of behaviour—head-hunting, peaceful cultivation, etc.—were doubtless responses to climate, soil, predators and so on, in the struggle for survival woven together by shared traditions often centred on magical interpretations of the group's origins and relation to the "supernatural". It is this unity cemented by mythology and in-group tacit communication which resists innovation demanded by altered circumstances or reformers. This slowness to change in a given culture as a well-known biological fact contrasts with the obvious flexibility of human minds to be moulded into such a diversity of societies. Clinging to the familiar and fear of the unknown and new are characteristic of babies, primitives and peasants. It looks as if patterns imprinted early are deepest and hardest to undo. This "backwoodsman" phenomenon is not unknown in advanced societies, where it can stultify even the most rational reforms in the name of the older group coherence patterns which had at one time favoured survival. Norman Cohn[4] has pointed to this element of "culture lag" underlying the Nazi ideology. In this movement some ancient Teuton culture myths came to be lived out. Many thinkers have regarded the accelerated technological change of our era as having outrun Man's capacity for social adaptation and control. This throws him back to no longer adequate but deep cultural imprints for coping with his stresses. Modern men have these old patterns slumbering below the surface, left there by the nursery years and the cultural prescriptions bequeathed by those who in love and wrath and piety were concerned to reproduce their kind.

2. PHASES OF DEVELOPMENT

Educative endeavour and social living would come to nought if it were not for those mechanisms and processes by which the child can reliably assimilate the parental influences. We take this so much for granted that an uneducable child (by reason of genetic handicap or brain damage) arouses much anxiety. Our knowledge about the social learning and internalizing processes in children took a great stride forward with the work of Melanie Klein and W. R. D. Fairbairn. The palimpsest of Freud's sometimes inconsistent theories based on sex instinct has been replaced by a concept according to which the motive force for social and emotional growth is the infant's striving to attach itself to a being (the object) which would give it support. This "object-relations" theory, supported by common sense, clinical observation and rigorous research, fits ethological and biological facts better. This is the baby's active reaching out for a loving mother to ensure survival. Bowlby[5] has done much to place this knowledge on a firm research basis.

This earliest love-affair is the foundation of future capacities to develop warm, life-affirming attitudes and secure personal relations if the mother or her substitutes make the appropriate responses. Infants' tolerance of frustration of vital needs is at first extremely low and emotional reactions to the object are total—extreme contentment or extreme rage and despair. "Good" and "bad" are experienced as absolutes without distinction of what is inside and what is outside the body. Growth of personality proceeds over the next few years through a series of conflict solutions between experiences of goodness and of badness of the love object, increasingly recognized as outside. Learning to be human is learning to put up with ambivalence, to tolerate the feelings of love and rage evoked by the contradictoriness and unmanageability of another real person. From the favourable outcome of innumerable encounters first with the mother and later with other members of the primary group, the gratifying and reassuring aspects of the relationship are more firmly imprinted on the memory. The child grows a basic sense of security and confidence that its object-seeking will meet with good responses. We can increasingly observe the feed-back in such a fortunately socialized healthy child's outgoing behaviour. A young person's capacity to love and give out accordingly comes from having built up this inner reservoir of assimilated adult love. The latter provides the antidote to the violent feelings which continue to be aroused by frustration of the child's developing self-will seeking satisfaction of its own drives. It is the loving and adequate handling of the child's hate and terror, by parents with *biologically appropriate* responses to the needs of the moment, which reduces the sense of threat of disruption which rage evokes in babies. The child learns to modify its raw destructive hate feelings by internalizing the good feelings of the love object as a *model* for identification. Aggression becomes "socialized".

In practice the simple answer to all the world's ills, which is apparently good mothering, is complicated by other factors. First, there is the innate endowment. Children and ethnic stocks differ in the robustness and intensity of their emotional potentialities and also in the rate at which biological maturation occurs. Secondly, mothers are not the only influences to which the baby is exposed. Other people come into relationship with it who may be far from ideal. Thirdly, the mother (countless mothers of all levels of personality from saints to furies!) is not in practice able to give all that her maternal response urges. She, with the other people round the child, is herself culture-conditioned. Her task (unless she is a WASP avant-garde intellectual, when she would have other problems!) is to secure conformity of her "product" with the requirements of the group. As an example, highly relevant to our main concern, I mention the virtual taboo certain cultures place on the expression of tender, dependent feelings towards, and "spoiling" loving responses to these by, the mother, even at earliest ages. Thus a good mother may, for the sake of "properly" bringing up her son, deny him much of her felt tenderness and warmth. Similar severities are brought to bear on the expression of childrens' independence, aggression or on toilet training, in blithe unawareness of the impact on the child. Indeed the very *state* of being a dependent infant, a minor, is often a source of conflict: part idealized, part ridiculed and despised. To these hazards to favourable personality growth must be added the disruptive events within the child's primary group. Broken homes, death or other causes of absence of one or both parents, which increase the insecurity of the remaining educators, are some of these. War, revolution, famine and unemployment have left many societies, not least those of European stock, with damaged and disrupted families which have passed on their stresses and anxieties to their young.

Turning now to what are the observed or inferred reactions inside young children, we first note that the earliest responses are thought to be innate. We know that there is much greater sensory awareness even at a few months to the stimuli and influences from outside than the infant can show because of lack of muscular co-ordination and brain capacity to sort out any but the crudest sensations of "nice" and "nasty". In this totally confused "mad" state there seems to be but one response: the infant has willy-nilly to "suffer" what the five senses make it feel. This is the beginning of *internalization* or introjection. As the discriminatory powers develop, so the infant learns to perceive first *part-objects* (the breast for example) as located outside, and presently the whole object, usually mother, with whom the *relation* of love-hate-terror is thus set up.

I must now delineate more precisely the "series of conflict situations" in the growth of personality mentioned a moment ago, following the Klein-Fairbairn model. We have identified two phases, of which the earliest is the *schizoid-paranoid*, the next the *depressive*, both occurring before the age of 3-4 and not wholly covered by the earlier Freudian oral-anal-phallic-genital progression more familiar to most readers. This mainly deals with zones of erotic sensitivity, while my description refers to the more fundamental *relation to others* which colours all emotional transactions including the sexual. The successful passage through these positions permits development into later stages. Arrest of development through failure to master these early emotional situations is a cause of deformed, in some way, infantile, insecure personalities struggling with contradictory inner forces belonging to the past, and leaving the individual less strong and integrated for adaptation to its present needs and tasks.

In the *schizoid-paranoid* stage, when both need for total satisfaction and frustration rage are at their crudest, the world and its human objects are invested with the same omnipotent and destructive qualities that the child feels in himself, because of the uncertainty of what lies outside and what inside. When the subjective experience of a frustrating, hate-evoking act by the love object becomes perceived, there occurs an internal psychic manoeuvre we call *projection* by which the bad object is ejected like bad food. This, the typical paranoid mechanism of denying that the badness is inside, gives this phase its name. The object that should have been good and soothing has turned wicked, poisonous. So the infant's automatic defence against this hate- and fear-laden experience is to split it off, deny its existence. Here is the hypothesized origin of the deepest disturbance in a human being's perception of the world. To preserve the goodness of the vitally needed object, he must forever try to banish its badness—really his own hate and terror—by projection, in order that life can go on. The earlier and the more complete this sense of terror that what should be loving will turn enemy and tormentor, the greater the feeling of inner persecution.

At the least, excess of such experience unassuaged by the love object's "correction" by good mothering will produce anxiously conforming, rigid personalities with loss of spontaneity and uncertainty of self-image. There will be a "fear morality", a readiness to scent insult or enmity in the other and a disposition to suspicion and solitariness. Clinically, these are the precursor qualities of those liable to later schizophrenic or paranoid illnesses. The capacities to develop warm loving relations as well as maturer forms of self-assertion will have been greatly weakened if not shut off. Good and bad remain split off from each other.

Here I am chiefly concerned with less total personality disasters than schizophrenic illness. But if the emotional basis of a person's *Weltanschauung* remains conditioned by being "stuck" at the paranoid level, he will, partly concealed under rationalizations, harbour a lot of mistrust of people and events—feelings Kafka depicted with such mastery: vague, powerful enemies "out there" closing in on the poor helpless self. I repeat that this is one typical outcome of arrest of a significant part of the developing person in this phase which normally leaves only small traces in the adult. The role played by genetics—and by real hostility, neglect or failure of parental concerns—is probably decisive as to whether the next stage is fully entered.

In the succeeding phase, which by similar analogy to potential clinical fate we call *depressive*, the infant has advanced to a capacity to recognize its love object(s) as distinct other persons against whom its hate-fantasies had been directed. There is thus a dawning of perception that the badness is also inside oneself. Anxiety changes to preserving these loved objects from the (still omnipotently perceived) effects of the child's own aggression. Here Klein and Fairbairn see the origins of the *sense of guilt*, of taking the blame for bad feelings and wanting to make amends ("reparation"). Projection still operates, but its content is changed to remorseful attribution of pain and hurt to the love objects and to an expectation of merited punishment and condemnation from them. There is here the potential for altruism and self-denial, but also for self-abasement and expiation. *Introjection* of the feeling complex surrounding the "bad" or frustrating elements of the love object now predominates. It is no longer ejected with the effect of seeing the badness only in the world outside. Since the relation is now to a real object, there also develops tender concern and capacity to grieve and mourn for the real or fantasied loss of the object. The good object is thus *felt as part of oneself*. Thence comes the power of *identification*, the most important mechanism in the transmission of the parental injunctions to the child.

The paranoid position only succeeds in preserving the need to save the ego as "good" by projecting all the badness back into outside figures, and is essentially self-centred, even solipsistic, withdrawn, in later years self-righteous and disdainful. The depressive position accepts the self's errors—perhaps too avidly—splits the ambivalence into "good' outside—"bad" self. The relation to the bad part of the love object thus becomes internalized as an inner voice or persecutor—Freud's "severe super ego", impelling the development of a too rigid sense of duty and subordination to authority felt to be critical, punitive and strict, but at other times loving, suffering, exhorting to virtue. The possession of such an "idealized" inner arbiter can result in severe conflict against its tyranny, which can be seen to issue in attempts at defiance, to do away with the burden of guilt feelings. This over-compensatory *manic denial* can bring behaviour characterized by exaltation, arrogance and even violence in negation of the deeper mood, a sort of "who's afraid of the big bad wolf?" outbreak of suppressed self-assertion well known to educators.

The capacity to own the whole spectrum of ambivalent feelings which brings a sense of freedom of thought and responsibility—a well integrated ego—is hampered also by too great a residue of depressive component. I hope, however, to have shown it as the raw material of the aspiration to moral progress. During this phase when the internalization of parental (cultural) standards becomes the child's model for relating to them and to the world, the sense of reward for conformity to these standards creates a feeling of belonging, a positive morality. At first he learns what is acceptable and what is forbidden by the pain of offending the parents "who love him". Later it is their internalized representation in his world of inner objects that constitutes his "role models" and more or less unconscious values—the deep imprints mentioned earlier. The transmission of the cultural heritage depends on the effectiveness of this early relational ground plan. On this base the expanding awareness of the child can, for good or ill, graft, build and store the varied and complex repertoire for adapting to its world of objects through its experience of love, hate, frustration and terror, which are increasingly worked into the stuff of verbal and symbolic dreams, fantasies and attitudes to people and things, some conscious, some deeply buried. It will be seen how an excess of hate- or fear-laden internalizations may condition and hamper this learning process in later phases, because of a dearth of good identifications.

One of the classical conflicts relevant to my main theme is that of the threat to the infant's need to feel "the one and only" to this love object, normally the mother. Rivals and intruders such as the father or siblings, are invested with much of the hate of the early ambivalence. The mother relation is clung to as "good" and fantasies of killing the monstrous intruding stranger who threatens the good object may be generated. But feelings about the mother as a traitor preferring others, or powerless to defend one, can also predominate. I am here, of course, introducing the Oedipus phase, which also has to be grown through in the journey towards personal maturity. Much here depends on the quality of parental solidarity and skills, as well as on culture values, as to how this well-nigh universal predicament is resolved or repressed, and these vary from family to family and culture to culture. This theme has been lately elegantly re-examined by the late Anne Parsons[6] in psycho-social terms. It is a predicament which seems to overlap both paranoid and depressive positions. It is now realized that splitting of significant objects into good and bad internalizations can occur even when the mother figure is as yet the sole perceived object. She may receive the hate investment of a threatening monster (cf. the Medusa's head, or Kali, in myth), with the father as the reassuring "good" figure, of whom the little boy, especially, can come to be the brave avenger (e.g. Hamlet). In the unconscious elaborations of this central family drama we can clearly perceive the germinal orientations towards authority, towards intruders, strangers, and towards sexual object-love. Repression from awareness of such early frighteningly destructive, omnipotent-powerless, object relations fantasies as the dread of being exterminated in retaliation for the wish for parricide, matricide—even world destruction—makes life possible. It also distorts and weakens by creating inner enclaves of "blind-alley" mental energies which pre-occupy the unconscious, requiring much psychic effort to keep them safely split off.

My purpose in dwelling on these early phases of human socialization is to provide a basis resting on clinical work and on child research from which to derive the intrapersonal motive forces which give their dynamism to various aspects of social and political behaviour, some very close analogues of clinical psychiatric phenomena. The child is father to the man because the internalized object-relations impart a latent "under-tow" to the growth into adult personality. That these hypothesized contents of the deeper, often unconscious, layers of the psyche are to a great extent the outcomes of conflict, between the subject's impulsions and the parental counter-actions, lends additional meaning to that adage. In so far as these object-relations are good, they speed maturation and tend to merge into the adult role. In this volume we have to consider those outcomes where some internal objects are of the "bad "kind. It is in them that there come into play the so-called mechanisms of ego-defence by which the inadmissible and repressed or split-off introjections are kept out of awareness or otherwise dis-posed of. The fact that they persist and exert pressure ("undertow") to gain resolution is a daily experience of psychiatrists, social workers and the courts. It means that the ego defences have given way under heightened stress so that the precariously maintained adaptation to adult life and human relations breaks down.

Whereas I have hitherto been dealing mainly with *predisposition*, I now have in mind *precipitation*, by which I mean those situations which trigger the breakthrough of the insecurely repressed, which now impels towards action. The danger or reality of such *regression* can often be shown as due to the stressful circumstances resembling or evoking strong emotive associations with the early object-relations. The emotions are now *displaced* or *transferred* from the original to less immediate or secondary figures and situations (e.g. from father to boss, from mother to wife). It is feelings that undergo regression to the infantile level, with correspondingly high levels of guilt, terror or overt hate. It is as if there was need to work belatedly through the unsettled scores of the original bad object-relations on the substitute figures. Stress precipitating regression may include organic disease (the childishness of long hospitalization), chronic poisoning (e.g. alcohol or drugs), social and economic calamity, or real threats from the secondary figures (e.g. working life), to name but a few. Space does not permit full exposition of this general psychopathology. Some basic patterns of psychological reactions to the regressive pulls do however require mention. (1) The subject identifies with the vindictive authority-image against his own bad feelings and impulses, that is, he retreats to the depressive position to ward off his hate against parent figures. (2) The subject feels persecuted and attacked and inflates his ego in righteous defensive self-importance (the paranoid position). (3) A blend or oscillation between these "masochistic" or self-abasing and "sadistic" or self-aggrandizing poles of wavering identity. (4) Chaotic confusion and withdrawal into "alienation" and nihilistic *anomie* of schizoid futility.

3. Some Extensions to Social Psychology

It has already been indicated that the requirements for "a good member" of a given social group will be influenced more by its culture norms than by abstract psycho-biological standards of mental health. No culture brings its offspring to adulthood without some distortions or loss of potentials for untrammelled maturity. But neither must my emphasis on the importance of early imprinting of conflict and distortion be held to imply that fortunate influences in later stages of growth cannot largely correct the deeper internalizations; or that catastrophic experiences in later life will leave a person, with a good early background, unscathed. Nor can we lay down universal standards of what is optimal mental health, since different societies demand different qualities of their "normal" citizens. The day of internationally agreed standards of mental health, permitting fullest and responsible unfoldment of the individual within a just and humane social order is not yet, however close the professions concerned may be to a blue-print for such desiderata.

A renowned physician and psychoanalyst, the late D. W. Winnicott, published an essay (by coincidence in the very issue of *Human Relations* in which my paper[2] appeared) on the "meaning of the word Democracy".[7] He argued that this word evoked for him the emotive associations of flexibility and maturity. It meant that in a democratic society leaders could be "got rid of" by many individuals taking responsibility after an inner conflict and decision expressed in a secret vote. One's inner self becomes, temporarily or continually, the arena of the political contest. Such socio-cultural adultness, a mark of control over dissent and bellicosity, he argued, was an achievement of only some societies at certain periods of time. It depended on there being at such times a sufficient number of individuals with the "luck" to have developed the requisite *personal* maturity (or healthy emotional development) to value and preserve the, to Winnicott, innate tendency to *social* maturity reflected in peaceful, tolerant, political institutions and machinery for effecting change and settling differences. There would, however, be X per cent of anti-social children not capable of valuing this achievement. Such a fraction could well be multiplied to $5X$ by, for example, a war and could sway the educational measures (through what is now called "backlash"—H. V. D.) towards more dictatorial methods, thus further damaging the chances for healthy maturation of the $100 - 5X$ per cent. There were further, continued Winnicott, a hidden Z per cent who react to inner insecurity by identification with the authorities, not from mature assent "based on self-discovery" but from *anti-individual* conformity and ego weakness impelling them to locate and control the conflicting forces in the external world, outside the self. Such people supported authority because they were not "whole persons" with self-generated convictions. They would by their fear of taking independent stands tend to push the social process away from the more mature, responsible, autonomous-choice contributions of "whole persons" in mature conflict resolutions. There would, lastly, be also Y per cent of "indeterminates" whom Winnicott does not further specify, except that "they can be swayed either way". They are presumably the "don't knows" of opinion polls—the "quiet lifers" or floating voters, who would not necessarily strengthen democratic responsibility. Winnicott's concern was to point to the precariousness of that politico-social "wholeness" which can tolerate the ambivalence of choice and of opposition to authority, as contrasted to the frank destroyers (X fraction) or the hidden anti-individual "Z" *authoritarians* (my term—H. V. D.) who have to support authority as an ego-defence against parricidal fantasies in their primary object-relations. In this sense Winnicott's is a statement of the difference between the political attitudes issuing from the paranoid phase fixations, and those in which parental symbols and substitutes are felt to respect and tolerate the subject's own right to individual choices and initiatives. Winnicott, a leading child-psychiatrist, also linked the achievement of such ego-strength to the background experience of a devoted, cherishing mother in a secure home and cultural climate.

It is permissible to correlate the variations in the authority structure in given social groups with the actual tolerance or severity and prohibitions imposed by elders on the basis of their own values and internalizations taken over from the group's culture patterns (of course with many sub-group and idiosyncratic differences depending on class, region, etc.) This will be a two-way process. In so far as the authority-wielders are also children of their culture, they will themselves have been conditioned by its moulding forces that prescribed and circumscribed the functions and limits of power "proper" to their roles, no less than for their subordinates'. As we know how the mechanism of *transference* works in clinical and other more limited areas, we can observe that this dynamism is at work in the displacement and substitution of primary love objects to the authority symbols of the society. It is a commonplace of psychology that monarchs, generals, politicians or policemen can embody parental images and receive corresponding devotion or execration from their subordinates. It is most important to reflect that in these conscious and unconscious interpretations of authority roles by the rulers and the ruled (at any echelon of the hierarchy) the basic mechanisms of introjection (taking in and identifying with) and projection (expulsion, negative identification) are likely to be involved. In other words, the reciprocal attitudes of citizens and their leaders will contain some infantile and irrational elements at unconscious levels, resembling those of children and parents. These could cut across rational and objective judgments of the merits of their actions.

The human need for dependence on, and goodwill of, objects that have the power to cherish or destroy has been stressed earlier. It is part of this need to keep the object good and gratifying, even where by objective standards the object would be seen as bad and depriving to other needs of the person. This process requires a dynamic restructuring of the ambivalence which we call *idealization*. As the term implies, this involves an abrogation of all hostile, even realistically critical emotions towards the object, who becomes "all-giving" or "all wise" (Tsar, Pope, etc.). To balance the account of that denial, the hostility is introjected and has to be kept turned against the self or against safe substitutes for the idealized figure. The latter receives all the self-abasement. Not until a person with this sort of incorporated authority-pattern comes to exercise a power role will it be apparent that the attribution of omnipotence to the ideal was part of an *identification* with that figure. The "swallowed" aggression emerges as the power role allows its exercise in the manner of the hitherto hidden bad aspect of the parent figure, with the idealized part of whom this unconscious fusion had occurred when the whole object had to be taken in. In some such way as this it must be that authoritarian cultures are passed on and intensified through the generations. The parental influences set the patterns. The more completely and the earlier the child is required to go through this process the more primitive and therefore paranoid the social climate. In assessing a society—say a nation —it becomes highly pertinent to ask in what institutionalized major ways feelings of guilt, arising from hostility towards authorities, are disposed of: (1) paranoidally, by the intrapsychic mechanism of fear of omnipotent retaliation and loss of love, or (2) depressively, by anxiety felt at the guilt of hurting the loved figures and incurring their reproach; a guilt and remorse morality?

There is never, I am sure, a complete either-or division between these two modes of impulse control. Thus, idealization and the consequential self-abasement are more depressive than paranoid. But the more the need to express dissent, anger and opposition lack tolerated channels, the more aggression against the authorities will be stored up. Since the authority holders of such a system themselves contain the

same tensions between persecutory love objects and fear-laden con-
formists, they will tend to enact their internalized authority roles
towards the powerless (children, employees, private soldiers, unidenti-
fied citizens) in the belief that they are hostile and must be contained
by force. This is the paranoid, persecutory system of police rule, smell-
ing treason everywhere. The more, on the contrary, the culture pattern
has succeeded in establishing an inner guilt sense as the mode of curbing
anti-social impulses, the gentler the external coercive pressures can
afford to be. The authorities in this case will work on the cultural
expectation that the subordinate is self-governing, wants to "do right".
They will trust him—and the police can go unarmed. It is this second
condition which seems to me an essential *psychological* foundation for
democracy, on which, however, I cannot here elaborate, beyond stating
that it must rest on Winnicott's "whole persons", who can accept the
human reality of other persons without attributing to them omnipotent
malice, which is characteristic of Winnicott's Z fraction.

In the paranoid authoritarian culture the split into a coercive THEY,
and a distrusted underdog US is the foundation, and the mutual projections are that the underdogs are only conformist through dread of
ruthless power, while the subjects equally dehumanize their leaders.
Both sides have to deny the hate which such a configuration entails.
The leaders are exercising their arbitrary power under the idealization
of "their people", just as fatherly love beats the weak, angry children
into submission. The revaluation of the oppressors by their grateful
subjects has already been mentioned. That oppressive governments
can push people with originally humane "guilt consciences" into regression by reactivating paranoid conflicts is well authenticated. Money-
Kyrle[8], who worked in my Unit on the selection of German personnel
immediately after the war, has made a valuable analysis of the problems
here only briefly outlined. I can now turn my attention to the German
scene in the hope that the application of the foregoing over-condensed
general theory to a concrete culture and some actual people it had
produced will make my viewpoint clearer.

CHAPTER TWO

HEIRS OF THE KAISER

The history of the rise of Hitler has been often told. My purpose in writing this sketchy outline is to set the background for the men I interviewed. I draw on many sources[1-7], among them my own earlier work, and also on quite recent studies by German scholars[8-10], which differ little from our Anglo-American war-time conclusions. These studies are all dedicated to discovery of the causes of renewed German bellicosity and ultimately of the cruelties and crimes the Nazis perpetrated, ending just short of national self-destruction. We had cogent reasons for trying at that time to comprehend the negative aspects of Germany, so surprisingly at variance with her creative achievements. Some of what I have to say on the regularities of German "character" and group climate is based on my own knowledge, and on many professional interviews with German prisoners of war 1942-45, whose life histories included the Wilhelminian period, well before 1914.

Wilhelminian Germany's was a paternalistic society with a rigid status structure persisting from the feudal era. Authority was transmitted from the pinnacle of the Kaiser through a step-ladder of aristocrats and liege-princes along one echelon; and of soldiers and bureaucrats along another hierarchy down to the smallest functionaries. At each level a touchy sense of rank consciousness demanded and received due deference from the lower orders. It was a society marked by much latent tension between classes and envy of the more exalted and powerful. For centuries Germany, nominally a part of the Holy Roman Empire, had been in fact a complex pattern of small dukedoms and other petty states, kaleidoscopic in their changes and allegiances. Loyalty to the "German nation", until Bismarck, lacked an effective central symbol except an "idea" based on the ancient Realm of Charlemagne and his successors as bringers of imperial and legal order to Europe.

It was the Prussians, the most authoritarian and austere of Germans, with their rigid military and feudal hierarchy, who clothed this idea once more with power and brought imperial unity after a series of successful wars of aggression, only 100 years ago. The Prussians' virtues: discipline, devotion to duty, industrious striving and, above all, soldierliness were rooted in a puritan ethic, and could become a model and a "moral corset" to the softer, more romantic Germans. The unification by Bismarck, not without some local resentments, has been compared by some authors to feminine yielding before a strong suitor. Thus on to a traditional, one may say primordial, patriarchal culture pattern common to most Europeans there was added the commanding tone of the new élite, the Prussian officer and official. In the era when the English fashioned their own preferred "public school" type, who was to be a tone-setter, the new German nation adopted the soldierly "*Herrennatur*" as the favoured social model to be cultivated and re-warded by society. It is in the nature of imitativeness and envious "upward striving" that the model influences ever wider strata of society —especially in so dominance/submission conditioned a culture as the German, where liberal and democratic values had been resisted des-pite the English and French revolutions and all that followed from these.

My evidence, supported by many authors, is that the typical Wilhel-minian family was both a mirror and the seed-bed in which these now generalized cultural patterns were transmitted in the moulding of the children. The father, even if he had to kow-tow to his superiors all day because "he knew his place", had his home in which to play undisputed master. The German wife was typically subordinate and relegated to her well-known sphere of "*Kinder, Küche, Kirche*" (kids, kitchen, kirk). It is my contention that this widespread pattern of authoritarianism in state and home was inimical to the growing of strong and self-regulating "democratic" personalities, as indicated in the previous chapter. The one-sided emphasis on paternal (male) domin-ance resulted in internal conflicts for the offspring that could only be assimilated by splits and contradictions in the resulting character structure.★

I derive the "typical" German male's oscillation between deferential conformity and harsh assertiveness from the pressures in the direction of "manliness" by the fathers, themselves conditioned by cultural influence, on exerting their patriarchal role. The damage is above all to little boys' normal tender attachment to their mothers. The young

★ The psychological sequence here delineated is, of course, also found in families and groups outside German culture. It is the regularity and intensity of it in the German context which gives it significance.

child must not draw his father's wrath (and jealousy at unconscious level) by being a weak, "spoilt" cry-baby—a term nowhere more despised than in Germany 60–70 years ago, since it includes the simultaneously idealized and devalued mother's feelings towards the child. The Oedipal tie is therefore not "grown through" to resolution but unconsciously prolonged by the introjection of forbidding, hostile aspects of the object-relation to *both* parents. One part of it is the repression of the hate against the intruding menacing powerful rival under a mask of loving and dutiful submission—almost a stereotype in life-history after life-history of German soldiers of all walks of life 30 years ago. The other part of the damage to confidence is the experience of what should have been the loving protectress as betraying the child and siding with the oppressor, herself a victim, only fit to be the docile drudge of the man. Here is already the prototype of power monopoly. There is no alternative to inwardly ambivalent, but outwardly perfect, submission to it. The child's picture of his world is reinforced when he sees his all-powerful father showing obsequious deference to even more terrifying dignitaries. In this way there arises a failure in balanced growth *both* of love capacity and of freedom for self-assured independence. The mother-seeking tendencies have to be denied. They become transformed into a furtive, guilt-laden collusion of mother and son behind the father's back, and ultimately into guilty adolescent confusion about sexual relations. Women become essentially debased but superficially idealized. Sentimentality takes the place of real feeling. "Mother was good, but father made all decisions" was a standard answer.

The revaluation of the depriving and threatening aspect of paternal authority is enhanced by the tendency, mentioned in the first chapter, to identify with the internalized aggressor, so that it becomes part of the personality to side with the stern authority and gain inner satisfaction in the sado-masochistic attitude of surrender to its power. The ego gives up its regulatory functions into the keeping of the authority who knows best. This manoeuvre produces the favoured social role of the eager loyalist. The self-image is that of the unruly, spoilt weakling who is proud to be hammered and tempered into a "real man" by harsh discipline, of which military service represented the acme. The resulting deficit in self-reliance and flexibility of the ego was at times conscious—as for example in the remarks by many a soldier interviewed: "We are so weak, we could never do without a strong ruler". More often it led to over-compensatory swagger, arrogance and bluster by which status and "strength" were unpleasantly asserted to those lower in the pecking order, by identification with the military model. Uncertainty in self-valuation, indicative of ego-damage, could further be observed in the violent fluctuations between feelings of group (national) omnipotence and personal impotence. This was expressed, to the astonishment of Allied interrogators in the Second War, in the stock phrase: "What could I do, I was only a little man?" (*Ja was konnte ich denn, war ja nur ein kleiner Mann?*) from corporals up to field-marshals— and even at the Nuremberg trials of the top leaders. We know with what "man-of-iron" postures these self-same "little cogs" could relentlessly bully and coerce when acting in superordinate roles as leaders, commanders or administrators, undeflected by any weak humanitarianism from the stern path of personal or national "duty". Men with this record could be seen pathetically self-pitying and eager to ingratiate themselves with us, their captors and therefore new authorities.

A brief excerpt from my interview with a Luftwaffe fighter-pilot officer in 1943 illustrates the foregoing on an aspiring member of the German élite:

This femininely handsome courteous youth was the son of a well-known general of aristocratic background, close to Hitler. We knew he had been responsible for machine-gunning a market town and was monitored to have boasted "what fun it had been". Our R.A.F. interrogator rated him as a "pansy type easily influenced by others". To me he described himself as "of course my mother's all", but thank God father's dominance had rescued him from her apron strings. Did his father send him to a boarding-school? "Oh no, that would be a great mistake! Then a father cannot shape his boy to his own liking. If I have a son I would devote myself *entirely* (his emphasis) to his upbringing." He joined the air force not only to follow his father but "of course" for the beauty of educating and moulding young men for their great destiny. Asked what he would have done had there been no air force, he said he really wanted to be an interior decorator—"I get the art from my mother" but "of course" that didn't count much. . . . Nor would he waste time on any daughter. . . . On the political side he had expressed his full agreement and justification for all that the Nazi occupation had done in Poland and Czechoslavakia after Heydrich's assassination,★ seeing that those benighted people "had permitted themselves dirty tricks" against the great German "Kulturvolk" who could not allow an insult to go unpunished.

★ See Chapter Three.

Such soft-skinned but not often so well-mannered young men abounded in our samples. They illustrate how the contradiction between a submissive relation to a dreaded father figure and being a "ruthless hero" can be resolved by romanticizing *group potency* and might. It was noteworthy that this cult of idealized manliness affected the more imaginative southern Germans more than the Prussians.

The worship of authority affected not only the young élite warriors. The process had spread downwards through military conscription. Dahrendorf[11] describes the new industrial magnates behaving like feudal lords and prasing the good effects of military training on their workers' efficiency and "regular habits". In the Second War we captured a republished diary of a factory hand from the Ruhr written during his service in the Kaiser's navy. I quote a few excerpts translated by myself:

> In 1917 the diarist comments on a Fleet Order by his Emperor: "When talking to his Navy he becomes tender-fatherly, talks of 'his boys'. . . . When he says 'I hereby command', then common sense struggles against the possibility of believing that here speaks only an ordinary man." In 1918 the writer is pondering a propaganda appeal by the Entente for a democratic revolt. He writes: "Our Kaiser—and our great General Staff—subject to a Reichstag! What would be left? Only a kingship like Denmark or England? Unthinkable!" Later, with German defeat looming, the Kaiser's image has lost its magic. The diarist tries to generalize the blame "on those above", but is already dreaming of a *really* good "*Volkskaiser*". When, just before the 1918 armistice the German sailors mutinied, he deplores this insubordination and longs for a "Man" (no longer called Kaiser) who shall arise and reunite the now warring Germans.

Here was what I am about to describe in a nutshell.

Historians know to what a dangerous degree this ethnocentric deification of the German state and its monarch was nourished since the Prussian rise after Waterloo. The influence of such a thinker as Hegel on the teaching and nationalist climate in schools and especially universities left deep imprints on the officials, lawyers and teachers who trained there. By comparison with the contemptuous hostility and envy towards other European powers (degeneracy, "shopkeeper mentality", etc.) anti-Semitism was still inconspicuous. In this chauvinism the German sense of weakness in the face of "big bullies" could be projected on to the political world screen, after the centuries of history when German lands had been exposed to French as well as Slav pressures. But the philosophy of war as the highest activity of man, and the divine right of the strongest to rule and to waive ethical principles in the pursuit of military power, brazenly asserted, had the marks of a regressive process. Omnipotence fantasy and *hybris* are psychological defences of dangerous import against inner feelings of constraint and submissiveness. Men with such feelings tend to compensate for them by identifying with group power under a great leader who becomes the repository of decision, responsibility and conscience—in effect, deified.

The weaknesses of these German characteristics were to be starkly revealed in the calamities that followed the defeat of 1918. The symbols of group invincibility and power—the Kaiser and his marshals—had gone. Parts of Germany were occupied by the victorious Allies who at Versailles imposed onerous reparations inspired more by revenge than economic realism, as Keynes saw. In place of the Emperor, a republican parliamentary state was proclaimed at Weimar, pledged to fulfilment of the Versailles treaty, to very modest armed forces* and to a Western democratic system. Our naval diarist's apprehensions accurately fore-shadowed the shattering effect of these changes, mainly but not exclu-sively, on the most fervent "patriots" of the tumbled regime. Recalling Winnicott's Z fraction, all those Germans, to whom conflict, opposition to authorities and loss of assured rank and status spelt a dissolution of their ego-defences, could not accept the new reality. There was no home-grown model for managing political conflict, for flexible impro-vization and self-help. The sudden removal of long-cherished boundaries of freedom which had been the guarantees of security was no liberation or new beginning for such men but only another destructive act of national humiliation by the alien Western victors. It spelt anarchy.

And true enough, in the first months there appeared the dread spec-tacle—and spectre—of the mutinous revolutionary soldiery and pro-letariat pressing for a "real" parricidal overthrow of the old order on the Russian model, then a bare year old. When these Left Wing mobs were venting their hate by tearing off officers' epaulettes and sacking military establishments, the dissolution of all that "decent men" had venerated seemed at hand. It was a signal for panic measures by the disinherited and disgraced. Fromm,[12] 30 years ago, had written of the fear aroused by a sense of unwanted freedom. To escape this fear, independence is given up for the sake of fusing one's self with others in order to feel support, "to seek for new, 'secondary bonds' as a substitute for the (lost) primary bonds". Those who could accept the

---

* Called the *Reichswehr*, limited to 100,000 officers and men.

new order could join various "democratic" parties (some dating from Bismarck's era of the consultative Reichstag) for this. Even these were, like the old Germany, a complex patchwork of ideologically intolerant "principled" groups that made flexible compromises and growth into a viable democracy difficult. But to the chauvinists and irreconcilables with their torn epaulettes and their lost father-symbols the unglamorous civilians who had signed the Armistice and now governed were the negation of German power and tradition. These furiously disillusioned ex-officers and their younger brothers—and indeed many older men too—quickly coalesced into various para-military groups, gangs and associations, styled Free Corps (Freikorps) pledged to uphold German "honour" and folkways that seemed so gravely menaced. By what? The Red proletariat now demobilized and influenced by Russian communists—and weren't the Soviet leaders mostly Jews?—the rich Versailles oppressors—and weren't they also "Jewish finance capital"? The Papist and their supporters—the Poles—all the foreigners who were as "always" poised to weaken and dismember Germany—and above all those treacherous un-German men of Weimar who were their puppets. The emphasis on one or another of these persecuting symbols differed according to background and provenance—the Rhine, or the Czech and Polish frontiers. It was at this early point that there occurred the first *paranoid denial of reality* by these die-hards: the famous legend of the "stab in the back". Not "we brave, true German soldiers" had lost the war. No, it was alien communists, Jewish war profiteers, Freemasons and Papists with their international networks who had sabotaged the home front and sold the pass. This displacement of hate and guilt of failure from the Kaiser's élite on to the composite, variously perceived, irrational image of pitiless enemies was clearly an effect of paranoid scapegoating, a deflection away from "good US" to "bad outside THEY" of the parricidal feeling aroused by the "God that failed", the father that had let down all his trusting faithful sons' expectations of power and glory, who had betrayed the motherland and could not control his anarchic rebelling children (as indeed Weimar never quite managed!). While more liberal men struggled to make a new start, and the socialist Left were expressing their anti-paternal feelings first in some rioting and later in legitimate political action, the irreconcilables could not bury and mourn the old soldierly father-image that had been the brittle source of their sense of worth and emotional security.

Here we can discern the fateful division in its German setting between those whose life histories had not vouchsafed them development beyond the paranoid phase, and those who had passed through the depressive phase and beyond, giving them the flexibility to adapt better to new reality by assimilating the loss of the old and re-entering into life. It is the former—Germany's "backwoodsmen" of the Z fraction—who had to keep alive their archaic loved-hated inner object, to defend it against evil intruders and persecutors.

Ernst von Salomon,[13] himself then an officer-cadet "with no hope left", has recorded his experiences as one of a group of Free-Corps desperadoes led by one *Kern* who was responsible for the assassination in 1923 of one of Weimar's ablest liberal statesmen, Rathenau, significantly for this group a Jew.* Their world had vanished, and they could only fight for their dream of "hundreds of years which saw the domination of the world by Germany". At first such gangs of veterans, and their younger brothers who had been cheated of their war experience, could find congenial work in manning the new Republic's undefended frontiers or carry on their private wars against Polish claims to Upper Silesia or the menace of advancing Bolshevism from the Baltic countries. Similar groups, sometimes with overlapping personnel, took part in the early attempts at forcible overthrow of the young Republic by Right Wing politicians, of which the most famous was the 1920 *Kapp putsch*, which was defeated by Republican troops. Such, however, was the political climate that senior generals of the Weimar (legal) Reichswehr secretly connived with the putschists, and after their defeat employed these self-same rebels to help break a general strike which the working class had called to hinder the Kapp putsch!

Thus, quite early in the Weimar period, the split in Germany assumed an ominous depth owing to the fact that the young state had a democratic government and parliament (Reichstag) but had left intact the human and institutional pillars of the Kaiser's regime—the senior civil service, the military "top brass" and judiciary, as well as the faculties of the universities. These were, of course, the men who had very recently stood highest in the national pecking order. They constituted, by and large, at least as powerful an opposition group against the purposes of the new regime as the more flamboyant para-military action

---

* Kern is stated as saying that his sole motive force was to destroy those who had allowed "his" Teutonism to be submerged, and force Germany to follow its path of suffering to its "destiny".

groups whose ideology they privately shared and whose growing illegalities they covered up. Backhaus[14] relates this weakness in the Weimar regime to the prestige as the upholders of "law and order" of this old élite which even the liberals and social democrats had been reared to regard with awe. This sapped some of their confidence in taking radical action for reform, including removal of their own enemies from the corridors of power.

This circumstance must be a factor in explaining the virtual impunity with which these die-hard, romanticized and increasingly violent swash-bucklers and veterans spiralled into lawlessness. Thus, the notorious "Marine Brigade", led by an ex-naval officer Ehrhardt, was several times declared illegal, but never brought to trial. After the Kapp putsch, at which they carried the old Imperial war flag adorned with a swastika as their banner, they went underground to form a terrorist network called *Consul*, under cover of various "harmless" patriotic, folkish and even trading organizations. They proudly claimed the assassinations of prominent liberal politicians as their work. Inside such gangs there was revived the practice of *Feme* trials. In medieval Germany this was the name for a secret assize court in which traitors against the Emperor were tried by high dignitaries in his name. The *Feme* murders in Weimar Germany had nothing in common with the original except the secrecy. The gangs staged ritualized illegal trials and summary "executions", aping field courts-martial, clad in Ku-Klux-Klan-like garb. They "sentenced" to death anyone accused of being an enemy of *their* Germany, including their own members or former members suspected of un-reliability or treason. Gumbel,[15] a liberal scholar and jurist, reports that between 1919 and 1923 there were in Germany 354 political murders by the Right, as against 22 by the Left. The Feme killings were typically carried out by very brutal methods in dark woods, etc., to add to the element of terror. From some of these Free-Corps and their underground emerged future Nazi leaders and murderers—e.g. Hoess (commandant of Auschwitz) and Martin Bormann.

Here, in my view, originated the scarcely veiled defiance and con-tempt for the lawful, weak and humane authority of the Weimar regime. It soon became the "patriotic", done thing in many minds, especially for the young, to be associated with these "defence and defiance" movements, going by romantic names such as Viking, Were-wolf and the like in which ethnocentrism, xenophobia and secret mili-tary training were cultivated. The majority of these were not themselves terrorists, but accepted the ideology of the terrorist extremists, who claimed they were the true Germany. The enemies of the state were not they but the legal Weimar authorities and their loyal police and magistrates. It is worth stressing the degree of paranoid projection with which these hate-filled underminers of their country's constitutional executive accused it of plotting and conspiracy with the various scape-goat enemies. If Weimar succeeded in bringing a few small men among the Feme murderers to court, there would be outcries of "terrorism" in the Right Wing press against the regime and judges, especially if they were Jews, were accused of unfair bias. The major figures, the Ehrhardts and Rossbachs or Reichswehr staff officers behind the illegali-ties, were at most heard as witnesses and could cover up the links.

In this severely condensed story of the emergence of the Nazis it would be unfair to omit mention of much real stress. In addition to the loss of status of the classes who thought of themselves as the embodi-ment of Germany, the disastrous inflation of 1923 destroyed overnight the money values of savings, pensions and so the security of countless middle-class people. It meant hardship and resentment as well as loss of educational possibilities for their sons. All the heroism and semi-starvation of the war had been in vain—only to be delivered over into the power of black marketeers (largely identified with Jews) and foreign capitalists and communists. What must be stressed is that the Weimar regime gave ample political and Press freedom to criticize and cam-paign legitimately. It was the psychological inability of the Right Wing to accept and work this very system, that created the atmosphere in which National Socialism could integrate and express the welter of "soldierliness", last-ditch militancy, Germanism, hate of bad authority figures and gang solidarity of the disinherited young in a millennialist dream of revival and renewal. It has often been stated that in Hitler's *Mein Kampf*, the Nazi bible, there was not a single idea not already current among the movements I have sketched, and out of which the Nazi party coalesced. The regressive slide into paranoid thinking and feeling was a spontaneous effect of stresses on a sizeable proportion of Germans whose brittle ego-strengths were unequal to facing a new reality, especially after four years of further military conditioning into abrogating inner autonomy. Their longing not only for a "Man" to lead them but for thus feeling great and secure again had already found tough gang-leaders as well as mythological sources of magic delivery. Hero figures like the Emperor Barbarossa (their Coeur-de-Lion), Henry the Fowler, Frederick the Great etc. became longed-for models; all manner of old Teuton pagan religious mumbo-jumbo and ritual folk romanticism flourished. The well-known "youthful revolt", that was the one permitted culture protest against the staid elders, was now wedded to German and perhaps especially Austrian dog-in-the-manger resentment and envy at the loss of privilege. Austria had, after all, also been a great Empire in which the German "masters" had now lost out to the "lesser breeds"—Hungarians, Czechs, Southern Slavs. Hitler's was at the same time a charismatic, magically persuasive and a "poor little angry underdog's" personality, whose inner fantasy life and oratory to express it seemed ideally suited to give some sort of emotional coherence to the different idioms in which many angry authoritarian "little men" had tried to formulate their violent denials of reality and betrayal by the wicked composite image of THEY: rapacious aliens, corrupt and permissive socialists, money makers and so on. Hitler's special contributions were first, his Austrian obsession with the malice of Jews, whose influence was for him ubiquitous, and at the same time diabolically powerful as well as diseased by degeneracy and sexual debauchery. Secondly, he crystallized the stab-in-the-back legend in such a way that to destroy this satanic power now strangling the good and incorrupt German soul and organism became the real patriot's sacred duty. He succeeded in dehumanizing all his enemies either into contemptible vermin or demoniacal ogres—or both. Thirdly, he systematized into a political programme what had been vague if widely shared wish-fantasies of revenge, restoration and potency. At last the dream of becoming really powerful by hallowed vicarious parricide could be realized. Here was our naval diarist's "Man of Destiny".

It is not difficult to see why the "nationalists" rallied to Hitler. The big men thought they could, by patronizing this ranting mob hypnotist, have revolutionary hatred deflected into nationalist channels. Once the "enemy" who had brought Germany low was no longer felt to be the old élite, but the foreigner and all his works (including Weimar), then let aggressive militancy rip. The generals and the magnates thought they could use and then discard Hitler. The little ex-soldiers and ruined lower middle-class men loved his flattery of their heroism and loyalty, and his insight into their resentment and envy of the rich and powerful who had not been impoverished by the war years—all the more if these were the pushing Jews who took all the best jobs. The young, cheated of their dreams of soldierly life idealized by their older brothers or youngish fathers, followed Hitler because he preached the uprising of the youthful and new against the old, greedy and effete.

It is harder to understand why working-class men were also drawn into the Nazi ranks, especially when the first objective of the Party was to smash the socialist, communist and liberal parties and unions of those very Germans who had achieved some degree of democracy and equality—in general those who did not share the fantasy world of the Right. Hitler's militant Party activists, organized long before he came to power into his SA troops★ on a local area basis, were largely used between 1925 and 1933 violently to disrupt their opponents' meetings, terrorize what they called the Red scum, and defend Nazi rallies from similar interruption. The working class as a whole knew that the Nazis meant to destroy their constitutional democracy. By 1931 the Left had organized its own uniformed fighting party militias, of which the socialist "Reichsbanner" was the largest. The SA, however, with all its mystique of being the glorious soldiers of resurgent German might, and composed of fanatics, were on the whole more efficacious. The very sight and constant suggestive effect on the German of marching columns with drums and band, with flags flying, was infectious to the "soldierly" element in the culture. These were the patriots who only wanted to bring order and greatness under a simple, inspired man. Even the National Government could not do more than ineffectually forbid uniformed marching, only to rescind it again. The whole phenomenon was too close to the culture pattern to be effectively resisted. But the deciding factor which gave Hitler his mass support by which he came to power constitutionally in free elections, was the great economic depression of 1929-31. Although this was a world-wide event, to German working people who had begun to see some improvement in the few years before, it was disastrous. Millions of youths and young men were unemployed and fell easy victims to the propaganda that Weimar had failed to give them bread and work. Those millions of new voters, not identified with any other loyalties, gave Hitler his Reichstag majority in 1933.

In preparation for this present volume I studied the life histories of some 60 old Nazi party fighters from captured files (of which more in Chapter Four). Unemployed urban workers were among these—including disillusioned Marxists. Many workmen were themselves ex-soldiers and proud of it, and many were state employees.

★ SA is short for *Sturmabteilung* or Assault Sections.

Backhaus[16] quotes a letter from Ernst Toller, a prominent Weimar period German communist and working-class leader, written to a French friend. In it he describes the "complete demoralization" of German communist party cadres by unemployment and loss of trade union support, wandering about as if lost. Toller continues: "The German has an anarchic core. Since the vagabond (Hitler—H. V. D.) has got hold of them, they have lost their reason. They are hankering after mischief (*Unheil*) of a kind your people can barely imagine. . . . Unemployment splinters them into a bunch of anarchists . . . caught by that adventurer who wants to . . . put on a show of mystical union movement for them. . . ."* Here from one of the "opposition", we get confirmation of the link between the dread of aloneness and anarchy (which Toller clearly shares as a member of another totalitarian movement) and the withdrawal from "real" revolution into choosing the security of a pseudo-revolutionary authoritarian "order". Wangh,[17] discussing the above phenomena, comes to a conclusion which has my full agreement. Given the wide diffusion of the German family pattern, there would be a proportion of working-class children whose parental object-relations predisposed them to authoritarian identifications, so that when the regime failed to provide their livelihood, they flocked to the swastika. Wangh writes:

> In 1930, at the decisive turning point between adolescence and manhood an entire generation stood hungry, bewildered . . . in the breadlines of the unemployed. . . . These had been very young children in 1914. . . .
> I suggest that these youthful followers reacted regressively to the fear . . . of 1930 because their childhood was encompassed by the First World War . . . subjected to particularly noxious influences . . . father's prolonged absence and his defeat as a soldier . . . his failure to protect his family from economic misery . . . the continuous and heightened anxiety of the mothers. . . .

This situation was not Germany's alone. But for Germans the combination of maximal Oedipal guilt stimulation with *real* hunger and other real deprivations overtaxed this particular nation's Z fraction. This stress-prone, abnormally father-longing and father-hating cohort could not deal with the new situation of 1930 precipitating loss of worth and security except by the regression to crude and childlike expressions of their social homosexuality—that universal link between fathers and sons.

* My translation—H. V. D.

46

Through their policies the victor powers bear some share of responsibility for this development. They did nothing until it was too late—and then they started to appease only when this enhanced the Nazi belief in the efficacy of power and blackmail. Germany once more showed her military, ruthless face. The élan was well-nigh irresistible.

Of over 1000 German military personnel tested by us, the fanatical Nazi core never fell below 10 per cent. The believers with reservations remained at a further 25 per cent. This sample included 600 or more interrogated well after our invasion of 1944.[18]

CHAPTER THREE

THE SS AND ITS WORKS

The "SS" was not the monolith popularly imagined. Only some parts of it concern us here. All the men I interviewed for this study had belonged to that section of the SS which carried out the greater part of Hitler's terror and genocide under the delegated authority of Himmler. Recent studies by Buchheim[1] and Höhne[2] have added clarity to the information available to Allied war-time intelligence on its role and deeds. In war-time Germany its operations were shrouded in secrecy. By loyal Nazis the SS were seen as their *corps d'élite*, by opponents as fearsome, sinister watchdogs of the regime—an image fostered by the SS themselves. My colleague Dr Wolfgang Scheffler will present a volume in the Columbus Centre series describing the growth of the "Black Corps" into a quasi-autonomous state within a state, a privileged enclave walled-off from their countrymen. Here I shall offer only enough material to make my interview reports intelligible without recourse to other publications.

Among the SA who constituted the Party's fighting mass formations, a small minority were selected to act as personal bodyguards for the leaders, and these became SS (short for *Schutzstaffeln* or protection squads). By 1925, when Weimar permitted the Nazi party to reform, these picked stalwarts were already marked off by greater discipline, earnest sobriety and "idealism" as befitted closeness to their leaders. This attracted a "better", even graduate, type of new entry. When Hitler made Heinrich Himmler their commandant there were 200 of them.

HIMMLER—HEAD OF THE SS

The rise and role of Himmler is the exemplary tale of how the "decent little man"under the impulsion of omnipotence fantasies could become one of the greatest mass killers in history. There was nothing in Himmler's early life to distinguish him from many "solid" middle-class Wilhelminian schoolboys. Born in October 1900, too late for the call-up, a son of a respected Bavarian headmaster, he was neither a battered veteran nor a victim of economic or status loss. I draw on several fuller studies [2-4] for the data on which to draw a "secondhand" sketch of this fantast, idealist, inconspicuous "backwoodsman" who gave the imprint of his ideology and power drive to his Black Corps.

Himmler's terrific "cult of manliness" must be seen as partly a function of his physical inadequacy: he was a myopic, narrow-chested fellow with a weak digestion, the laughing stock of his classmates. His youthful diaries show him much preoccupied with the yearning to be athletic, powerful and of superior self-assured bearing. The second influence was the patriarchal, strict Catholic home which made him a striver and a sexual prig, fighting against lust, guarding his pre-marital chastity and deploring relaxations of propriety in others—even the nakedness of little children! Inhibited in all social contacts, he dreams of becoming an officer. But the Reichswehr will not have him, so he joins a Free Corps while at Munich University as an undistinguished and slightly ridiculous student. In 1922 we find him in Roehm's gang, whose banner he carries into Hitler's Munich "putsch" in 1923. During the two years that the Nazi party was banned Himmler is in a "Völkische" cover organization. He is taken up as a "useful" little eager beaver by Alfred Rosenberg, the Strasser brothers and the Kaiser's last war lord, General Ludendorff—prominent early Nazis. From this contact Himmler emerges as a fully fledged Party zealot and ideologist. His lack of success in the normal world is compensated by the ego-enhancing doctrines of Hitler's inner circle that, like him, dreamt of the day of glory and preached the superiority of German genetic stock, the destined rightful heirs to world dominion. He absorbed Darré's ideas on "blood and soil" of the German settler, the saviour of Europe from lesser breeds and from the effete rule of Western and Jewish capitalists. He—Himmler—would fashion the new élite of Hitler's coming Nordic Empire, and his SS would be the seedbed. Pure in blood, procreating large blond families, they would become the knights-in-arms and frontier yeomanry of the millennial Reich.

When the Führer in 1929 conferred on his faithful henchman the title "Reichsführer SS", by now 280 strong, Himmler set about feverishly to translate Darré's and Rosenberg's ideas into practice. He sponsored an office for "Race and Settlement" problems with which was linked a pseudo-scientific research centre for inheritance, chiefly in order to select SS men and their brides on his racist model. The new breed were to be warrior-yeomen close to the earth, despising modern culture and leaving political and value judgments to their lords to whom they would give entire loyalty (Treue). It was a model compounded of the crusading Teuton knights who colonized Prussia and beyond "with fire and sword"; of Frederick the Great's giant Potsdam grenadiers—his faithful guards he would call "my children" —and of Tennyson's "Theirs not to reason why". In pursuit of this image, so clearly an idealized picture of the composite paternal object-relation (complete mastery over perfectly manly, docile hero-sons) Himmler tried to fashion the SS as a chivalrous "Order", with ideological training centres and retreats in mediaeval castles, oaths and initiations.

With this Nietzschean dream of being the grand master of the "supermen" of the future went Himmler's organizational talent. Between 1929 and 1932 the SS had grown from 280 to 30,000. Though still a tiny minority in Roehm's SA which was soon to be numbered in millions, differentiation had to occur. The chance came when an SS troop was used to suppress an intraparty rebellion. The Führer now established the Black Corps as a separate entity, with the implicit role of watchdogs over the mass party. In addition to bodyguards there now was a *Party security-service*. In 1931 Himmler had appointed Reinhard Heydrich to develop this new branch.

HEYDRICH AND HIMMLER

In Heydrich, born in 1902 in Saxony, the Reichsführer nursed up one of his most notorious and feared lieutenants. Forced to resign his (Weimar) naval commission by a court of honour on account of moral cowardice over an irregular liaison with a woman, this tall blond narcissist and status-seeker was persuaded by his ambitious mother to join the SS as a "gentlemanly enough" alternative to being a real officer. As seen by Aronson[5], Heydrich was a vindictive character with personal anti-semitism based on his step-father's alleged origins. Seeking power through his brilliant organizing talents, he built up the SS Security Service (SD) by creating an extensive personal dossier system and informer network. When Hitler came to power, Himmler, with Heydrich as his lieutenant in this area, became responsible for internal security, starting with Bavaria. They soon extended their hold over the entire police system of Germany, including Goering's secret

State Police (known by its German abbreviation of GESTAPO), a new branch of the old "legitimate" police—not a Nazi party organ. By 1934 Himmler had the Gestapo, and by 1936 the Reich's Security Police (SIPO) in his hands as a part of the SS. Now it was not only Party malcontents but the whole population who had to fear Himmler and his SD and Secret Police Chief Heydrich, promoted to SS general at the age of 30. In 1934 when Hitler decided to liquidate Roehm and his chief aides as a potential rival centre of power against himself and the army, he entrusted this task to the SS with himself at their head. This broke the power of the old SA and established the SS as the chief instrument of the Führer's will.

THE PARTS OF THE SS

(a) From the original "*bodyguard*" functions there grew not only a special "Life Guards regiment Adolf Hitler" commanded by a Free Corps swashbuckler Sepp Dietrich who is said to have shot Roehm personally. In other cities similar para-military formations performed similar security and guard functions at the sole disposal of the Party chiefs. It is from these crack units that the *Waffen-SS** was later developed—that "army within an army", all volunteers, which Himmler may have intended as a counterweight to the normal armed forces whose loyalties were always suspect. In effect, these units which grew into divisions became operationally a part of the war-time field force under military command, though administered by the SS. These troops have little to do with my theme, except that cross-transfers with the security forces (of which more below) occurred from time to time. In Himmler's mind they may have been his future dedicated élite to guard the coming Reich.

(b) The category of *general membership* of the SS also changed its functions from the early days. It became the "done thing" to join for both fanatics and (after the 1934 events) for opportunists and band-waggon climbers in all ranks of society. It functioned as a manpower reservoir feeding the specialized branches of the SS; as a source of support and prestige for Himmler's empire against the claims of numerous Party rivals who suspected and resented his spy-network. Through the many "nominal" members in business, university and professional circles, group life was radicalized and brutalized by these pace-setters

* Armed SS.

of Nazification. The influence of the general SS waned with the coming of war.

(c) *The Political Police and the Einsatzgruppen.** The incorporation of the police forces of Germany in the SS meant that Himmler had taken them out of civic responsibility under law, of which they should have been the guardians. What had been a *Rechtsstaat* (a state based on law) remained so only when it suited the Nazis. It will be recalled that Hitler was the leader of the converging streams of self-styled "outlaws" of the Free Corps and Feme murder days, who brought with them their gang morality of obedience to the leader and contempt for lawful authority. The SS, in particular, took a personal oath to Hitler and to his Reichsführer SS. This essential rejection by Nazis of the legal order and its continuing institutions for the protection of human rights was scarcely veiled. The exemption of the Nazi leadership and its coercive organ, the SS-cum-police, was made explicit when Hitler, during the Roehm purge, proclaimed himself the sole source of "law". As in all totalitarian systems, lip-service continued to be paid to the principle of legality as a sop to German public conscience and sense of order, and to present the arbitrary actions of the Nazi government and Party at home and abroad in the best light. This would also explain the great and sometimes farcical lengths to which they went to justify, camouflage or deny these actions, representing their victims as the offenders against law and order.

I do not know what proportion of the Weimar-appointed policemen had crises of conscience when the merger came. They did not have to join the SS as such, but Himmler "hoped" that those who "met his selection criteria" would do so as sworn henchmen. He was their boss. From various sources, e.g. Lerner[6] we know that a considerable proportion of Weimar police officers were already Nazis as private persons before 1930 and listed in Party élite directories, as were judges and civil servants, etc. Any others would not have lasted long in their posts after 1933. Goering has recorded his purging of the Prussian police and replacing them with SA and SS men,[7]a process Himmler and Heydrich continued. Many new men came from the (originally Party) SD, now to run the terrorist security services of the whole country—and indeed German communities abroad penetrated by Heydrich's network. In his hands ideological arbitrary ruthlessness was fused with the unquestioning, blinkered loyalty of traditional German civil service

* "Special Mission Groups".

mentality. Some of the most zealous top executives of political and racial persecution graduated to their SS heights from long professional service in the old Weimar criminal police, as for example Heinrich Müller and F. Nebe. Müller became head of the Gestapo before he joined the Party; Nebe the Chief of one of the *Einsatzgruppen* in Eastern Europe. We learn that to the terror machine doctrinal fervour came second to professionalism and reliability as "cogs"— that fateful readiness to serve any authority just because it *was* the authority.

Until the war of 1939, Heydrich's terror, exercised by the threat of sudden arrest and "protective custody" in a concentration camp, was largely against Germans, but secret SS and SD cells had been operating, long before the 1938 annexation, in Austria. These produced not only the Feme-like assassins of Austrian Chancellor Dollfuss but later many important administrators of terror, e.g. Eichmann, Globocnik and Kaltenbrunner.

When in 1939 Hitler invaded Poland, Heydrich's machinery was ready to implement his decrees. In the wake of the armies followed the *Einsatzgruppen*, subdivided into a number of *Kommandos*. These were mobile units composed of SIPO and SD(SS) men. Some commanders were SS, others career policemen. The groups were invariably headed by SS generals—some originally police, now assimilated. In addition to counter-intelligence and policing functions such as any army would set up in its rear, these special task groups had the main, but secret, mission to round up and kill all potential leaders or intellectuals who might create a Polish resurgence. As Hitler's grandiose dream of massive German settlement (Lebensraum) grew into his central war aim in the East, so the transfer and decimation of whole populations now living there became all-embracing. The army commanders had to accept and indeed provide logistic support for these activities, officially designated as operations to secure their rear from "Polish terrorists", etc. The regular army often knew and condemned the brutalities of these SS detachments whose methods at that time were those of mass shootings in remote spots over open trenches the victims had to dig first—not to mention the scenes of horror and desolation as the convoys of the doomed were corralled and herded to their destruction. Some protesting army generals lost their jobs, even though they pleaded chiefly in the name of preventing the demoralization and brutalizing of young German soldiers who were outraged by these mass murders, ordered and obviously justified by "high official personages of the SS and police"[8].

My just quoted source emphasizes the extent to which the SD had, before invasion, prepared the ground in territories containing German ethnic groups by covert organization of local armed militias ("*Selbstschutz*"). These fanatical Nazified people were used a great deal for informer purposes and for actual pogroms and shootings. Many were then enrolled in the SS for permanent police or concentration camp service. Some of the SS generals themselves are on record as fearing for the morale of their men in these operations. Some devolved as much of the killing as possible on to these local militiamen with their smouldering hatreds; or tried to mount the mass murders as if they were "lawful" military executions. One advocated fostering collective guilt: "the blood of victims will cement comradeship".[9] These patterns of *Einsatzgruppe* brutality were repeated in the West, the Balkans and Russia. Instead of ethnic Germans, local fascist groups played the role of auxiliaries to their SS masters, denouncing political opponents and especially Jews, once Hitler's decision was made to speed their extermination.

As occupation of foreign countries became static, the *Einsatzgruppen* became the security-services under a "HSSPF" (Chief, SS and police), largely independent of the governors or gauleiters, just as in Germany the SD functioned as a law unto itself, often resented by the less extreme civil administration.

(*d*) *Concentration Camp Guards.* Concentration camps (hereinafter called KZ after German colloquial usage) were set up in 1933 by Goering in Berlin and by Himmler in Dachau (Bavaria). They were manned by militant—and also often unemployed—SA and SS men now enrolled as "emergency"police to guard the many categories of "enemies" rounded up by the SD: leaders of the Left parties, editors, Protestant and Catholic clergy, liberals, but also "undesirables" of which homosexuals were a named category. The network grew rapidly after Himmler took charge in 1934. This low-prestige rabble of fanaticized or just job-seeking party-troopers had to be turned into a semblance of a smart SS body to meet his criteria. They also had to take the oath of unquestioning obedience required of all SS volunteers, in so far as they were not already SS. This made them part of the élite above the law.

Himmler appointed a rather discredited party roughneck, Eicke, his first inspector of KZs, with the task of training and indoctrination of the core staffs that would man the projected permanent camps. With totalitarian "double-think", the camps were intended to "reform" as well as detain. Dachau became the *alma mater* in which Eicke played his sinister, norm-setting role for numerous KZ officers, drawing on his own record of brutality and chicanery derived from Free Corps and Feme days, combined with an old grudge against the regular army. Not without opposition by the Reich treasury, Eicke had by 1935 created a force of 3,500 dedicated warriors on the national payroll, and based also on Sachsenhausen and Buchenwald, making a further depot at Linz in 1938. Eicke managed to induce some sense of higher mission, far above mere conscripted soldiers, in these stepsons of the regime, and also to incalculate clearly the double-standards: "clean hands" and legality, no arbitrariness but complete discipline on the surface; in reality—implacable brutality and hatred against the "enemy"—all categories of human beings Hitler had ordained as unfit to survive. Until 1939 these were largely Germans—the Jews and Gypsies came later, after which it was to be the turn of all Slavs, selected West European and Balkan opponents.

There was an unconscious understanding of the ambivalent father relation in Eicke's methods. First he gave them a distinctive badge— the skull and crossbones, proudly calling them Death's Head units (*Totenkopfverbände*) which had a pre-1933 vogue among SS.[*] To break them in, the TKV (as abridged) recruits had to undergo the worst excesses of barrack-square bashing as well as insult and humiliation, scarcely easier than that meted out to inmates. Next they would be paraded to see "official" flogging and torture of prisoners, and were watched for signs of compassion or revulsion that would be punished and derided as "dereliction of soldierly duty". Moral scruples were called weakness or "cowardice before the enemy", threatened with "dire consequences". They were all the Führer's soldiers fighting a ubiquitous enemy; their historic task must be done in the SS spirit of self-surrender without the selfishness of private emotions. And then when he had terrified, exhausted and shown them his pitiless hate and devotion to his Führer's cause, he would become all "comradely", spend the evenings plying them with beer. He knew what had to be internalized. They all called him "Papa Eicke", a great scout.

[*] And in the old Prussian cavalry, whence Britain copied it for one of its regiments.

LICENSED MASS MURDER

The turning over from being frightened underdogs to identification with their Death's Head Papa reached its fullness once these KZ cadres, always the rejects from other branches of the SS (except some Einsatz-kommando recruitment), began to operate on foreign soil, away from home influences, from some scrutiny by SS critics concerned over their poor quality. Then these men, promoted far beyond their capacities, with their old *Rabauken**-mentality, put into action Papa Eicke's real teaching. Himmler had to make a strict code for his SS to appease his critics in state, Party and army. He instituted SS courts to deal with infringements of "correct behaviour" towards detainees. They had to sign every three months that they had not mistreated any prisoners. But they knew what in fact was expected and would earn commenda-tion, and what moral obloquy and in-group contempt any suspicion of "softness" towards their "enemies" would bring upon themselves. And Himmler had instructed his SS courts to deal leniently "with offences into which the perpetrator had allowed himself to be drawn by excessive zeal in the struggle for the National Socialist idea".[10] The split in the system between the "high-minded" exponents of race policy and the reality of brutal cruelty they had conjured up in the TKV was such that the fine gentry of the SS and the Party had to project all this destructiveness into these men.

As the war drained more and more fit men away, TKV replacements came chiefly from the unfit and useless, and from those ethnic Germans in the occupied lands over whom Himmler as head of "Race and Settlement" claimed tutelage. It was also part of SS policy to sup-plement KZ manpower by letting German common criminals serve their sentences in them and employing them as "trusties" (*Kapos*) with overseer and informer functions. Just as in the Soviet "labour camp" described by Solzhenitsyn,[11] so in Nazi KZs these gentry formed a camp élite whom it paid the political detainees to appease and bribe in return for not being denounced and for a few extra scraps to eat. The Kapos had power to blackmail either way. The degradation of many inmates by entering the informer network themselves to improve or save their lives was part of this system.

The organization and horrors of life and death in the KZs are by now well known. In accordance with Nazi policy their functions varied: some were mainly detention centres; some holding camps for

* *Rabauken*—a contemptuous term by which the snootier members of the SS described the old SA roughnecks or "toughs".

the slave labour increasingly used in German defence industries; others specifically designated as extermination camps. In some KZs inhuman medical experiments were done on inmates, not only by SS doctors. The KZs were the static units "processing" the multitudes fed into them by the activities of the SS police security groups all over occupied Europe.

THE "FINAL SOLUTION" OF THE JEWISH PROBLEM

By this euphemism Hitler called the murder of every Jew he could lay his hands on. Until 1938–39 his venom, shared by many of his followers had been limited to economic and legal deprivations, bad though they were. He let many Jews emigrate. Physical violence had been mainly sporadic on the part of SA toughs. Plenty of Jews had suffered KZ treatment since 1933, but as Marxists, liberals, "degenerate" artists, etc., rather than *qua* Jews. It was not until 1941 that Hitler personally gave the secret order to include the Jews in the categories in which the Polish élite and Germany's own mentally handicapped had preceded them. It staggers the imagination to know that even the resulting Jewish holocaust was only a prelude to a much more complete "cleansing" of the world of a large part of the Russians, and doubtless Latin and other "sub-men" who littered the space the Master Race wanted, once victory was theirs. Norman Cohn has documented the process of "demonization" of Jews in Germany.[12] I had personal experience of the paranoid depths to which this delusion had eaten into many a German soul—most startlingly in Rudolf Hess.[13] Though this gigantic operation was carried out in a cold, matter-of-fact, bureaucratic spirit, I think we must assume that the majority of SS and Nazi activists shared violent racist beliefs with their Führer as their central justification and instilled them into their simpler followers.

The operation of exterminating Jewry was entrusted to Heydrich as head of the State Security office* in 1941. For some years before this, SS Colonel Adolf Eichmann had been doing the preparatory work, just as other faithful SS/SD bureaucrats had been busy on the "Roman Church" or "Freemasonry" or "Gypsy" desks. Already in September 1939 Heydrich had held a top-secret conference at which he briefed *Einsatzgruppe* commanders on their work in Poland. In addition to Poles the EGs were to round up and confine all Jews from the now "liberated" ex-German areas (Poznan, Danzig, etc.) into a few large

* *Reichsicherheitshauptamt* (RSHA), created by Himmler in 1939.

Polish towns and also concentrate Polish Jewry into these catchments. This became the action creating the "ghettoes" of which Warsaw was only the best known in Western wartime news.[14] The cover story was the "resettlement of 'alien' (fremdsprachliche) elements" beyond the boundaries of Greater German ethnic space into their "own" Gau (Nazi for province)* on grounds of racial purity and of military security. With greatest security, Himmler's HSSPFs in Poland created a series of vast KZs which were the real destination of the endless convoys which were beginning to roll east, and out of the ghettoes. Their very names still arouse a shudder—Maidanek, Treblinka, Chelmno, Sobibor—and the largest—Oswiecim (Auschwitz).

From 1941 the primitive mass-shooting over trenches of the Polish campaign was to be superseded by a well-planned military operation, with Eichmann's office as the nerve centre in Department IV B4 at RSHA. It involved, besides the various SS/Gestapo units to carry out the tracing and arrests of the victims, the co-operation of many civil officials at ministerial and local authority level; transport staffs; scientists to devise more effective ways of killing and architects to design giant crematoria. The operation, maintained at maximum tempo through more than three years, is estimated to have employed 250,000 people, not to mention the diversion of money, transport and material from shrinking military resources. Few of the many asked questions or failed to play their part. They accepted the cover stories that accounted for the goods trains overfilled with agonized human beings or the columns of "arrested" civilians trudging the streets at dawn. Such was the need for psychological denial that not only the Germans who took part in or witnessed these events were glad to believe that these were people going for resettlement" or to work in the "new Eastern factories". The stories even deceived many of the victims right up to the moment of entering the gas chambers labelled "shower-baths". But this all is now well-known and authenticated as one of the most spectacular triumphs of paranoid omnipotence fantasy when it can command blinkered and faithful administrative robots.

Economic Activities of the SS

Besides the division concerned with Reich security under Heydrich and (after his assassination) Kaltenbrunner, Himmler's SS empire

* Cf. Soviet models of Birobidjan for their Jews; or Apartheid's "Bantustan".

contained other great departments—e.g. General, Waffen SS, Legal. It also early developed its own logistic service, which under his powerful lieutenant, Pohl, grew into a vast business enterprise. Two elements of it interest us here. First, that the SS was the agency for expropriating and administering the estates of its victims, both in life and after death. "Enemy property"—Polish, Jewish or other "enemies" possessions and real estate were turned over to the Reich. So were the gigantic collections of victims' personal belongings: clothing, valuables, spectacles, children's toys, taken from them on arrival at the camps (always with meticulous receipts!)—and gold dental fillings after death. The police units and the KZ staffs were respectively involved.

Secondly, there was the growing demand for "slave labour" for industrial plants built in Eastern Europe to be out of range of Anglo-American strategic bombing; for military roads and works and indeed for the labour of the camps themselves—not limited to maintenance. Camp inmates were coerced to perform the gruesome tasks of removal and burial of the mounds of corpses, especially before the completion of crematoria. It earned them brief respite before it was their turn. For Himmler it created the conflict between faithful execution (*le mot juste*!) of his Führer's extermination decree and keeping the fitter detainees alive to work. In certain camps, therefore, selection was made on newly arrived convoys into "immediate death" (the old or enfeebled and women and children), and "fit for labour". At Auschwitz, at least, this task was in the hands of SS medical officers, who stood on the arrival ramp and pointed right or left like Roman Caesars.

In TKV hands death always won. The slave workers, whether Jews, Russians, Slovaks or Gypsies, would be so driven and so undernourished that within months they would qualify for the "final solution". With typical pedantry all KZs had sick bays, often staffed by physicians who were inmates—but always headed by a TKV man, often with minimal medical skills. This situation offered great opportunities—rarely for humaneness, nearly always for more subtle cruelty. Indeed, it was a favourite mode of disposal. It became "mercy killing" and could be certified as death from natural causes. Where inanition or ward dysentery was too slow, a shot in the back of the head or injections of lethal substances hastened them. The medical death certificates meticulously kept and sent to higher echelons were always "correct".

LICENSED MASS MURDER

Euthanasia

Hitler's first essay in mass murder was not an SS project, though some medical men who willingly co-operated—including well-known psychiatrists—were privately SS members. It aimed at freeing the nation's economic as well as genetic resources from all chronic mental patients and severe physical or mental defectives. With the usual high-minded rationalizations inside the project and complete, if inefficient, secrecy to the outside, volunteer medical and nursing teams were set up in several places; the coaches with drawn blinds began to roll and crematoria to smoke in the heart of Germany. The gruesome programme, begun in 1939 when Hitler believed his people would be preoccupied by war, had to be discontinued in 1941 owing to public outcry, not least by church leaders. By then between sixty and a hundred thousand helpless German children and adults had been murdered. But the centres continued to be used for those for whom no bell tolled: selected inmates of KZs in Germany or foreign forced labour, whether ill or merely "undesirable".[15] The programme was an early example of the lawless murderousness of the Nazi regime. Moreover, "mercy-killing" became thus another sanctified piece of double-think, while the technical lessons learnt and the machinery devised were utilized with much greater "cost effectiveness" and more secrecy in Poland. Here, together with the seasoned personnel now skilled in gassing, lethal injections, etc., they were placed at the disposal of the notorious Globocnik, HSSPF for Lublin (Poland), a leading organizer of anti-Jewish operations.

Could SS Men Withdraw?

A brief reference to this important question must be included here. At their trials SS as well as other war criminals pleaded duress,* but this was disallowed by both Allied and (later) Federal German courts. The German military code based on the older "Rechtsstaat" continued to carry a paragraph 47 under which soldiers were entitled to resist a superior's order contravening the moral and criminal codes. Obedience was to be always subject to overriding regard for the Law. What of "outlaws", the *volunteers* who had abrogated legality and sworn obedience to their Führer? There seems to have been no difficulty in

* "Befehlsnotstand"—duress under need to obey orders.

withdrawing in peacetime. Nearly 8,000 SS, including 146 from the TKV, did so in 1937 alone. In law they had nothing to fear, since the SS was, at least on paper, governed by its own code forbidding commanders to take arbitrary action against subordinates—Himmler needed powers to control his own lieutenants and maintain the "lawful" face *vis-à-vis* the outside world. Nor would he have wished to retain men no longer identified with the SS. None the less the extralegal basis of the special sections of the SS here described made them both "soldiers" under oath and above moral law in the Party sense. Humanly speaking it was the harder to opt out the deeper they were in. Indoctrination on top of original Nazi convictions made them not men who would stand up to authority—or they would not have opted for Party shelter. The worst that could happen, given the internal group *mores*, would be ignominious discharge, humiliation and chicanery. And in remoter places the bounds of the SS code were often overstepped by cruel commanders against men who "chickened out". The heirs of the Feme would not have scrupled to frame such men on false charges and have them shot or thrown into KZs. A request for transfer to a front line unit was always open; or the civic courage to question orders. In general, once the war was on and the TKV and Security SS involved in "guilty secrets", the brutalized group ethos made withdrawal, except for ill health, practically impossible—and many such men indeed broke down and not a few killed themselves.[16]

Höhne refers to the grotesque levels of self-pity which went with the "bestial deeds" of the security squads; I append a few quotations from higher SS leaders:

(a) "The people really worthy of pity were we, the liquidators, because our men were in a worse nervous condition than those who had to be shot". (Commander, EG 4a.)

(b) "How could anyone object to a few Jews being liquidated— or even to the prescribed removal of gold fillings by specialists?" . . . "I protested when it was suggested that our men became sexually excited (angegeilt) at these executions. . . . It is regrettable that over and above this unsavoury work (üble Arbeit) we also have mud slung at us when we are merely doing our duty." (Gestapo/SD commander in Minsk area, referring to criticism by his Gauleiter.)

Himmler himself showed not only much self-pity over his job but suffered increasingly from "stomach cramps". His chief of staff reported that on a visit to Minsk, Himmler nearly fainted when witnessing the shooting of 150 Jews. Later, Himmler made many speeches within the SS praising the courage and virtue of "German men" who had done these things and—"apart from a few instances of human weakness"— had "remained decent". To a crack Waffen SS unit he compared their clean job with the strain of "having to hold down hostile populations of low cultural type, to shoot, cart people about and drag howling women around"....[17]

By 1944 Himmler had achieved a mystical level of idealizing his men. To an SS college audience he spoke of the SS as alone capable of "the highest form of activity"; loyalty was all . . . coupled with the supreme virtue of obedience "which can sacrifice all pride, all honours, all that we hold dear".... Words of a Guru addressing a monastic order! Even Heydrich, not usually credited with Nazi fervour, is recorded as claiming that "posterity would one day be grateful for what the SS had shouldered as a sacrifice for the German people".

Here then was the grandiose delusional basis of the SS's mission as the chosen instrument of the saviours and cleansers of the world.

CHAPTER FOUR

THE VARIABLES SOUGHT IN THE INTERVIEWS

In this chapter I describe the gathering of the background sketched in the preceding chapters into an interview schedule of working hypotheses that was to be tested in the encounter with actual men.

I will begin by restating the purpose of my present study as questions the interview data might answer.

(1) How did my interviewed subjects compare with my wartime samples of men in terms of the relation of personality traits to Nazi fanaticism? For this part I had my already validated method for distinguishing fanatics from non-fanatics among German soldiers.

(2) An ideological fanatic or devotee is not *per se* a systematic mass murderer of helpless human beings, even though he may be a dedicated soldier or party activist. Was there anything identifiable and characteristic in the life histories of these mass killers that had favoured their descent into ever more atrocious acts of violence? As luck would have it, I was able to derive some hypotheses as to what king of people meeting with what kind of experiences were likely to become KZ or *Einsatzgruppe* terrorists before I saw my interviewees. By courtesy of the Wiener Library I studied a set of over 60 self-descriptive "party histories" written by old Nazis for their party archives in 1936, which had fallen into U.S. hands.[1] These writers were people closely matching my subjects in social and general characteristics 30 years earlier.

(3) What inner motive forces and what outer, institutional pressures and aids not only moved these human beings to volunteer for the terrorist services of the SS but kept them in their roles as either manual killers and torturers or as "armchair" executives in the system over months and years? There also arise the subsidiary questions: what happened to the inner worlds of these men after the collapse of the morale-sustaining sanctions of the regime? What modes of dealing with their burden of blood-guilt had they developed? For this part of

my schedule I used some unpublished hypotheses by Nathan Leites*
that we had discussed many years ago, unrelated to any ongoing research, but based on what we knew of Nazi and Soviet methods of
terrorism.

I shall now fill in some detail of the hypothesized variables which
were to be tested by my interviewees. I hope that this procedure will
also amplify the highly condensed statements of the previous three
chapters.

I. THE HIGH F SYNDROME

This concept, based on a set of validated ratings of personality traits
significantly correlated with Nazi fervour and fanaticism, has been
described by me in a number of papers. [2, 3, 4] At first the term "High
F" merely signified to me a high score on a set of political attitudes held
by German prisoners of war interviewed by British interrogators in
routine morale studies, already mentioned. The remarkably stable
distribution curve for the five classes or degrees of fanaticism (F for
short which could also mean Fascist) we used, followed a nearly regular bell shape (based on 1000 men between 1942 and 1944).

F I (the highest)	11 per cent
F II (Believers with reservations)	25 per cent
F III ("unpolitical", Winnicott's Y group)	40 per cent
F IV (divided, or passive anti-Nazis)	15 per cent
F V (active anti-Nazis, "democrats")	9 per cent

I drew the working hypothesis from this curve that an active political
ideology could only in part be accounted for by indoctrination and
group conformity. I assumed that the closer the ideology fitted the
given man's personality needs and dynamics, the greater would be its
emotive pull. The Nazi and near-Nazi "High Fs" were likely to be those
who, as argued in Chapters One and Two, had remained "stuck" in
unconscious paranoid or depressive positions with poor ego-strength
or sense of personal identity. I decided to interview a random sample
at depth, ignoring their "politics" which someone else would score.
The variables to be searched for in these further interviews were de-

* Nathan Leites, the author, among many other writings, of *Ritual of Liquidation*,
was a former colleague in UNESCO Social Science Division and in the RAND
Social Science Department.

signed to test this assumption. They related to background and family history and to clinically observable characteristics which as a psychiatrist I regard as the outcomes of such childhood damage.

The hope was that I would obtain meaningful and "consistent" configurations of personalities that went with High F scores. I was able to conduct, between 1942 and 1945, 138 such detailed interviews on freshly captured German soldiers, sailors or airmen, using the schedule which follows.

My *background* variables were (*a*) *demographic*: age, rank, service, educational and class status, regional, urban-rural origins and parental religious affiliations; (*b*) *psycho-cultural*: (i) which parent dominated (as well as the usual data on loss of parents from various causes); (ii) harsh or permissive home atmosphere; (iii) related to the preceding, patterns of guilt-and shame-inculcation, discipline; (iv) deeper attitudes to father, expressed directly or as reflected in evaluations of later authority figures and feelings about deference, obedience, rejections etc. (The excerpt from my interview with the air-force officer in Chapter Two, p. 37 is an illustration of this sort of data collection); (v) deeper attitudes to mother, direct or displaced. For these background data, abstracted from rich qualitative material of long relaxed conversations, I listed alternatives graded for "mental health" or "adultness" by the standards accepted by the consensus of psychoanalysts and dynamic psychiatrists.

The disposal or fate of the primary parental object-relations was expected by me to be highly significant. In other words—this was an attempt to assess how each man had dealt internally with his Oedipus situation, and with what feelings.

I predicted that there would be an internal consistency of these background data with (*c*) certain *personality traits* selected for rating. I will first list these: (i) taboo on tenderness—self explanatory; (ii) split in attitude to women: "sexual—debased" versus "pure—idealized"; (iii) cult of manliness—a shorthand term for a tense idealization of soldierly virtues, sport, comradeship—a variety of "social homosexuality", but also including evidence of overt, clinical homosexuality as the dominant sexual alignment; (iv) tendency to projection (paranoid defence), including a feeling of being persecuted, singled out, observed, etc.; (v) the varieties of disposal of primitive aggression (hate, sadism) in the subject; (vi) anxiety or insecurity, in any of its protean clinical forms, including hypochondria or fear of illness; (vii) feelings of inadequacy, inferiority; (viii) the presence of clinical depression; (ix) observable guilt feelings; (x) ambivalence; (xi) narcissism; (xii) schizoid features.

Unlike the background data which we could only infer as being present or absent, the directly observable personality traits I had selected were scored in intensity ratings of 1 (gross), 2 (perceptibly heightened) and 3 (normal limits). An exception was "Sadism" (aggression) which was recorded under headings without intensity scores like the background data: (a) overt, direct (evidence of cruelty, cold murderous, etc.); (b) harsh, domineering, threatening; (c) indifference —calm unmoved acceptance of the brutality of others and the suffering of victims. These three ratings were grouped for statistical purposes as "anti-social". Ratings: (d) "self-assertion without viciousness, stands up for himself"; (e) gentle, conciliatory, submissive; and (f) squeamish horror and guilt at suffering or brutality of others—were together classed as "social" modes of dealing with intrapersonal aggression. (On this scale our young air-force officer was rated (a)) The ranking here expresses a rising degree of moral self-scrutiny, with (d) considered the healthiest, while (e) and (f) are "civilized", if exaggerated, reaction formations against brutality. (xiii) We also recorded the man's religion, with an expectation that a high proportion of those scoring High F would be "Gottgläubig"—that specifically Nazi "belief in God" which was far from Christian.

These were the personality variables I wished to rate in order next to compare the ratings with the political or F scores obtained by another skilled interviewer, using a schedule with defined pointers to degrees of Nazi fervour. The 138 were picked for me by the chance of capture and stay in a transit centre possessing the necessary facilities for monitoring as an additional check on the interviews. Until the mass captures in N. Africa and Italy the men came from destroyed U-boats, from baled-out air-crews or were taken in our small raids (Dieppe, Norway). There was, therefore, a preponderance of "élite" personnel. A brief breakdown of the demography of our five political categories is perhaps useful.

F I were usually under 35 years old, typically of lower middle class. Rural "backwoods" origins (Thuringia, Bavaria) predominated over Prussians and big cities—very few came from Berlin and the great seaports.

F II were nearer to fervent "nationalists" of the Kaiser period; often better educated and sophisticated, they admitted some defects of the

Hitler regime but more on grounds of inefficiency or wartime short-comings than out of ethical or other conviction.

F III (the "don't knows" of the polls), the biggest fraction, was made up of minor civil servants, small artisans and farming folk, preoccupied with personal problems, home, order and the quiet life. "I don't get mixed up with all that—we've had the Kaiser, and then Hindenburg and now we have Hitler, but we still have to get the cows milked" was a typical attitude. A proportion of Regular serving soldiers and sailors came in this group.

F IV were highly ambivalent and disillusioned people who had often welcomed Hitler earlier because of the promise of order, work and a restoration of the Fatherland's prestige. They had now an emotional and ethical bias against the Nazis and the war, in which they served with loyalty and stoicism because they were "German soldiers". It was a sample overlapping in composition with F II, often over 35 in age.

F V, the active anti-Nazis, were a mixed group who had in common chiefly their consistent opposition in thought, feeling and sometimes deeds. There were trade unionists, Marxists, adherents of the Catholic and Evangelical churches, principled liberals, "aristocratic" conservatives, staunch individualists and cosmopolitans, and—the young sons of such backgrounds.

The results of comparing my personal ratings of those who scored high with those who scored low on Nazi fanaticism are set out in the Table below, as statistically examined by the method of χ^2 or tetrachoric correlations.* This picture shows a spread of the variables along a range, rather than polarization into black and white, even on those variables that turned out to be discriminating between the personalities of those rated High and those rated Low. For economy I have shortened the Table to show only the results which were statistically significant. Several of my selected variables: the traits of guilt feelings, ambivalence, narcissism, inferiority feelings, depression and schizoid splitting and parent-dominance among the background data failed to distinguish low from high by statistical standards. I had only expected "submissiveness" to be so general as not to be worth including.

The statistically valid cluster among my variables formed a most interesting and consistent configuration or syndrome of traits, the more so when I learnt four years later that the monumental American study by Adorno and his co-workers had arrived at almost the same picture

* This was carried out by Edward A. Shils, at that time on the staff of SHAEF.

TABLE I

COMPARISON OF POLITICAL, AUTHORITARIAN RATINGS AND PERSONALITY VARIABLES OF GERMAN PRISONERS-OF-WAR

| | F rating total numbers | | | F ratings as a fraction of one | | | Probability | |
	High I, II	Low III, IV, V	Total	High I, II	Low III, IV, V	Total as unity	χ^2	(0·05 or less = significant)
Man's religious adherence								
1. Roman Catholic (strict)								
2. Protestant (strict)	17	26	43	0·40	0·60	1·00	27·8	Between 0·01 and
3. Nazi (Gottgläubig)	30	5	35	0·86	0·14	1·00		0·001 (statistically
4. Atheist, etc.								significant)
5. Indifferent	18	40	58	0·31	0·69	1·00		
	65	71	136	0·48	0·52	1·00		
Father cathexis Father:								
1. Mature object choice								
2. Persisting father identification	58	52	110	0·53	0·47	1·00	10·3	0·00137 approx. (statistically
3. Partial identification								significant)
Anti-Father:								
4. Rebel								
5. Mother identification	4	20	24	0·17	0·83	1·00		
	62	72	134	0·46	0·54	1·00		
Mother cathexis								
1. Still attached to mother								
2. Transferred to female partner	32	62	94	0·34	0·66	1·00	21·5	Less than 0·00 (statistically
3. Transferred to Führer								significant)
4. Transferred to State or Service	33	10	43	0·78	0·22	1·00		
	65	72	137	0·47	0·53	1·00		

TABLE 1—*continued*

	F rating total numbers			F ratings as a fraction of one			Probability	
	High I, II	Low III, IV, V	Total	High I, II	Low III, IV, V	Total as unity	χ^2	(0·05 or less = significant)
Tenderness *Too*							6·7	0·00964
Present	37	25	62	0·60	0·40	1·00		(statistically
Absent	23	40	63	0·37	0·63	1·00		significant)
	60	65	125	0·48	0·52	1·00		
Sadism Anti-social (*a, b, c*)	42	26	68	0·62	0·38	1·00	12·63	Less than 0·01
Social (*d, e, f*)	21	46	67	0·32	0·68	1·00		(statistically significant)
	63	72	135	0·47	0·53	1·00		
Homosexual trends Gross Perceptibly heightened	46	39	85	0·54	0·46	1·00	4·1	0·04288 (statistically significant)
Normal	18	32	50	0·36	0·64	1·00		
	64	71	135	0·47	0·53	1·00		
Projection Gross Perceptibly heightened	45	30	75	0·60	0·40	1·00	0·88	0·00301 (statistically significant)
Normal	21	40	61	0·34	0·66	1·00		
	66	70	136	0·49	0·51	1·00		
Anxiety Gross symptoms Perceptible symptoms	49	43	92	0·53	0·47	1·00	4·2	0·04042 (statistically significant)
Normal	16	30	46	0·35	0·65	1·00		
	65	73	138	0·47	0·55	1·00		

Notes 1 Where the total in any column does not add to 138, it means "no inference possible" in the remainder of the subjects.

2 Very few qualified for scoring "mature object choice" in either the High F or the Low F groups under "Father cathexis".

3 The term *cathexis* means the emotional investment or linkage of or to a significant object, at conscious or unconscious level.

of the "authoritarian personality"[5] amongst American subjects as I had found in the German study here described. Unknown to each other, the Adorno team and I had selected almost identical variables on closely similar theoretical assumptions.

The syndrome of the High F German scorer, examined under the conditions described and shown in the above table, can be summarized as follows:

(1) The man was likely to declare himself "gottgläubig", or else a nihilistic atheist (this he shared with the Marxists!);

(2) He showed evidence of an unresolved bond with an internalized father-figure colouring several of his other significant traits. As defined in the project plan, this primitive identification becomes his unconscious model for dealing with his environment as if he were (a) such a punishing, dominant, even omnipotent person in relation to his inferiors (children, women, subordinates, out-groups) as well as (b) himself subject to an inner compulsion to behave with deference, obedience and submission to superiors, because they represented re-projections of this internal "super-ego" model.

I hold that some of the personality traits scored above result from the psychic "mechanisms" (as Freud called them) used to bind and deflect the hate and fear part of this internal conflict.

(3) There is a dearth of deep positive relations to maternal figures and attitudes; institutions and groups receive the need to belong and be taken care of instead.

(4) There is heightened intolerance of tenderness* with a tendency to despise and deride it. This trait I link with (3) as part of the compulsion to counteract acceptance of a female influence under the need to display

(5) The cult of manliness which in Table I I called homosexuality, and on which I shall enlarge below. Its general meaning and effect on personality should already be clear from my allusions to "Prussian virtues" in the earlier chapters.

(6) The preponderance of "anti-social" sadism is striking for the High F. We had seen a small sample of it in the remarks of our air-force officer, who, when he felt unobserved, expressed his "fun" in machine-gunning towns and also voiced his agreement with the perpetrators of

---

* This is close to the trait or variable which the Adorno study[6] called "anti-intraception", following H. A. Murray's[7] original "intraception", meaning a capacity for imaginative, empathic, emotive warmth.

the murderous policies of his government. Poles and Czechs deserved what they got for "their dirty tricks". This links easily with

(7) The tendency to project and see hostile intent outside the self, thus readily feeling persecuted, discriminated against or unjustly hated. The other does "dirty tricks", is a terrorist, etc.

(8) The last of the variables on which the study discriminated between the High and the Low fascist scores was neurotic anxiety; in the former chiefly shown by dread of their captors and by a variety of psycho-somatic symptoms indicative of psychological stress which finds a bodily outlet so as not to face the feeling itself. One may call this also a form of projection—to one's stomach or bowels—in avoidance of the shame of appealing direct for parental help or mercy.

I should also briefly stress the salient differences in the rating of the *low scores* with whom, I am sorry to say, this book is not concerned. These were less tense and defended men, who had sincere Christian beliefs or easy going tolerance; kindlier images of the fathers and *five times* as many anti-paternal Oedipal attitudes, upholding their women, and scored low on their reliance on the service (the group) as their "home".

There was less of the cult of manliness and denial of tenderness and anxiety, though military training had had some effect. Most significant was the reversal between "social" and "anti-social" ways of expressing aggression, though projectiveness was less clearly different: it was turned partly against their own fanatics and leaders and partly against the Russians—the universal bogey.

The distribution of traits was expected to be over both sides of the line drawn between high and low. Among the latter were some ex-Nazis (F IV) and many "unpolitical" dark horses who were also, after all, Germans. The feel of the low scorers on contact was very different.

What was a new finding was the configuration of traits highly correlated with Nazi fervour and contrasted with more relaxed, humane, individualized German personalities who did not hold the ideology though they often mouthed one or another aspect of Nazi indoctrination. The configuration of personality variables with Nazi fanaticism now became for me the *High F syndrome*, in most ways identical with the Adorno group's "authoritarian personality".[6] In its German variant this syndrome is a cultural artefact, rather than a genetic affliction. An illustration may help to clothe these abstractions with flesh and blood, though I must severely condense.

(No. 90 in my 138). A captured bomber pilot, Flight-lieutenant S., interviewed at length in April 1943. 25 years old then, he was single and much decorated for valour. He was proud to be descended from "old peasant stock" (echoes of "blood and soil")—the "salt of the earth." One of eight siblings, his eldest brother was killed in the First War. He claimed an "ideal family background", despite his father's poverty and subsequent compulsion to give up his farmstead. "We were strict and hardworking—not like these French who neglect their farms and live solely '*pour l'amour*'." The Italians too were contemptible. His father died when S. was 9, and his mother when he was 12. He was then in an orphanage till age 17, where he had a secondary education. The Nazi Party and joining the air force (1938) was "like coming home". He rejected his Roman Catholic faith and became "Gottgläubig". "Military, serious flying—not just sport".

From my attempt to collect a life history there resulted a long and unsolicited harangue from between clenched teeth, with intervals of biting his nails or picking at some raw spots on his face. It was a bitter attack on the British for starting the war under Jewish orders, for the R.A.F. "terror" raids (cf. Chapter Two), a degradation as compared to the Germans' humane precision bombing demonstrated over Coventry! (There was for him no irony in this.) "Yes Germany *had* to burst out—a soldierly people of 100 million, thank God, will not be ground down" (demonstrated by his thumb on the table).*

"When Russia is liquidated—then mercy on this island!" "We will descend on you with every device—your few troops are not battle-seasoned!" When he uses the words "mein Führer" his voice drops almost to a love sigh. He talks of "passionate love" for him. "He has made us great and created a worthy armed service."

There is a pitying superiority in this man's tone when explaining how forgiving and magnanimous Germans are: they have not avenged themselves on the French for the Ruhr,† but indeed treated them with kid gloves. "Of course if there are those fools who cut military cables, etc. (he meant French Resistance men), they must expect to be put against the wall."

On the whole he is quite patronizingly kind about the U.S. and British as "soldiers", but deplores the follies of their democratic system. No, thank God, he is not married—what would a flying man do tying himself up . . .

* Even Hitler never boasted of more than 70 millions!

† The French occupation and "terror" there after World War I are meant.

there are "little girls"—lots of them, for the Forces are rooted in the population—of course he could choose any of them! Pity—those spots on his face —"some impurity of the blood—I won't let them heal". Fussy about his teeth which flash. Always a mountaineer—the good mother earth up there, but none of that degenerate St Moritz life. "We are hard—hard on ourselves— *draconic* and decisive in running our affairs", he says. "Look how radically we have dealt with the Jews—at last someone has seized that nettle firmly."

His restless, anxious and overbearing behaviour; his dogmatic and arrogant lecturing on the superiority of German arms and soldierly prowess with which he felt himself at one; his love-sick adulation of Hitler as if he was a personal love-object; his denigration of almost every other nation (including Austrians and British); his lack of any human love object but instead a worship of nation, service and Party; his complete endorsement of cruelty and inhumanity towards enemies—and especially Jews—give him a very high score on all the High F syndrome criteria: Gottgläubig + Oedipus solution (Father cathexis): 3 (because not a completely docile, but rather "mutinous" type, common among Nazis); Mother cathexis 3 (to Führer and also could be 4); Tenderness taboo +; Sadism (*a*); Manliness cult (HS) I.; Projection 2 (not attributing *all* aggression and hostility to others, but heightened to include Jews and French); Anxiety I. Also Narcissism I. Libido Split I. Doubtless his insecure and orphaned background helped to form this picture.

Space does not permit citing other vignettes of this series, and I will only add that as the war progressed to the increasingly glaring disadvantage of German arms, the other side of the paranoid attitude became more obvious. Thus in a captured private diary of a petty officer from a U-boat, the entry for 26.1.45 (when the Soviet forces were capturing the Baltic littoral) written at Gydnia, near Danzig:

> I always ask myself: whatever crimes have we Germans committed, why must it be precisely we who have to suffer all these horrors? Precisely our people, the most industrious and cultivated country of the world? Envy and malice, the revenge of these thrice-accursed Jews from whose greedy claws we have freed ourselves, who sought to poison our nation like a plague spot. And in the rest of the world they have succeeded. I believe in God and therefore in our victory, in our just cause, and that one of these days these scum and war criminals will be bitterly punished for it. (My translation— H. V. D.)

The passage occurs at the end of a harrowing account of German refugees being hurriedly evacuated by sea before the Soviet advance. We shall see this self-pity for being persecuted as a recurring theme in the SS men I interviewed for the present report. Other "High Fs", interviewed in the closing period of the war, threatened to "go over to the communists" and pillage and destroy, in a fantasy of scorched earth vindictiveness, comparable to Kern's statement (quoted in Chapter Two) that he could not bear the collapse of his vision, but must destroy.

Such was the psychological model of the High F syndrome which formed the basis for my assessment of the SS killers.

2. The Biographies of 61 Nazi Party "Old Fighters"

My scrutiny of a set of "naïve" self-descriptions written in 1936 by militants with an eye to winning Party merit not inhibited by captivity and fear of the disfavour of enemy authorities, came as a valuable source of insights early in the present project. Several elements constitute this value: (*a*) the concentration of these men on their subjective motivations for their Nazi party activism and on their party "career-development"; (*b*) a fair degree of demographic detail about themselves; (*c*) the fact that some 21 out of the men reported themselves as volunteering for the SS, including five who specified KZ guard and auxiliary police duties. This study, including my content analysis of their self-presentation to their own leaders, gave me a scale or model for very similar life histories of my present sample.

The 100 or more *curricula vitae* came from the Hesse party headquarters. Thirty-nine were illegible or too short, which left 61. The reason given by the Party bureaucrats for collecting these essays was the accumulation of archives for a Party history of the time before Hitler's accession to power. Clearly, by some of these high-flown 2-6-page-long descriptions of their own doughty deeds, as well as praise and adulation of their local and national leaders, the veterans hoped to impress the latter and gain recognition or perhaps paid jobs now that Hitler was in power.* These were indeed revelations of the ways of thought and feeling of mostly simple Nazis including reactions to post-First-War stresses. Here, I said to myself, were the sort of men whom 6-8 years later I had interviewed as prisoners-of-war, but now writing as they wished to appear to their father-figures. As mentioned,

---

* W. Scheffler, in a personal communication, suggests that the Party's real intention in collecting these personalia from these "Rabauken" elements was to keep tabs on them after the purges and virtual eclipse of the SA, whose task was done.

VARIABLES SOUGHT IN THE INTERVIEWS

all the writers lived in Hesse-Darmstadt, a mixed rural/urban area, parts of which were under French military occupation at one time after World War I.

I shall now briefly abstract the findings of this study as a source of new variables.

The data below are based on 61 biographies, arranged in simple enumerative tables.

TABLE II

AGE AT FIRST JOINING, OR FIRST ACTIVITY IN PARTY

I (aet 13-17)	II (18-21)	III (22-25)	IV (26-30)	V (31-35)	VI (over 35)	VII (Unknown)
18	9	10	3	3	12	6

This Table shows a bimodal shape: the under-21s and the over-35s, typical of the "old soldiers" and the "hungry children" intakes into the Party.

TABLE III

CLASS BY OCCUPATION OF FATHER

I Landed aristocracy, former Imperial officers, etc.	NIL	
II Professional, academic, higher civil service, university students	4	
III Merchants, hoteliers, business executives	2	
IV Minor civil service, clerks ("White Collar")	7	
V Artisan, small trader, shop assistant	20	(33%)
VI Skilled industrial workers, truck drivers	10	
VII Rural labourer, small holder	4	
VIII Unskilled urban worker (e.g. watchman, messenger)	2	
IX Non-commissioned regular armed Forces	5	
Unascertainable	7	
	61	

TABLE IV

URBAN/RURAL, FORMATIVE YEARS

City over 60,000	Smaller towns	Rural	Unknown
5	42	7	5

TABLE V

INFERENCE ON HOME INFLUENCES*

Authoritarian, father dominated	Relaxed, egalitarian	Broken home, orphanage
11	1	1

The remaining 48 documents could not be assessed for this factor, though many expressed views typical for the High F syndrome.

TABLE VI

RELIGIOUS AFFILIATIONS

This was also a failure: There were: 1 sincere evangelical; 2 sincere R.C.s; 1 "atheist" and 9 "Gottgläubig". The remaining 48 could not be scored. The proportions are nonetheless suggestive.

We now come to more central factors in my search for motives impelling the writers to join and "suffer for" the young Nazi cause. Of their background stress I abstracted the following list, mostly concerned with families of origin, but not entirely.

*An attempt to abstract data comparable to my interviews—not very successful.

VARIABLES SOUGHT IN THE INTERVIEWS

TABLE VII

SOCIAL STRESS

1. Front line wartime soldier feeling disgraced (This group is almost exactly that of Age Groups III, IV, V, Table II.)	15
2. Unemployed, family impoverished	9
3. Expulsion from occupied zone with loss of security	20
4. Cannot stop soldiering ("finest hour" motive)	5
5. Too young for war service and making up for it	21
6. Identification with father's views	7
7. Protest against father's views	7

(Obviously some of the cohort scored under several headings, e.g.
1 and 4, or 2 and 3, or 5 and 6, etc.)

We next come to the more personal or inner motivations, pointers to which were provided by the manifest or latent content of the essays.

TABLE VIII

PERSONALITY POINTERS

(a)	Submissive character, hero-worshipper	22
(b)	Need for affiliation and gang comradeship	28
(c)	"Manliness", love of being a soldier	18
(d)	Anti-bourgeois, anti-older generation rebel	13
(e)	Smarting under national humiliation and weakness	19
(f)	Paranoid scapegoating (further analysed in Table IX)	43
(g)	"Millennial" fantasies and hopes	10
(h)	Urge to act out brutality, sadism, love of brawls	26
(i)	Economic or status gain by joining Party	4
(j)	Need for good order and discipline	9
(k)	No clues	2

Again, there were often several combinations of these factors, such as (b) (c) and (j), but also of (d) and (f), (e) and (f) and so on. The combination (e) and (f) made me cast my net a little wider, and I constructed the next table out of 58 mens' ratings for paranoid scape-goating as under:

TABLE IX

HATE PROJECTION TARGETS

1. Solely general anti-Semitism ("Jewish poison", etc.)	17
2. Solely anti-Marxist and anti-democrat	11
3. "Economic" anti-Semitism ("Jews have all best jobs")	3
4. Anti-capitalism ("people's" or national socialism)	7
5. Ethnocentric or undifferentiated generalized hate (Jews, Marxists, Catholics, Allied powers, "un-German", etc.)	25
6. Anti-Versailles, anti-Dawes, anti-Young plans (i.e. Allied reparation schemes)	13
7. No inference possible	6

Though there was some overlap in these categories, they seemed to divide the predominant attitudes into economic, ethnocentric and anti-victors groups. I have to resist the temptation to quote examples of all the categories. Some general observations may however be useful.

(a) The most rabid "pure" anti-Semites described themselves as having already been such before encountering the Nazi party, and joined because the Party affirmed their attitudes and promised action against the Jews.

(b) There was in Table VIII under rubric (h) the group whose accounts of their service and affiliation to the party (usually in the SA) were almost entirely devoted to detailed and vivid descriptions of brawls and violent action against opponents, with few Party clichés. These men tended to dehumanize their enemies: "The Jew", "The Commune" (meaning socialist or communist groups); "The Blacks" (in this context denoting the Roman Catholics)—even in small towns where they would know many of their opponents personally. Those who described themselves as "now serving as KZ guards", i.e. as "auxiliary police" of the SS, displayed the greatest gloating, enjoyment of blood drawn from "the commune" in the whole collection. They were the "Rabauken".

(c) Any injury or occasional death inflicted on the Nazi groups was invariably described as having been "provoked" by the "Reds" who were then "crazed beasts", "rabble". Police actions, including prosecutions against the Nazis, were nearly always called "terror". This, we should recall, was when the Nazis were in open defiance against the Weimar regime.

(d) Some of the more literate histories show an escalation of brutality from mere marching or eviction of hecklers at meetings to the use of coshes, pride in secret "arsenals" including pistols, in pursuance of "gaining power in the streets". The picture I gained of welding these local SA and SS groups (which at first were under the same leadership) into an increasingly tough, vindictive and also disciplined body by constant marching in uniform, with drums and band, mass rallies and shared memories of people killed on both sides, was impressive evidence of how a group induces regression (here called "hardening") and a sense of persecution in individuals.

(e) The effect of the annual Nuremberg party-rallies, when detachments of local party organizations marched past, were inspected and harangued by Hitler, was impressive. A good proportion of the writers stress the "unforgettable", magical moment when Hitler looked (or they felt looked) into their eyes, or squeezed their hand. The merging of the "only a little man with my childlike faith" in the collective of the drumming, stamping, great parade shouting "Siegheil", with the aspect of the radiant figure on the dais with its massed flags, is stressed again and again as the supreme experience of devotion and self-surrender for the sake of which the writers were prepared to suffer persecution by the Weimar regime and by the opponents when back home again.

Anything so elevating to one's sense of corporate power, and so healing of narcissistic wounds, must be good, and all its opponents and detractors bad.

3. The SS Fraction of the Old Fighters

The likeness of some of the 61 pre-1933 histories to those I had obtained from my sample of sentenced killers made me review closely the records of 21 Old Fighters who recorded membership of the SS. There were four who were KZ guards by 1933 (the year Hitler became head of state), one who went to an SS officer school (Junkerschule

Vogelsang); one, a senior man, who joined Himmler's SD, and so on. Here were similar men in the fullness of their Party fervour, flushed with recent political victory and more than 30 years younger than their confrères when interviewed by me. I thought it likely that my clients would have felt many of the same emotions as they eagerly offered themselves to the SS. I subjoin Table X of how they came out on the variables I used. I shall quote some of the more characteristic sentiments of a few, in default of obtaining such avowals from my own sample. The lower-case letters, figures or roman numerals in the columns are those denoting my variables in Tables III, VII, VIII and IX.

While in most of the statements an undercurrent of anti-Semitism could be detected or inferred, the SS fraction in Table X was at this epoch more overtly concerned with "the Reds" or "the Blacks" in various forms as the hate targets. Doubtless this was because during the time of the struggle for power both local indoctrination and Party focus was on those who opposed them: the identification of all such enemies with the "Jewish world conspiracy" was latent. That 9 of the 21 SS men were inhabitants (some expelled) of the French occupation zone also stresses the xenophobia of that time.

Some excerpts from the statements will make the Table more real, e.g.

Case 7. "Father came back from four years' military service with poison in his heart" and became a socialist, later communist party member. The son (the writer) led a communist youth group; his brother was in "Spartakus",* but the "Reds" tried to frame him. So both young men switched to Nazi discussion groups. "I was too young, but just the feeling and blood made me find my ideal and my longing in *Germany*!" "A peculiar prickling in the blood" when the Deutschland anthem was played, but above all the "thought of the Führer" and the *person* of the Führer". He joined the Party at 17. Mentions how after beating up Jews "we followed them right into a neighbouring farm". "The group leader was always 'Papa' to us." His own father boxed the lad's ears for belonging to the Nazis, aged 19.

As SS he guarded Hitler personally once for a meeting, and helped him on with his coat. "A fanatical veneration like a will to full surrender." "I wonder if he noticed what went on in me as I helped him?" . . . "We had broken with *everything*; nothing could any longer impress us except our Führer and his Idea. . . ." "The holiness of his idea . . . and he found believing disciples. . ." "that meeting was more like Divine Service. . . ." When Hitler

* A militant communist group of 1918-20.

TABLE X

SS MEMBERS AMONG OLD PARTY FIGHTERS (1936)

Serial no.	Year of birth	Class origin	Social stress Table VII	Motivations Table VIII	Hate targets Table IX	Dates of Party & SS affiliation
6	1882	VI	(1) (2) Ex-Navy: lost job as "Nationalist"	(e) Soldier, disgrace (f) Need for order (j) Scapegoats	(5) All Left and Jews	1924 Party, SS Joined SD
7	1910	V	(7) Father returned from war as "Red"	(a) Hitler-worship (d) Anti-bourgeois (f) Scapegoats	Mainly (2) Anti-Marxist	1926 SS—1932
12	1909	V	No evidence	(a) (b) (c) (f) (g) (h) "The 1000 Year Reich"	Mainly (2) Anti-Marxist	1923 SS Officer School
16	Ex-soldier ? date	V	(1) (3) Deported from French Zone	(b) (c) (e) Very ungushing	No evidence	Pre-1923 SS soon after
17	1905	V	Mainly (5) and (6)	No detail Very ungushing	Anti-Weimar	Early Party Full time SS 1935
19	1910	VI	(5) (7) Father was local Comm. Party boss	(a) (b) (c) (f) (h)	Mainly (2) but also (5)	Party 1927 SS 1931
20	1898	IV	(1) (4) Free Corps Feme man	(b) (d) (f) (h) mainly	Mainly (1) Also (6)	Party 1921 SS and Police ? date

TABLE X—*continued*

Serial no.	Year of birth	Class origin	Social stress Table VII	Motivations Table VIII	Hate targets Table IX	Dates of Party & SS affiliation
24	1909	VI	"Transfer from Marxist camp"	Mainly (*a*) and (*j*) ("order")	Entirely Marxists	Party 1927 SS but left for SA!
29	1906	V	(3) Deported from French Zone (6) National fervour	All factors! but (*h*) is high	(5) Rabid Hates everybody	Party 1924 SS "Major", Death Head; KZ service in 1933
30	1898	VI	(1) Old cavalryman Hate of employers (3) French Zone (5)	(*d*) Hates old bourgeois parties (*f*) Very paranoid No evidence	Mainly (2) and (4)	Party 1927 SS 1931 Ranking
31	1886	V	No detail, inn-keeper of Party HQ	No evidence	Mainly (6)	Party 1928 SS KZ guard 1933
32	1910	V	(6) Son of above	Entirely factual, at least (*h*) ? (*i*)	? No evidence	Party 1928 SS KZ guard 1933
35	1907	V	(2) Unemployed, sacked as Nazi	(*b*) Gang solidarity (*f*); (*i*) Jobs in Party	Mainly (2)	Party & SA 1925 SS 1929
37	?	?	No detail Party and SS	Says "always good member"		Party 1926 SS 1931

TABLE X—*continued*

Serial no.	Year of birth	Class origin	Social stress Table VII	Motivations Table VIII	Hate targets Table IX	Dates of Party & SS affiliation
43	1905	?	No detail	(a) Führer's will (c) (f) Very rabid (h) Very strong	Mainly (1) Also (2) and (6) Extreme hater	Party ? SS 1925 Corporal
46	c. 1900	IV	(3) Deported from French Zone (6)	(b) (f) Anti-French	Mainly (2) (6)	Party 1922 SS 1929
53	?1910	III	No evidence, well-off	(c) "Hitler's soldiers". (f) (h) Strong	Mainly (1) and (2)	Party around 1927 SS 1930
55	1903	II	(3) French Zone dweller, well-off	(a) (c) (f) (i) Status in SS	(2) Mainly anti-Red and anti-R.C.	Party 1926 SS 1927
56	1898	VI	(1) "Old Soldier" Shunned by workmates as Nationalist	(a) (b) V. strong need. (f) (i)	(2) Mainly anti-worker (4) Also "Socialists"	Party 1922 SS 1924 "Officer"
61	1908	II	(3) French Zone dweller (5) Missed being soldier	(b) (c) (e) (f) (h)	(5) (6)	SS 1926 Corporal in University coll.
63	1906	IV	(3) French Zone dweller	? "Werewolf" at school	Mainly (2) (6)	Party 1928 SS 1932 University

suffered the 1932 electoral defeat, No. 7 wrote: "Best smash everything to pieces . . . rage sought a discharge . . . so when I passed a shop . . . 6-7 Jews stood impudently blocking the sidewalk; by-passing simply didn't come into question—so I just sloshed the owner. . . ." He cannot understand the action of the Weimar police in warning his group leader for a "harmless" statement: "When it hopefully smells of blood and iron we shall all be in on it. . . ." Or when No. 7 himself had shot an opponent in a street battle and was arrested, he complains that he was "treated like cattle". The socialists' attacks on Nazis are always "cowardly murderous hands" of "the Red mob".*

(In 1934 not only Roehm, but other former Nazi luminaries like Strasser and Heines were liquidated by Hitler.) This is how No. 7 comments after fulsome support for and cruel gloating over the Führer's act; he says "They were destined to die before they were even properly ('richtig') born."

We note the escalation from sentimental readiness to defend his Führer to using firearms against the "enemy", whosoever is so deemed —even old Party members. The next interesting case for our purposes is:

No. 20. Born in 1898 in West Prussia as son of a bailiff. The writer was a demobilized sergeant (Feldwebel) who felt the disgrace of defeat and blamed "the Jews" who had "dragged everything that could be sacred to a German into the mire". He re-enlisted to "defend my homeland against the Poles". He was in an "illegal" defence organization called "Schutz-und-Trutzbund" ("Defence & Defiance Association") from 1919 to 1921 when he became a Nazi with a very early Party number (this ranked high!). "I was the first to undertake anti-Jewish and 'Völkisch' propaganda in my town S. . . ." He even indulged in scuffles with Jewish holiday makers on the promenade at a Baltic seaside resort. An early member of the SS, he joined the police as a Nazi "plant", and used his position to inform the SS and even lent his pass to the assassins of the Weimar statesmen Erzberger and Rathenau. "The successfully accomplished affair Erzberger gave us a great boost . . . in our parlance he was 'executed' ." He also tried to blow up a statue of the (Jewish) poet Heine. "I was proud to have been associated with Kern in the Rathenau execution" ("dabei gewesen zusein"—leaving his exact role a little vague).

One cannot imagine this man to have had any loyalty problems when Himmler took over the German police forces.

No. 29. Born in 1906, this man writes as a "Sturmführer" ("junior lieu-tenant") and instructor for his troop of 8 SS men. "We need no thanks, we remain fighters . . . our memorial is the Reich . . . in grandeur, might and

* We recall Gumbel's analysis of the relative figures of killings by "Left" and "Right".

majesty (Herrlichkeit) ... which we liberated at the 11th hour." We learn that his home was in the French zone, a place of ... "Marxist darkness ... the tread of "Welsch"* soldiers, German front fighters beaten and arrested by foreign soldiery ("Soldateska"—a Nazi cliché) ... German women and girls raped, partly by niggers and Asiatics. ..."† He is incensed at Schlageter's death (executed by the French for terrorism and sabotage). "I was proud to be the first SS man in the occupied zone. ... Our Flag was inscribed 'May an avenger arise from our bones ... may they hate us so long as they fear us'." "And this became fact ... wherever our SS troops appeared it became the joy of those with a spark of patriotism and the terror of our opponents." "They were real chaps ('Ganze Kerle') ... every night as I donned my brown shirt I felt ... this is my shroud (Totenhemd) ... we have closed our account with life ... we wear the death's head. ..." He greatly relished this sense of being an avenging man of death, so paranoid that he detected a "mocking smile" on policemens' faces. He recalls the "flaming speeches" at the summer solstice festival (when early Nazis and Völkisch were apt to congregate on local hill tops and light bonfires—H. V. D.), of how Nazis were the heirs of 1813, and how theirs was "the sacrifice of the noble in spirit". Germany was "democratically infested" ("verseucht") ... the crowds in Frankfurt who opposed (or rather whom the Nazis interfered with—H. V. D.) are described as "sub-humanity" ("Untermenschentum") "the impudence and cowardice of this brood...." The SS are his fellow "sufferers" ("Leidensgenossen") hated by the Jews, the "internationals" and the authorities ("Behörden") ... "mocking criminal faces "jeered at him from a train ... Germany was full of "Judenknechte" (serfs of the Jews) ... "Jews, Welsch and Reds" were as one in their chicanery of Nazis. Perhaps this man's greatest indignation is reserved for a Catholic priest who had blamed the Nazis for the death of a young SA man in a street battle. When this cleric also refused to allow an SS funeral ceremony to follow the Catholic burial rite, our writer launches into a veritable millennialist's threat and curse of this "false priest". "If our Lord Jesus Christ were to come again on this earth ... He would chase such false priests out of the Temple." Our man claimed to be a good Catholic.

We again note the spiralling of this man's sadism. As his SS group grew, by 1929, he mentions being "merciless" as his troop's way of dealing with opponents. "The Jewish question was my favourite topic." The opposing groups are always either "cowards" or else "paid by international Jewry". When he is sentenced for a breach of the peace he is furious—it leads to the sentence "This murderous state, this Jews' republic, must be annihilated (vernichtet)!"

---

* German for "gallic" or French—always pejoratively used.

† The stationing of French colonial troops in the Ruhr was greatly resented by Germans.

LICENSED MASS MURDER

About the time when Hindenburg* was re-elected in 1932 and the Weimar government forbade the SA and SS to parade in uniforms (possibly made them illegal) he writes: "The Reds in his (Hindenburg's) entourage used their chance against us." He calls the prohibition against the SS wearing uniform and acting as stewards at meetings "an act of terror". It was the Jewish double-dealers who had persuaded the despicable German public not to vote National Socialist. This brings him now to include "Spiesser" (scornful term for conventional, conservative citizens, not unlike our "square") among his rich bouquet of hated categories of mankind.

On the morrow of victory, 1933, he is already armed and helping to round up and beat up his opponents, as an "auxiliary" policeman, with a special loyal homage to Himmler not left out of his document. He is seen next in charge of an early KZ for active politicians of the Left. Gloatingly and with contempt he describes how in that salubrious environment they changed and "confessed Adolf Hitler to be their true leader".

This man illustrated how the intensity of multivalent hate, and its paranoid projection would become constellated into a virtuous and superior sense of a reforming, cleansing mission, not least against his own contemptible fellow citizens. The passages about the uniform with the death's head as his own funeral shroud, and about the "noble suffering" of his companions are, I think, of great significance. There is a chilling sense of murderousness in this primitive sado-masochism, the reality behind that horrendous German concept "Kadavergehorsam", cadaver obedience, constantly bandied about throughout the Third Reich. It was easy to feel what Freud meant when he attributed the aggressive tendencies in man to a "Death Instinct".

The SS group of 21 were not alone in those mixed expressions of submission and violence. Equally florid Führer-worship and delight in recording their aggressive fantasies were found in the autobiographies of many others of the 61. In this study of the old fighters we could get some idea how mass killers might have become possible in Nazi Germany. It also afforded a glimpse of what sentiments they hoped would please their Party bosses.

4. Terrorism as a Way of Life

In Chapter Three I said that there was a difference between the sporadic (although at times roughly co-ordinated) violence of SA groups (and

* A revered father-figure, Field-marshal of the Kaiser!, who (like Eisenhower in the U.S.A.) served as President of the Weimar Republic until 1933.

their socialist and communist opponents' militant formations), and the long-term, quasi-professionalized role of a KZ guard, a member of the Gestapo or of the *Einsatzgruppen* which functioned routinely and mainly in cold blood, much as any "state enterprise". It was the wish to understand how men at various levels in this organized "job" could cope with its destructive and murderous reality which made me gratefully take up Leites's theoretical scheme for use in interviews with terrorists. I will outline this schedule as adapted by myself in searching for significant factors in my interviews. The assumption was that Europeans with 1500 years of Christianity behind them, however hardened and outwardly unconcerned they seem, have had to achieve a step-by-step psychological adaptation to killer roles. The two preceding schedules could take us as far as understanding in some degree how a proportion of German males had been motivated to cross the threshold of being considered for terrorist roles.

It will be apparent that some of these motivations carry over in more organized or "chronic" form into the inner capacity, the dynamic to sustain the role activities demanded. We have seen that the SS authorities concerned, from Himmler downwards, were aware of the problem and had planned institutional and leader support by indoctrination, gradual "inoculation" and guilt deflection methods to deal with it. In the final analysis it is the individual terrorist, manual or administrative, who has to adapt socio-psychologically to the demands of his task.

Here then is my classification (based on Leites) of possible ways in which the "practice" of officially sanctioned terrorism may meet the inner needs and stresses of these people.

I. CONSCIOUS FACTORS: These all depend on the experience of the leadership as symbols of the "good" aspect of the ambivalent father image, and on positive identifications with its purposes and ideology.

1 *Submissiveness:*

    (*a*) "Cadaver obedience", idealized as the highest virtue.
    (*b*) Feeling a dread of departing from the Führer's will.
    (*c*) Being praiseworthy in being totally loyal and punctilious in whatever is ordered; earning promotion.

2 *Aggression and hate:* in this context not repressed.

    (*a*) Avenging past wrongs and humiliations done to the group (nation, class, family) by the victim's group, real or invented.

(b) Identification with omnipotent power and superiority.

(c) Proving hardness and tough manliness.

(d) Experiencing conscious sadistic pleasure in cruelty, including sexual urges and "childlike" spontaneity of doing what one fancies.

II. MORE UNCONSCIOUS FACTORS: Here we assume that the repressed or split off, denied relation to inner bad objects is receiving substitute expression and satisfaction.

3 *At Paranoid (Projective) Level*, in which guilt and badness are projected to others.

(a) Victims as despised, sub-human, representing a repressed dependent weak self.

(b) Victims as disturbing, demonic, powerful, representing both split-off threatening father and own parricidal hate (devil inside).

(c) Victims as vermin or infection, requiring "cleansing"— symbolizing bad "anal" and sexual self.

(d) Fear of own authorities as ruthless, hence need to conform (overlap with 1b and 2b).

4 *At Depressive Level*

(a) Terror as denial of conscience and guilt—"bravado" or defiance, "going the whole hog" with the damned.

(b) Paradoxically, terror "from a sense of guilt"—relief to kill a scapegoat and not the really hated figures. (cf. Crime and Punishment).

(c) Terror as means to break tedium, sense of unreality, affectlessness, pointlessness, "depression".

(d) Terror to escape from thought, words, doubt into "action" (especially in conjunction with 3b—fear of superiority of victims at level of encounter).

(e) Terror (killing) as defence against despair and suicide (a variant of 4b).

This table could also be read as implying various forms of ego-weakness, of curing a sense of personal impotence by exerting naked power on helpless victims by shared and sanctioned group action.

In a further table Leites classified also the kinds of terror practised: with or without torture; with "bare hands" or in elaborate de-personalized ways; with or without mockery at the victims: e.g. as "sport" or as "pleasure". Part of Leites's analysis was concerned with the typical Soviet (Russian) legal principle of obtaining admissions of *guilt*, with the need therefore to "crack" or "break down" resisting victims. No such semblance of quasi-judicial process remained during the Nazi mass exterminations. The official policy was "humane", i.e. rapid impersonal "despatch", conveyor-belt fashion. The individuals' acts of cruelty and fiendish inventiveness of physical and moral torture and chicanery were "not in the regulations". We knew that they were condoned, as "zeal" in line with the utter dehumanization of the victim classes. I have described some of the efforts of the SS machine to mitigate guilt and despair in their "manual workers", almost to maintain "face".

Such efforts are variants of *psychological denial*, partly for the sake of the outside image of the terror operations, but easing self-deception for the men whose sense of identity was so greatly a matter of how their milieu saw them. I summarize some variants:

(*a*) Euphemisms: "Final solution" for genocide; also "resettlement", "special treatment"; the terror as a "cleaning-up operation"; securing the army's rear.

(*b*) projecting responsibility "upwards" until nobody, not even Himmler, but only the Führer's will is saddled with the guilt. The plea of "only obeying orders under oath and duress" as a little cog.

(*c*) Group division of labour: Eichmann "only arranged the transports"; somebody else "only kept order"; or "only" helped to push the victims into the gas chambers ("never killing anyone personally"); or "only" turned on the gas jets, etc. This can result in a welcome sense of "only a little man" doing a routine, concentrating on efficiency, never on the result.

(*d*) Thus terror operations become "normal" jobs, as already hinted earlier—like a factory routine that "happens" to be connected with an abattoir or a crematorium.

(*e*) Misdemeanours or hostility are fastened on the victims to lighten guilt and justify aggressive action: if an inmate "complains" (even correctly by regulations) he is deemed insubordinate; if he is caught stealing or bribing to get a little extra food, he becomes a criminal—

so temptations are made available. The famous plea of "shot while trying to escape" is in this area. The victims are labelled "terrorists" or plotters.

(*f*) Terror represented as "reprisals" against others: this is applicable both for *Einsatzgruppen* in occupied villages, or for KZ personnel *vis-à-vis* all inmates of a barrack or a section where someone has broken real or imaginary regulations.

(*g*) The fiction that the victim has "really" hurt himself, and in any case "deserves" his suffering.

(*h*) Falsification of death records, of a quasi-medical kind, which are formally ratified by a legal representative who merely signs without inquest. Alternately, at a later date—*no* records are kept. "Who knows what happened in the far-off Polish forests."

Such fictions help to protect the individual terrorists' separate self-image, for example, *vis-à-vis* their parents or their wives. "Fritz is doing something terribly secret and important somewhere in the East."

In addition there must be, however, more effective mechanisms without so much denial and fiction. For these we can only be on the look-out during the interviews. We know from the literature how much individual and group bravado, guilt defiance, sense of being a privileged élite with a special mission, and downright terror of SS sanctions against themselves kept these KZ teams together.

PART TWO

CHAPTER FIVE

THE FANATIC?

INTRODUCTORY

Now that we have reached our interview material, a few indications of how this was obtained are in place.

Permission to proceed was negotiated at a high governmental level between our Trustees and the Federal embassy in London. In due course the names of prisoners in a number of German gaols who had volunteered to speak to me came through to me via the Embassy. I now made final dates with the governors of the prisons concerned, which, thanks to the reliability of the modern car, I could keep throughout. I have elsewhere expressed to those gentlemen of the Federal German service my warmest gratitude for their unstinting help and friendliness in putting quiet, comfortable rooms at my disposal as well as the official dossiers, court proceedings and judgments by the various High Courts of the German Länder governments in whose jurisdiction the various men were tried, sentenced and kept in custody.

I had, in several cases, already some advance information on the roles and deeds for which these interviewees were charged as criminals, by reading newspaper files on individual Nazis, kept in the Wiener Library, London. In passing I should like to stress the excellent level of objective reporting of the court proceedings by organs of the German press which tallied to a surprising degree with the official documents.

I started on each man by reading these documents so that I had the objective accounts of their histories and indictable offences, duly elicited according to the rules of evidence. In addition, each man had been invited to write for me his own *curriculum vitae* and his subjective statement of his part in the events in which he was implicated according to the criminal charges. These two accounts will precede the report on the interview(s) made by myself. They will be condensed summaries, as the official dossiers run into many pages, and are repetitive (e.g. witness's statements and examinations). My own reports were dictations from notes made at the time, and recorded within hours. It was not permitted to take recording apparatus into the prisons. To this extent the accounts of my interviews fall short of the most rigorous requirements of psychiatric research technique, though they are comparable to the normal interview material on which most clinicians in our profession would base responsible diagnoses, including giving evidence in a court of law.

The interview technique is, save that it was in German, the same as I have used and perfected over 40 years of consulting practice. While the elaborate schedule of variables I am searching for is in my mind—even before me in brief tabular form as I sit with my respondent—the interview is unstructured and free from direct questioning, and the "answers" on which I feel able to record the presence of a certain trait or factor in the background or history may emerge as a result of a number of communications scattered through the conversation extending over several hours. I have to reply with some comment and observations which help the interviewee to feel that I am in touch, the completely passive bearing of a classical psychoanalytic interview would defeat its own object. The manner in which this was done will emerge from the content of the reports which follow.

While I have not distorted or disguised the official records, I have suppressed the names and places of activity of all but one of the subjects. The highly informed could probably identify them. My object is not to highlight individuals but to bring out the genotypical elements in the executants of certain mass crimes, to support or controvert the hypotheses made in advance on the causes and meaning of these actions. In contrasted print in the body of these reports will be my commentaries and glosses relating the individuals' material to that of others or to theory developed in the first part of the book. I should also add that an attempt was made to estimate the mental mechanisms of denial, splitting, rationalization and so forth by which in the aftermath of their murderous activities, and especially in the Here and Now of their encounter with a total stranger and representative of the "outside world", the men tried to forget, explain, justify or otherwise assimilate their now far-off experiences. It has to be said also that by comparison with what can be learnt of the details of childhood experiences, etc., in clinical practice, there was in these men a heavy blanketing of emotive themes, not only in relation to their SS careers and deeds.

Though they were few and by no means representative of all aspects of the SS activities under discussion, they managed to illustrate quite a broad spectrum of variants in our theme which I have indicated by the title given to the reports on each man.

THE FANATIC?

Seen in a prison in the Bonn–Cologne area where he was serving a "multiple" life sentence for a large number of individual murders of KZ inmates in Camp S at which he had been an SS Hauptscharführer (roughly warrant officer) with the role of a "Rapportführer" (a post in most KZs just under the Deputy "Commandant of the Penitentiary Camp" involving close contact with the prisoners—somewhat like a "Regimental Sergeant Major" and very powerful). During his trial together with another SS TKV NCO from the same camp, the two men were described as "the most dreaded and bestial characters" in that KZ by surviving inmate-witnesses. Many of the victims were German, not Jewish or foreign, anti-Nazis, intellectuals, etc.

Summary of evidence and sentence The judge of the Bonn Court described *S2* as having acted from excessive fanaticism. He said: "S2 was not a sadist but the prototype of the unmoved, feelingless and determined murderer". Already in 1939 Rapportführer, he had for years been nicknamed "Iron George" throughout the SS. His father was a railwayman in Upper Silesia* where S2 was born in 1911 and spent his childhood. In 1918 the parents refused to opt to become Polish citizens under the plebiscite award of the area to Poland, and were expelled in 1919 or 1920. They migrated to a town in Westphalia but S2, then aged 8, was left behind with an aunt "in order that one day he could claim back the title to their house and small holding". He was described as the best scholar in his class. After leaving school S2 was apprenticed to a smith and turner, and duly became a skilled tradesman. By 1930 (when he was 19), it had become clear that the Polish authorities would not permit him to claim and work his patrimony. S2 emigrated to Breslau (now Wroclaw), where he had an uncle. The latter was the leader of the local Nazi party and a great fanatic. S2 had no job to go to. In 1931 he was already distinguished in the town as an aggressive and impulsive street and meeting-hall fighter in the SS. The Court summing-up next mentioned that he caught the eye of various important Party bosses while on escort duties with the local guard troop (see Chapter Three). His bearing and keenness earned him a place at the SS Junkerschule (junior officer school) Vogelsang in 1933. Here he met his wife who was employed there. After finishing this

---

* Territory to which the Poles laid claim after 1918, the scene of much German resistance.

training he was sent for a first post to KZ Esterwege, and thence to S, where, the judge said, "S2 perfected his techniques". This was a man who "not only obeyed orders from above but even anticipated them and interpreted the spirit of various edicts of destruction in the most brutal possible ways." The judge said that the split in this man might never be explained for he was at the same time a "model husband and a loving father" of his three children, who would have "tears in his eyes if he had to chastise them", according to his wife who testified on his behalf.

The trial revealed that S2's killing went far beyond the shot in the back of the head or gassing which were the prescribed SS-Gestapo techniques. He had set up whipping blocks for merciless beatings, he was known to have trampled victims to death on the ground; he had used the method of inserting a fire hose into a victim's mouth and running water in under pressure until the man literally burst; he had flung people into cesspits and watched them drown there; one man testified that he had set his beard alight. Short of killing, S2's "punishments" had been based on pack-drill: making elderly, frail or starving people double across the camp parade loaded with very heavy sacks of cement, and then kicking them or whipping them if they collapsed— and all this to the blare of martial or gypsy music. Deaths were reported with complete deadpan bureaucratic detachment. "Another departure (Abgang)—collect."

The judge commented that, while in remand, S2 was said to have been undergoing some transformation as evidenced in his favour by the prison chaplain (pastor). "While he showed no contrition, at least his consistent bearing 'was worth more' than his fellow-prisoner's crocodile's tears." (*Here we seem to be seeing a general German—probably also British—cultural preference for the "stiff upper lip".*) Partly this signified that S2 did not deny the charges, but was reported to have replied to the evidence and the question What had he to say, softly with "Yes, it could have been so." (Jawohl, so kann es gewesen sein.) That is, the judge gave him credit for taking responsibility and facing reality. He was sentenced to lifelong penal servitude in February 1959.

The journalists (Stuttgarter Ztg. 9.2.59; Bonner Gen. Anzeiger, 7.2.59; Dortmunder Westdeutsch. Tageblatt 17.1.59) described this erstwhile "Iron Man" as "broken", listening with bowed head to the recital of his deeds, as if "moved", and also remarked on his near-zeal in being co-operative at the trial, almost as if enjoying having the tables turned.

Curriculum Vitae This is not reproduced here as it contained nothing not already noted or stated verbally during our long interview.

Interview (in chaplain's office). The prisoner through the governor had begged permission for the pastor to be present—this was a surprise on arrival. As his initial anxiety and suspicion wore off, the chaplain asked S2 if he now minded being alone. The pastor left us alone later, when S2 felt more secure with me.

This is a lean, medium-sized man now aged 56, with a raw-boned hatchet face and intensely luminous dark eyes, bushy eyebrows and dark, barely greying hair growing low on his temples and forehead—a pretty ugly looking fellow and far from a Nordic type. He makes intense and immediate contact, as if to capture me by his manly, straightforward candour. There is a real press of speech, with no need—almost no chance—to ask questions. He knows—he'll come to that in a moment—first to explain how he cannot trust people, as I might go and publish things which will harm his family.

He launches into an entirely unsolicited, very well connected and possibly mentally rehearsed discourse or harangue infused with considerable strength of emotion. One cannot deflect him from wanting to tell his story—as if to help himself to get it integrated. I am a participant in a monologue delivered with much vividness. How at 8 his people went and he was the little representative of Father. How at 10 the Poles "stopped us learning in German" and only Polish was supposed to be spoken at school. "If your teacher heard you speak German he sloshed you one." So all the German children became rabid anti-Poles, and the Evangelical Church community (German in contrast to the R. C. Poles), led by their pastor, became the resistance centre.

One wonders if that is why S2 wanted to have his pastor with him when alone and faced by a potential enemy now. He brushed aside my attempt to ask how it felt to be left alone by his parents—this was not something that worried him. His parents had been "prima". He had his marching orders from Father to stand fast on his Germanism, to defend it. It was his master, the smith, who told him to clear out. That man had been a sailor in the crew of the Kaiser's yacht *Hohenzollern*, a Free Corps man against the Poles and now a leader of the underground resistance. In Breslau S2 would find work and good Nationalist friends. I now hear how he found his uncle to be *the* leading Nazi (Ortsgruppenleiter) of Breslau, and a totally committed fanatic who infused S2 with his fervour as a lad who had always looked for a Father—the Evangelical community, the "good master smith" and now his uncle had given him this sense of belonging to the right people. "There was no difficulty in persuading me to join the Party and the SS" whose members at this time (late Weimar times) were an undercover reserve unit for the Reichswehr, whose officers spent time giving them secret military training, *not* under Party auspices. "All of us lads joined this instinctively against the Poles and Czechs." He had ample time for all this and plenty of marching and street fighting against the "Reds", because he was unemployed. "It could not happen again now in Germany because all the young men are much too busy and well paid." This was the period when he acquired his reputation and soubriquet of Iron George —"one just wasn't afraid of anybody and we lads all liked fighting". It wasn't always the SS who got the best of these brawls. He did not spend much time re-contacting his parents—the SS was now his reference group.

Then came Hitler's take-over in 1933 and a call for "Old Fighters" trained in arms, who could drive cars and were good shots, to join the *Verfügungstruppe.** He reiterated the data (from the Court summary) of how he stood out by his smart bearing as bodyguard to lots of important leaders, including Himmler and Heydrich and Bormann. It was in this unit that he met and became a friend of Hoess (later to become commandant at Auschwitz). S2 was picked as a bodyguard to accompany Hitler, Himmler and their top SS entourage for the trip to Bavaria in 1934 to liquidate Roehm and associates. He witnessed most of what went on but did not do any shooting—this was reserved for "officers". At this point S2's face suddenly became twisted with fury. He said: "When Hitler proclaimed himself the supreme judge at that time why did not the 15,000 judges of Germany rise as one man and say 'you can't do this!' There were only about 1000 well-armed and well-trained SS men in the special units in the whole of Germany. No—it was those guardians of legality who betrayed the lawful state and allowed us people to forget about laws!" S2 continued with much venom for some time citing more examples of the spinelessness and abdication of the lawyers. He himself had reported to a magistrate a case of mistaken identity, when a man had been sent to a KZ in error.

* The SS guard troops at the disposal of the local Party leader.

The judge had simply replied: "What does it matter about one more or less?" "So of course we sworn SS men forgot about legality. What *Hitler* said was right and we believed it." S2 already felt he had, by his inner knowledge of the "iron necessity" animating the inner circle, somehow broken with his "civilian" life—he was on the inside.

The next stage in this process of becoming a committed insider was his posting in 1935 to Esterwege KZ. (*Here the court record differs from his account to me—and his sounds more convincing.*) It was, as he said, a very select body he was now joining, under the direct training by Eicke "whom they all called Papa". Here was the training school on how to deal with enemies of the people (Volksfeinde). *He described this training exactly as Hoess had done in his book.[1] This was the concurrent use of flattery, sense of being Hitler's elect, with a show of utter severity and constant indoctrination that the TKVs' task was the most privileged and onerous of all—the unremitting vigilance of the guardians of the new Reich against its cunning and relentless enemies "who were behind the barbed wire". The newly enrolled "volunteers" of the SS, who had responded to this challenge, were then systematically introduced and inured to sights and sounds and methods of "punishment" of these "enemies". First, the whole company paraded to watch a flogging—without moving a muscle, and next an execution. The "doyen" of these punishments was an old pre-Nazi prison warder who had done the same job before World War I. Hoess described going hot and cold all over. Ocular demonstrations of what happened to SS men who transgressed, either by being too soft or by "corrupt" dealings with prisoners, were included. Eicke would publicly, on full parade, tear off their insignia and have them imprisoned. Hoess (on p. 79 ff.) confirms that Eicke's intention was to make his SS men "basically ill-disposed towards the prisoner". They were to "treat them rough", to root out any sympathy . . . engendering in simple-natured men a hatred and antipathy for the prisoners an outsider would find hard to imagine. "This influence spread through all the KZs and affected all the SS men who served in them, and indeed it continued for many years after Eicke had relinquished his post as inspector." Hoess describes, like S2, only more eloquently on paper, his conflict between his conscience and his SS role. "I should have gone to Eicke or to the Reichsführer SS (i.e. Himmler— H.V.D.) then, and explained I was not suited. . . . I felt too much sympathy for the prisoners. I did not find the courage to do this. I did not want to make a laughing-stock of myself. I did not wish to reveal my weakness. . . . I had voluntarily joined . . . the active SS, and I had become too fond of the black uniform. . . . My admission that I was too soft for a job assigned to the SS would unquestionably have led to my being cashiered or, at least, immediately discharged. And this I could not face."*

We shall see later how Hoess, as well as S2 and others, came to terms with their roles they, at least for a time, still rejected inwardly.

S2 said: "I then still felt a bit of conscience when the notion of 'shot while trying to escape' was explained to us, as a way of disposing of certain inmates." He took his scruples to a higher SS officer—a doctor, "whom he loved like a father", and this man in a most impressive way told him that as an SS man he must overcome such doubts and learn above everything to obey. S2 again explodes to me with rage: "Here were all these judges, and they just signed the death certificates which we turned in to them without a question. We had lost our sense of right!" He felt he was now privy to a lot of secrets, and it was no use pitting his private doubts against the leaders who knew best and trusted him.

In 1936 came the military re-occupation of the Rhineland, in breach of the Versailles Treaty—"and nobody took any action!" Clearly the leaders were right. Himmler, noting S2's zealous, devoted soldierliness during more escort duties on triumphant tours of the liberated country, had him posted to Vogelsang, one of the SS sanctuaries and higher indoctrination schools. Here S2 received 6 months of most intensive schooling. With some emotion he said: "Here we lost what was left of the Ten Commandments." "We were told all the time we were the elect, we were to be the Führer's and Himmler's special instrument for creating a new Reich. They became our conscience, we lost our personal moral self-determination." Here he also met his wife, thoroughly approved by Himmler because a good Nazi maiden privileged to work on the domestic side of this SS seminary. He let slip that he had always been a pure living lad and highly proper.

S2 was now a highly regarded man, and was sent to a further 6 months' course in Berlin which he called "Abwehrsicherung" (Abwehr = the German term for Military Intelligence, Sicherung = making safe, security). Here all the highly classified secret information, only accessible to the SS special security troops, was systematically entrusted to his class. *It is of course doubtful if this was literally true, but it is significant that this type of person at NCO level was in this way made to feel very important, trusted and irrevocably committed as privy to hush-hush policy matters. It had the desired effect on S2.*

"I was now married, and I had passed this course, so I was now right for the KZ service. I now held secrets from the rest of the population, I was in the know about the coming war." When he was assigned to camp S where he was to spend much of his SS career, it was commanded by a notorious torturer, Koch. Koch was succeeded by a certain Baranowski. About him S2 remarked laconically: "the man who taught us the fire-hose method." It transpired that a good deal of the grandiloquently named "Intelligence security" course was in fact devoted to ways of making sure that the potential spies, saboteurs, enemies of the state and so on were duly and terrifyingly overawed by the SS's/Gestapo's omnipresence and ruthlessness. At this course high SS officers explicitly taught the future camp officers various terror methods—and, S2 added, "these were the methods which had already been employed by the Feme executioners". He added wrily: "these old outlaws (Vogelfreie) were now the power in the state and had brought their old tricks with them."

One of the things he had to sign was never on his own initiative to beat or injure a prisoner—"but the real intention of the authorities was well known to us". Simple shooting was not terrifying enough. For effective terror there had to be more brutal methods. The KZ populations had to know that their guards would use these on them without flinching. He added: "It allowed thousands of Jews to go quietly".

Clearly, S2 had grasped and identified with an, in one sense, quite cynical calculation of how a ruthless, dedicated, small body of men could control vast masses of cowed people—and had agreed with it.

He now enlarged on the double thinking that lay behind the hypocritical SS rule "never to act without orders" and the training he had received in refined torture and gross brutality. Your superiors were likely to punish you for "not acting energetically". (*We recall here the indulgence towards "zeal".*) What was a man to do, S2 said. There was no retreat. Everything was covered up. He repeated, the examining magistrates never enquired, never penetrated the KZs beyond the officer's mess and simply signed the lists of deaths put before them. There was Himmler, whom he often saw in the camp, shouting: "Decimate them! I want results!" Each man had to set an example to the younger ones in hardness and ruthlessness in doing the Reichsführer's well-understood secret will. This was the catastrophe of believing in the "Führerprinzip"—if you were a leader you must do better than your subordinates and show you flinched at nothing. It was left to you how you carried out the orders to get rid of people—these orders were never written down, they came down from higher-up. S2 now expressed his supreme contempt for the Gestapo chief, Müller, who just sat at his desk and never soiled his hands. S2 said he had seen an SS man arrive one day in charge of a fresh convoy of prisoners, and the next day he was brought to the same camp to be shot himself. He did not know why. It all became routine, one slid into complete indifference. As an illustration he recalled the occasion when he was summoned to attend a conference at which the killing of some hundreds of captive Soviet army political commissars was discussed and decided upon. There were five SS generals and one civilian, whom he took to be an army general incognito and who never opened his mouth. The five SS generals vied with one another in ingenuity. Only ways and means were debated, no one expressed any misgivings on the principle of preparing this slaughter. S2 was there because he had to devise the "ways and means" as an old hand. His narrative during all this continued with the same sober vividness.

I now remarked that his tasks seemed to have lain with Slavs. He replied that until the (so-called) Crystal night (when a young Jew had killed a Nazi diplomat in Paris and a pogrom was laid on in Germany) Jews had not even figured as a special category in KZ classification of inmates. True, in the camps in Germany there were plenty of Jews, but they were held as members of a political party or in some other category of national enemy. Only from that day in 1938, so far as the camps were concerned, were the Jews suddenly classified as an ethnic group. S2 added: "The SS, as such, had no special feeling about them." (*This seems a surprising expression, ex post facto, of the bureaucratizing of the KZ murder business—like a post office which by an administrative decision has to open traffic for a new type of commodity.*) S2 said: "From now on we knew that soon the destruction (Vernichtung) orders would come, as the SS command began systematically to prepare KZ staffs for it. You see experience had already been gathered with the methods on other categories of inmates and in euthanasia." And now, he said with some depth of feeling; "we suddenly had phenomenon Eichmann, another of these pure office bureaucrats who never saw what the likes of us had to carry out". In 1938 S2 could see the war coming because of the secret plans, under the code name "Cleaning House", for the SS. The roles of the Einsatzgruppen and the Gestapo in rounding up all potential and known criminals, "asocials" and saboteurs now became for him a worthwhile patriotic goal—securing the rear.

Here the zealous assent to the ideological purposes of the regime, almost lost in the working out of the grisly tasks that followed from it, seems to be clear. This man is not a soulless robot—he was with his leaders up to the hilt, even though his task was a rotten one.

He remembers disliking what he called "the dirty deal" between Germany and the Soviet Union in which he had a task of handing over mutually unwanted communist personnel. (*It was by this deal that many old German C.P. leaders were extradited by the Kremlin—possibly in exchange for known Soviet agents in Germany.*)

S2 said the more he took part in these secret operations, the slenderer became his chances of transfer to a more normal unit. "I knew too much to be let out." "We in the KZs were a completely isolated clique. In each camp the initiated, the men in the know, were at most 25 men. We knew the intentions of the leadership and we were completely trustworthy to carry them out". (This was said with very considerable pride.) S2 followed this by what sounded equally genuine retrospective remarks (too rapid to set down verbatim) that he knew what a godless and lawless group the top leadership of the Gestapo/SS were. He instanced it by the inhuman decision to decimate (he liked the technical term: "dezimieren") the Polish intelligentsia and élites. (I remarked that's where he had started—in his hostility to the Poles—he hinted "that's where it's got you".) He was scathing about the role of the OKW (Supreme H.Q. of the Armed Forces) in this: "these gentlemen just washed their hands of the whole affair and refused all responsibility in mock righteousness". He became very worked up when he added: "The SS bore this on their heads. I have to stand up straight and face it that I was one of them!" At this point I asked S2 did he then believe in the eternal German Reich and the plan for world domination? Yes, he said, "until I was captured by the Americans. Their interrogator wanted to break me by pushing lighted matches under my nails—and then told me that Himmler had run away and poisoned himself!" Until he knew this was true, S2 had always believed that the SS "would stand together as one man, and stand up straight for their deeds". Hadn't Himmler "told us all we were the elect of the earth to whom the future belonged—and then he shows he was a coward who killed himself". (*This clearly was S2's moment of truth. Until the news of "his" leader's ratting he had dwelt in the belief that he belonged to a monolithic order of "death or glory".*) By this time his spate of spontaneous self-description had subsided and one could interpose more questions. I asked which of the leaders had really drawn such loyalty and inspiration. S2 replied: "*Himmler* was hated in the SS, but feared because he was such a mean-minded pedant. He could bawl you out for a comma in the wrong place, he acted like a petty tyrant." Not so *Eicke* who was a leader of men and a soldier. He could be hard, but he would, after strenuous training, relax and call for beer all round and be comradely. Even *Heydrich* knew men and had a certain gentlemanly way of dealing with subordinates. (*These are the apparently perennial specifications of all soldiers and lower orders for requirements of good man-management. Under this heading Hitler was not even mentioned by S2.*)

S2 now turned to talk more about himself. He was at pains to show me that he at least had not ratted: he had denied nothing at his trial; when things were near the end in the war, he could have faked his record, documents and uniform. But he never disguised himself or went underground. He wore his death's head insignia to the last. The complications of orders worried him: he was detached from his KZ duties at a certain stage when slave labour was required, to fetch convoys of Jews from Riga (Latvia). "Here we wanted these people for industry, and at Auschwitz they were gassing them!" He seems to have been assigned to take charge of a slave labour "construction brigade" on the Western front after D-day. (It was in this way he was captured by the Western Allies.) He said contemptuously he "told these people not to resist capture", though as an SS man he had orders to resist to the last.* He had a low opinion of the slackness of the British who first captured him. With some ideological humour he said "They didn't want me for being a KZ torturer", but because at his SS station there had been another unit engaged in faking Allied documents and forging British bank-notes. He implied that's what interested the British. And anyhow he had no trouble in escaping, but he was recaptured by the Americans who, learning of his mission to Riga, handed him over to his "spiritual peers" (Gesinnungsgenossen)—the MVD (Soviet Security Service). S2 had nothing but praise for their methods, more subtle as well as more "legal" than the Gestapo's—but, he added, they had years more experience. He was taken to Riga, the

* Our first prisoners on the French coast were in fact just such "construction troops", Latvians, Ukrainians, Russians in German uniform.

scene of his anti-Soviet crime in acquiring citizens of Latvia for the KZs, and he was condemned to death by a Soviet court martial. "I wasn't like those among the SS who laughed on hearing my death sentence. I went rigid with fear. In the condemned cell I began to try and sum up my life. I found I suddenly came back to the Ten Commandments and the little prayers my mother had taught me. I recalled much of the Bible I had learnt as a child—yes these were the rules men had made so that they could live together, but which my people (the Germans) had forgotten. It wasn't that I became exactly religious in the old sense. But something happened to me, especially when I was suddenly reprieved by the Russians." But this was not the end—the MVD had by now found out his record as a KZ guard—and this meant being sent to Vorkuta (the ill-famed Soviet "KZ" in the Russian Arctic). He could now experience the regime from the other side of the wire, and from the way he talked of it this was to him a restorative of his sense of justice. "Fortunately", he said, "I got into an international camp with all kinds, from venerable Tsarist-day old professors to Eastern Europeans and some disgraced Soviet Party big-shots. This was better than being with Germans, because those who were war prisoners all spied on each other and reported everything to their Russian guards." I remarked that the KZs had not been without such informer systems. "No, no", he exclaimed, "the Russians were fairer than the SS"—he had never seen a Russian guard strike a prisoner; executions were always on a written verdict of the courts martial— there was no arbitrariness. The MVD, however, made an effort to enlist him in their service, but he refused—"one such system was enough for me" he said. So he was "left to die", on the lowest rations and hardest work. When Stalin's death became known in the camp there was a huge uprising of inmates in which he took part. Again, this seemed to confirm for S2 the Russians' greater humanity, for, instead of being shot the commandant suddenly released him, having told him he appreciated his honesty. "My greatest mistake was not to stay in East Germany, but to choose the West," where he was promptly arrested to face the present sentence. He took leave of me in the friendliest manner. (End of Report).

Commentary on personality In the above record there appear scarcely any obvious statements of the variables I had taken such pains to systematize before these interviews. Why, the general reader may well ask, was a seasoned psychiatrist needed to elicit this straightforward narrative? This is fair comment, to which the answer is that we did not know how "easy" or "normal" a notorious mass murderer and sadist, in the same class as Kramer, "the beast of Belsen", would be to talk to. S2 made an appealing, boyishly open, naïve rapport with me. This strange trust that if he was frank people would value or love him was the strongest factor in his personality—he used the trick with me as he had done with his successive father-figures. He was already a docile, devoted "pet" of his prison pastor's. This does not mean that the chaplain was indulgent or in any way "permissive". During a private chat with the reverend gentleman I learnt that he did not think S2 had sufficiently repented, "though he was trying", considering the vileness of his deeds. This attitude between us, discussing S2 like a naughty boy, and my originally thinking of him as a docile dog who had attached himself to a good but severe master, was the psychologically most surprising and important discovery—totally unexpected by me. The non-professional interviewer might have got all the story in the same way. My role was to evaluate this material—or more exactly this man, as I saw him. Apart from his initial suspicion and wish to have the pastor with him, S2 showed little overt paranoid anxiety—it was more as if the young child wanted his daddy to be with him when visiting the dentist. When he saw that I was not dangerous he let himself go and proceeded to "vamp" me with his "honest, boyish" attitude. Here was the most typical basic German trait which has been stressed by all students of that people: this is the wooing of the Father-figure's love and approbation by manly bearing, eager devotion and subordination. He could not be got to talk of his original parents. He had written his actual father off and went for the substitutes, after being left all alone at 8 with an aunt to be a big, strong boy. He scarcely mentioned his wife or children—they seemed not to count. His thirst for masochistic "faithfulness" (Treue) was what had sent him on the descent to increasing obedience to his affiliative group and its leaders' orders. He would always do what such figures expected—even if privately he objected a little. In his career he had been passive—allowed "them" to post him. He had never had the right to choose. When the Soviet MVD paid him back in kind he was not put out—he was now *their* dog, and they were kinder than his propaganda had painted them. When the SS—after Himmler's ratting—ceased to be the reference point of his *Treue*, he became the good inmate of the MVD system, earning the Vorkuta camp commandant's good marks.

In his Bonn gaol he was equally helpful, compliant, brightly eager to please—"no trouble" to the staff.

The predominant need for such favours, pandered to by his sense of being entrusted with more and more terrible secrets by his superiors, promoted, given privileges, was obviously much stronger than any moral scruples which came only from his mother—Sunday school stuff, only recalled under fear of death, now perhaps brought out to please the pastor and the new German masters. This was a glimpse S2 permitted into what lay under his strong and personally effective defence of being the trusty and eager "son". This defence was clearly based on having split off his childish need for protection from his mother and, like an orphan, relied on institutions and their heads to provide his security in return for unquestioning service. The hate fraction of the ambivalence involved in such a renunciation and resolution of the Oedipal dilemma had equally clearly been enormous. If we rate S2 along the lines of my tables of variables, the most important items visible, I guess, even to the non-technical reader, were his High F resolution of the Father-tie by remaining almost totally dependent on the strict, "loved" figure; transferring most of his mothering expectations to institutions—the SS far more than any other. He scores high on "cult of manliness and homosexuality". On his sadism we have very convincing evidence. What was surprising—and I repeat this impact of his person on me—was the childlike lack of guilt, of any suffering—not even the paranoid, self-pitying persecuted feeling such as I had seen and was to see in other SS killers. In *this* case I think the adults had left him with a ready-made social split he could use to distribute his love and dependence needs (good object-need) and his hate and persecution needs (bad object-relation). It was the "bad Poles" and the "good Germans". It wasn't daddy and mummy who didn't want their boy—(and what a monstrous piece of inhuman behaviour it was to use this small boy as a pawn in a potential property claim!)—no it was the beastly Pole who drove the parents away. No wonder S2 could not discuss all that lay behind this 50-year-old event. At the very least it was strong presumptive evidence of devaluation of him by his parents. The tenderness taboo and parental coldness is a reality and hurts children. S2's behaviour has something in common with a prostitute: his good parent-figure is now the one who currently feeds and protects him, however much they may abuse him. This is the *mercenary* mentality shared alike by harlot and "Landsknecht", the man who hires out his brawn and his lust for killing because he does not belong to anyone. We score him very high on this ambivalent splitting. Thus we may well ask, as the question mark in this chapter heading does, whether S2 *really* was a fanatic. Did he really hate the Poles—or was it the German Sunday school in Upper Silesia that favoured this displacement? "All the lads" shared this hate target. Unlike some of my other clients, the personally paranoid fervour (such as in my quoted bomber pilot) was lacking. "Right—from tomorrow we have a new class of enemy—the Jews: the regulations say so." The day before yesterday it was the Commies, and yesterday Roehm and his SA conspirators. The bosses say shooting is too tame—show the inmates what ruthless chaps we can be—bring out the hose ... keep them freezing on the square ... etc. The parent-substitutes have a lot of targets and never-ending use for his primitive, scarcely guilty sadism—but not a fervent hate.

I think I have said enough to show how I evaluated this man at personal level: an individual whose need to belong had been perverted, while the resultant anti-parental hate had been displaced to authority-approved targets. His sense of fair play is also very childlike: he knows that he should not have pulled the fly's wings, and what they do to him is what he deserves for it, like a child who does not resent a "fair cop". We must, then, be prepared to face the full horror that some of these murderers were not super-aggressive villains, but morally defective children who surrendered their decisions to objects for attachment. If there is a fanaticism in S2, it is in the quality of subordination, need to belong, not to question what the reference object of attachment wants. This is the "*Kadavergehorsam*".

We need quickly also to look at the social factors that may have facilitated S2's career from a turner's apprentice into a historic killer. We have his petty state railway official father, a loyal nationalist of the Kaiser epoch; we have the Silesian border mentality with its traditional fear of the East. Then come the dispossession and loss of security by political treaty—and the irredentist revenge teaching. The ready father substitute and affiliative group meet him in Breslau to cure his loneliness and severe resettlement problem. So he is a Party member and SS activist gaining approbation as Iron George with the ruthless, unworrying lust of hitting. Only it must still be in a "good cause", in which his anger and need to show himself a "real little man" can find virtually guilt-free outlet.

S2 also illustrates the path along which by gradual conditioning the cadres of the TKV KZ-teams were hardened and themselves dehumanized by exploiting their personally enhanced cultural need for dependence and subordination to father-figures, for the love of whom they were prepared to stand originally averagely "decent" moral instincts or virtues on their heads. The arrogant claim by the Nazi leadership, nowhere more brazen than in the SS, to be above the law, and their contempt for moral and legal scruple took S2 some time to assimilate. His fury at the "15,000 judges", and later with the Allies, for keeping silent and allowing Hitler to "get away with it", to abrogate the Ten Commandments, made poignant hearing. In psychological terms, the good parents who should have kept their sons straight had abdicated. He must now love the foster-parents who had use for him and trained him—men fairly close to him—not Hitler or Himmler but his master, then his uncle, then Papa Eicke, and the "wise" SS doctor—their views and authority were not to be questioned.

S2 was continuously motivated by almost all the predicted factors I enumerated as maintaining the morale of these killers. Obedience, identification with the secret as well as overt aims and rationalizations of his leaders and teachers, feeling fatefully dedicated to these and having given his conscience into their keeping; but also feeling righteous in avenging his hurts at the hands of Slav enemies, gave full scope to his omnipotence feeling and capacity for violence—more childlike than sexually sadistic. To still what simple Sunday school scruples there had been, he was able to use the defences of "duty", of manly hardness, of routinization, of using terror to cover up his doubts and prove that "one could do it and remain decent". It was "house-cleaning", it was part of the war, he was a "soldier", and the authorities were responsible and had to save the country. S2 had been, nonetheless, apparently a rare phenomenon in the hundreds of trials—he had not in fact abrogated all responsibility but accepted it in open court. Was this itself high moral rectitude—or was it the supreme indifference and conceit of the true professional? "I've done this—I am not going to stoop to deny it—you see what a cool customer I am!" His bearing in court does not support the latter theory—rather that when, first in Soviet and then in Federal German hands, his crime is brought home to him, he "stands straight", because the new masters obey other laws and want him to be decent by their standards. This behaviour reminded me of a captured German air force sergeant who in the British transit camp where I worked during the war in 1943 said to his buddies: "At the moment I am no longer a Nazi, but a German soldier I remain." He, too, was under another authority and need not conform to the Nazi *mores* any more, but the built-in personal attitude of subordination as "honour" was deeper than this and he abided by it.

Of S2 I could say that his emotional development had only one dimension—to obey and adapt himself to the overriding need for being acceptable to the demands of any parent figure that he could perceive as loving or protecting him. If this was the Devil himself then he would sell his soul and his primitive and unsocialized sadistic toughness to him. He was the ideal recruit for Himmler's needs by the latter's stated desiderata, which I quoted in Chapter Three ... "a man who despised most developments in modern culture because he had no judgment in such matters ... also left all political and social judgments to his superiors ... essentially a destructive man, ready to act on the vilest and most stupid orders. . . . ."

In the brief citation from Hoess in the body of this case account, we saw that Hoess, though the scion of an old officer family, showed this same tendency, which carried him to even greater status in the TKV hierarchy. Though Hoess had a much more secure economic background, the severity and tenderness taboo in his upbringing were similar. He claimed he was indulged—even given a pony—but between the lines of his pre-execution autobiography of his early years one could see his love-hate alienation from his martinet-father who was unremittingly moulding him to total obedience and dutifulness to all elders: parents, teachers, priests. "I always fought shy of any sign of tenderness much to the regret of my mother and aunts. . . ." "I was never able to confide in my parents." He rejected his little sisters for their sissy ways, played jokes on them, teased them till they cried. "I had veneration for my parents, but not love like other children have for parents. . . ." By the time he came to school he was feared—implacable until avenged; at 13 his father died and Hoess was "not much affected by this". Yet from his military—now fanatically Catholic—father he had internalized the model of a totally dedicated being: he had been vowed to the priesthood, to being a missionary in lands where as a young officer his father had "battled against rebellious natives ..." with "sinister idolatries". By 16 he is in the army, sent to Turkey and Iraq, where his new Father-figure is an "ice-cold captain" of his squadron, with whom he felt "a far more profound relationship" than with his real father. Hoess, coming home a blooded warrior full of contempt for the traffic in religious cant and its hawkers in the holy places of Jerusalem; knowing how to keep an iron mask to conceal fear, anger, etc., now experiences the dispossession—his mother having died, various uncles had disposed of his home and expected him to become a priest. So he had "nothing more to do with them", and his hatred for these kinsfolk, family, his background, is expressed in joining the "outlaws"—Baltic Free Corps, Rossbach's gang, Feme murder and all the rest.

As in S2, we read of the gradual escalation of his capacity calmly to accept terror. In Latvia the sight of charred bodies of women and children still made him shiver (these were executed in a primitive action—à la Lidice or Pinkville). But what counted more was that he had "found a home again in the comradeship of my fellows. Oddly enough, I, the lone wolf, . . . drawn towards the comradeship which enables a man to rely on others in time of need and of danger."

Later, sentenced for his part in a Feme-murder, we can see young Hoess being the model prisoner. Admiringly he writes[2] how in his Prussian prison . . . "life was strictly regulated down to the smallest details". Discipline was on severe, military lines. The greatest emphasis was placed on the punctilious discharge . . . of the exactly calculated task. . . . For Hoess it must have been like being back with father! He is able to say with evident satisfaction that the enemy could not fault him: "I conscientiously carried out my well-defined duties . . . to the satisfaction of the foreman" (in the prison workshop—H. V. D.). "My cell was a model of neatness and cleanliness, and even *the most malicious eyes* (my italics—H. V. D.) could see nothing there with which to find fault." I placed the paranoid undercurrent in this smug attitude of the prig in italics to show its link with suppressed hate of the Father-figure. We have already seen how his own more civilized guilt feelings were eroded by this fear of falling foul of the authorities to whom he had given his loyalty, in our terms his need to be approved. He says: "For a long time I wrestled with this dilemma, the choice between my inner convictions . . . and my oath of loyalty to the SS, and my vow of fidelity to the Führer. . . . Should I become a deserter?" Then he re-assures himself that KZs are necessary and "true opponents of the state had to be . . . locked up" to safeguard the rest of the people from their evil deeds. "Nevertheless, by remaining in the KZs I accepted the rules and regulations that there prevailed. I became reconciled to my lot, which I had brought upon myself quite freely. . . ." And further ... "The Party ruled the state, its successes could not be denied. The means and ends of the NSDAP were right. I believed this implicitly and without the slightest reservation. My inner scruples about remaining in the concentration camp, despite my unsuitability for such work, receded into the background now that I no longer came into such direct contact with the prisoners as I had done at Dachau." This was when he became a "desk murderer" on promotion. His dehumanization of the "enemy" was completed by constant references back to the doctrines on race, social Darwinism, etc., which could make him, too, feel a just, stern guardian of his in-group, futilely telling himself that he was not a cruel or unfeeling man; and pharisaically dissociating himself from the "rabble" he had under his command in which the prisoners, of course, came off even worse than the SS rank and file, whose sadism and cruelty he could not abate but only deplore. And he knew what Eicke could do to SS men who faltered. Even higher SS officers were never promoted if Himmler had reason to think they still had bourgeois scruples.[3]

Hoess, in the end, makes a worse impression than his humbler fellow-student, S2, who at least does not indulge in self-pity and unwavering moral superiority which Hoess recovers after the brief conflict with his conscience is over. He now becomes the misunderstood martyr to duty, good intentions and the malice and incompetence of his superiors and his subordinates. "I became a different person at Auschwitz ... the sense of comradeship, which up to then I had regarded as something holy, now seemed ... a farce. The reason was that so many of my old comrades had deceived and double-crossed me. . . ." "I withdrew further and further. . . . All human emotions were forced into the background." This is, to the psychiatrist, a fairly predictable deterioration of behaviour under the cracking of defences against increasing guilt feelings that have to be paranoidally projected in order to preserve the remnants of brittle self-esteem and sense of "goodness" that Hoess clearly needed. In the end he squarely execrates Himmler for being the man responsible, and having an "iron will" no SS officer could have resisted. In his peroration, with death "in a shameful manner" looming ahead, he can still feel only that he was an "unknowing cog in the great extermination machine created by the Third Reich". He remains convinced of his goodness and that he was "never cruel". But greater than any of these fears for his reputation is the dread of his tender emotions for his family and his secret doubts being published to the world. He would still rather have been regarded as a good SS man and even a blood-thirsty beast, than a cissy.

It is a well criticized hobby of psychiatrists to make deductions on the personality structure of historical figures. I will indulge this tendency and try to compare Hoess's mind, from the record he left, with S2. These two men at their different levels represent one sort of SS killer—the principled, in their terms "high-minded" and duty-ridden henchman of the regime who had ethical norms based on Christianity but had allowed their morbid sado-masochistic obedience, and their zeal to stand well with every sort of authority figure, to obliterate individual conscience and civic courage until it was too late. Both then, when already arrested (Hoess was awaiting trial by the Polish government), showed a kind of dawning of hitherto stifled negative evaluation of their erstwhile uncritically idealized heroes whom they now saddled with the guilt of their own crimes. I have commented on S2. To sum up Hoess's impression on me as a psychopathologist, I would say that he was more paranoid and defensive to any implied or actual criticism of his ego than S2. Everybody around him was "out of step"; his superiority amounting almost to solipsism (in which his horses, and to some extent his wife and children, seemed included as part of his self) was cast-iron. He always knew better and could get no help—just as when he was a little boy he could not make anybody understand him. Low, murderous or greedy motivations were in everybody, only he was pure and noble. This immense narcissism was part of his deep and early personality split which, in paranoid level fashion, saw things as black and white. His "white" was the one-sided idealization of his military father and grandfather, followed by a series of men whom he credited with the "ice-cold" superior manliness and soldierly virtue he believed himself to possess. The father, it will be recalled, had "dedicated" Hoess to the priesthood while a little boy, but none the less had never made any warm contact with his son. It can be said that in order not to feel murderous towards this omnipotent figure, Hoess idealized and identified with him. He was thus carrying inside himself an inner object of the most exacting kind, driving him, making him a perfectionist, feeling very isolated and surrounded by "people without feeling". Hoess transferred the feeling of being offered up to a great cause from the Church to the SS. Even though almost everyone in it—certainly the leading figures, not excluding Eicke—comes in for a lot of criticism (retrospective), the sacred mission, with himself as one of the elect, is never given up. I think this capacity for preserving this idealized image of his in-group despite its deeds, nay, agreeing with the necessity for those deeds, stamps Hoess as the more bigoted and irredeemable. One of the most horrifying traits in this picture is Hoess's plea that try as he might nobody would let him improve the lot of the prisoners with whom he felt so much "sympathy" (on strength of his own 5 years in goal as a Feme-murderer). He was, it appears, unconscious that this "helplessness" in the face of evil was first and foremost in himself, in his deeper ferocious assent to murder derived from his early implacable hate. His autobiography is essential reading for all students of political fanaticism.

Dr G. M. Gilbert, clinical psychologist at the Nuremberg War Crimes trial and attached to the prison, where *inter alios*, he also interviewed Hoess, could also link Hoess's "schizoid" detachment to the sense of being "spiritually a minor"—while his religiously fanatical father was regarded as a higher being to whom one cannot talk, with whom one could not share.

Gilbert[4] questioned Hoess specifically on whether this profound detachment extended even to his marriage. After assuring Gilbert that he was "entirely normal", he emphasized his preference for being alone; he loved his wife "but a real spiritual union was lacking", and his wife knew it. "Things looked normal outwardly, but I guess there was an estrangement". Hoess reiterated how "normal" his sex life was, only to continue that after his wife learnt what his job was, desire for coitus became rare. In fact sex had never played a great part in his life—momentary affairs, rarely any passion. Hoess's self-sufficiency and life-long solitariness—an onlooker—had not even led to masturbation. For him his Nazi faith became a complete equivalent of his childhood Catholic piety. He had taken, for example, the anti-Semitic writings of Goebbels, Rosenberg and Hitler as doctrinal truth not to be questioned. The source of his unquestioning obedience was his rabidly devout father who never beat him but forced him into religion. Instead of beating Hoess as a boy, the father's punishment was prayer. It made father responsible for his son's misdeeds before God as the boy's guardian. "The thing that made me so stubborn . . . was his way of making me feel I had wronged him. . . ." This is as far as such a bigot and high-minded puritan could get to becoming aware of the split between the love for his father and the hate this spiritual coercion engendered. Beyond this he chiefly made the point of his cadaver

THE FANATIC?

obedience to Gilbert. As a concession he added: "You can be sure that it *wasn't always a pleasure* (my italics—H. V. D.) to see those mountains of corpses and smell of continual burning". But Himmler "was so strict about little things and executed SS men for such small offences". This made it certain that he was acting according to a strict code of honour. Himmler had ordered it and *even* (my italics—H. V. D.) explained the necessity. Hence there was only faithful discharge left to Hoess.

We recall how interested Hoess had been in the "mud and blood" of the wounded and dying hospital convoys of German soldiers as a boy; how ambivalently identified he was with his victims as "prisoners" of which he had been one himself under Weimar as a Feme-accomplice. There is once again the strong probability of the operation of that extreme form of sado-masochistic trend I commented on in the last chapter in reference to the SS man rhapsodising about his uniform as his funeral shroud. With the powerful investment of masochistic submission implicit in the cadaver obedience, the poverty of positive sexual and love ties except to leaders ordering killing and sticking it out in the mud, we are justified in assuming the presence of unconscious *necrophilia*—full or semi-sublimated sexual attraction to the dead. This was already implied in the theoretical schedule I drew up before steeping myself in these cases, under the rubrics of the inner emotional needs served by the SS career in KZs. It could be both an acting out of, and a punishment (by the masochistic component) for, parricidal hate, a denial of guilt by displacement to despicable, evil victims; and a relief by reason of the unconscious libidinal satisfaction to overcome the sense of inner apathy, incapacity to love, hence affectlessness; and as it became more and more of a routine addiction under the aspect of duty, it absorbed more and more of that libido, until nothing else seemed real.

CHAPTER SIX

TWO NORM SETTERS

1. The Tormentor Tormented

The second case I present is of an officer in the TKV, who was the head of the "protective custody camp" (Schutzhaftlager) of Auschwitz from its inception until 1944 when he was transferred to command less notorious camps in occupied Western Europe. This is the only man in my series of whom it could be said that his pathological mental state—but in no sense clinical insanity—was easy to see.

I shall call him *Captain A.*, allowing him his highest assimilated SS rank (Hauptsturmführer) during his service. He was immediately subordinate to Hoess, the commandant of Auschwitz. His role was that of chief executive in all matters appertaining to the inmates, while the commandant had wider duties towards staff, the farms, etc.

I had a foretaste of his highly suspicious, persecuted frame of mind when the prison authorities told me Captain A. had agreed only to meet me, but had refused me access to his official dossier and record of his trials and convictions. He had, since his apprehension by the Federal German authorities in 1959 already been tried separately for crimes committed (1) at Dachau KZ, (2) at various smaller camps where he had been commandant since transfer from Auschwitz, as well as (3) at Auschwitz. Captain A. had also refused to write a personal *curriculum vitae* for me.

Preliminary Information This record is an abstract from voluminous press reports gathered in the file of the Wiener Library. The press coverage of Captain A.'s trial was very full as this was one of the earliest of the big concentration camp trials. The newspaper reports were largely based on lengthy excerpts from the court proceedings including the judgment. The account demonstrates the initially voluntary step of joining the SS followed by the descent into increasing commitment to the point of no return.

A. was born in 1906 in a small Franconian town, the son of a butcher's and slaughterer's assistant. After average performance in primary school he was apprenticed to a painter and paperhanger, making the grade of journeyman (Geselle), but then failing to get employment in his trade. He took any job he could get—waiter, hotel servant, salesman, all over Germany, especially in various North Sea bathing resorts. When aged 26 (1932) he joined the Party and the SS "without conviction", because he was again jobless and because he could now wear his brother's uniform, after the latter had been thrown out of the SS, "without further outlay". Captain A. soon joined an instructional course for auxiliary police, in which he enrolled after Hitler became Chancellor. He served first in his native N. Bavarian town, and in September 1933 he was posted as a guard to KZ Dachau among the earliest batch of volunteers. This was the period when Eicke was setting Dachau up as the model and training centre for the future cadres of staff for the KZs. Here A. was "hardened" by Eicke. He was described in the SS records as "having proved himself (bewährt) and was quickly promoted. In 1939 he was Hauptscharführer; by 1941 he was Untersturmführer (lieutenant), by 1944 captain, and a commandant after leaving Auschwitz. In evidence it was shown that at no time had Captain A. asked for transfer out of the TKV and KZ service, e.g. by volunteering for front-line service in the war. This fact decided the Munich court that tried him to classify him as "co-actor" (Mittäter) and not merely as accomplice (Gehilfe).

Captain A. had originally been arrested in 1959 to face charges arising from his earlier KZ activities. His trial for Auschwitz came around the New Year 1964, when he was already serving life sentences for these pre-Auschwitz cruelties and killings. His first murder was at his "alma mater" of Dachau. After the organized nation-wide anti-Jewish pogrom of 1938 (usually called "Crystal night"), he shot an elderly Jew whom he found in a washroom "contrary to orders". Next came a "shot while trying to escape" murder by A., then still a Rapportführer. It was common practice to hound inmates to the edge of the trench marking the permitted limits and then shoot them for transgressing these. He pleaded in defence that he had orders to keep good order and discipline in the camp, whereas the discovery of the old Jew in the washroom, where he should not have been, had surprised and frightened A. and constituted a "disturbance" (Unruhe), and anyhow the pistol went off accidentally. Most other charges he side-stepped by the repeated phrase "I cannot recall anything of the kind" (Ich kann mich an Derartiges nicht erinnern).

The charges for Auschwitz, where he was the second senior, were not "limited" to routine, i.e. the mass extermination "conveyor belt".

There was damning evidence of keeping the barracks unheated in winter "because they were not kept clean enough" by the inmates. He was a flogger, and seemed to have had a special animus against Gypsies, whom he would force to practice "sport"—the heavy barrack square drill mentioned in Chapter Five—and then beat the falterers, starved, ice-cold and ill, with his stick to "cheer them on". For the sake of amusing his subordinates, he would organize man hunts (Treibjagd), ending at the camp limits with the shooting of the human quarry. On one occasion he killed a prisoner with the aimed throw of a bottle.

At Auschwitz Captain A. was in charge of the arrival ramp for the convoys of deportees, supervising the selection process, seeing that "good order" prevailed on the way to gassing. He also had similar duties at the emptying of the gas chambers of the corpses. His evidence was often given as a collective "we". The prize statement was when directly asked at his trial whether he accepted responsibility for sending people into gas chambers. "We did also help shove" (Wir haben ja auch mitgeschoben). *This impersonal semi-denial of his top responsibility for this manual work somehow conveys the impression, especially in its German words, of there being others who really did this, only he had to do his little bit to help.* But he would also say: "Well what should we do . . . we had been ordered to." His main attitude in the trial was that he was innocent, a victim of duty. "Where I am posted there I do my service." He said he was glad "he did not have to go into the stables often"—a reference possibly both to the overcrowded barracks and to the farm outbuildings in which shootings were carried out before the main extermination plant was built, which replaced such "manual" killing. At the trial he put all the blame on his commandant Hoess (already judicially executed by the Poles), and others no longer alive: "they are the ones who should be in the dock." At such statements he was reported to have become very excited, sometimes tearful; on one occasion he exclaimed; "I don't know what they want from me", under cross-examination. "The men who only sat at their office desks and telephoned" were the ones who were to blame, not small fry like him. At the end when the presiding judge had, in summing-up, shown that the state prosecuting attorney had demolished A.'s defence, he shouted "Words fail me" when asked what he had to say.

The evidence also showed that Captain A. had gone underground after the collapse of Nazi power. He did not return to his family but lived a hunted outlaw's life under assumed names and identities. He became a farm labourer and later an institutional stoker. He had contracted sexual unions and had to pay maintenance for two illegitimate children.

The Interview   Captain A. was seen in a Bavarian prison, for a whole day, in 1967. He was the first "officer" in the series, and rather unreasonably I had some sort of expectation of a more polished or self-confident personality. In fact this turned out to be the most repulsive among even this group: a huge, fat, coarse "butcher" with bloated features and thick neck. His pale grey eyes had a hostile expression which could only be called baleful as well as suspicious. His complexion was "beery" and his voice screechingly hoarse, like a worn-out sergeant's. With his reputation for sudden temper attacks and sense of being singled out, I had asked the deputy governor of the prison whether I needed a guard hovering somewhere near for my personal safety. I was assured that Captain A. was not violent against persons! All the more disconcerting was it when A. himself insisted on being looked after by a warder throughout the long interview—a gentle young officer who managed both to efface himself and none the less be a chairman—more so than the chaplain of S2 had been. Captain A. was so distrustful that he would not even sit down until I had by a simple transference interpretation shown that I understood his fear: "Here was a man from abroad who might be an emissary of all that A. regarded as hostile, and perhaps meaning to denigrate him in the world's press." I also promised that his name would not appear in anything I wrote, and tried to establish my "professional" status.

It is difficult to convey the paranoid feeling emanating from this man—and doubtless from me towards him in view of his known history. He was the only one of my group of SS men I would describe as approaching "clinical patient" level. Thanks to my early transference interpretation, repeated several times in varying form during the first hour, I was able to secure from A. a relatively coherent statement of his suspicion of me expressed in objective terms. In content this was the poorest interview in the series, but psychologically perhaps the closest to what might be expected of such a killer. I refrained from writing even brief notes, as it would have raised his paranoid fears, and it took all my attention to keep contact and to follow his hoarse and indistinct Bavarian utterances. This was the roughest, most uncouth of customers, with a continuous challenging defensiveness, as if to say "What more now is going to be pinned on me—wasn't it clear that

I am the most unfortunate and unjustly abused man?" I said I was interested in him as a man of his time—how he had got to his present predicament. When we got to past history, he began with his unemployment which, like 6 million other workless in Germany, had forced him to retreat to his home after learning his paper-hanger's trade. Most of the time he again used "we" as if including all his underprivileged unseen comrades. Thus: "we" were forced to join the Nazi party, as it gave "us" something to hope for. "They promised us something and it came to pass." Asked why A. should have chosen the Nazis rather than one of the more obvious working-class parties, he could not even understand how this was possible. He said: "90 per cent of us were Nazis—didn't I know the Party had 7 million inscribed members?" This was a fair example of his level of thinking. At 61 he still had the blinkered one-track adherence to "the only possible" social group to which to belong, stated with a fanaticism which even in this setting was terrifying.

I encouraged A. by saying he was now telling me just the sort of thing I was interested in, and could he go back even earlier. He now told me that his father, the butcher's assistant, was away in the army during the 1914-18 war, while his mother died in 1915, when A. was 9 years old. He and his three brothers and a sister had to go to their grandparents. When I said this must have been sad, he quickly came back with "grandmother made up for the lost mother", as if these things were of no significance. With a sheepish smile he parried my further probe about disrupted homes by saying he could not remember such things. One of his brothers was killed in the Second War—and wasn't it terrible how the small and the poor man always had to suffer—and still does—at the hands of "German justice" (*which seems a blunderbuss term to cover all regimes*). He becomes worked up and shouts angrily: "Look at these SS high-ups and leaders! They should have stopped those crematoria from being built." His chief target is *Hoess*, "who was a *really* bad man"; but beyond him a nebulously conceived hierarchy in the SS Chief Security office (*whose chief, Kaltenbrunner, the successor of Heydrich, at Nuremberg brazenly denied that this had any responsibility for the KZs and Final Solution measures!*) When I remarked that in his book Hoess had described himself just like Captain A. as being under orders and acting on compulsion from above, he became very angry. "That man (Hoess) couldn't get the camp started fast enough, he was driving everybody and shouting at us all day." Again A. brackets himself with the underdogs, saying they were now the scapegoats for the misdeeds of the higher leadership. When I say that many of the latter have already been tried, executed or given severe sentences, Captain A. says: "And that is where it should have stopped. Wasn't it enough to take revenge on the people who planned the system, and let the small fry go free? And always this hounding—extending the time limit ever longer for the apprehension and trials of SS men!" (*This is where his indignation has shifted from the old to the new masters. He is correct in that the Federal Parliament at Bonn had several times moved the statute of limitation forward in time on public demand.*)

A. now becomes almost confidential: "Shall I tell you who is doing it? It is all those perpetual witnesses who go from trial to trial, their despatch cases full of hate. And do you know that they all regularly get together in New York and work out what they will all say in their evidence? And of course they get all their expenses paid for attending the trials. These are the people who hate, not me and my comrades who only did their duty and were under duress ourselves!" Oh yes, he could be kind to prisoners too. He didn't hate Jews—the Jews hated Germans. With near tears he cites as an example how, when he moved his family into the house assigned to them at Auschwitz, he was entitled to a maid servant. So what did he do but pick a nice young Polish girl internee who was forthwith released, and her prison garb taken off. She served his family faithfully and did not even desert them when they had to leave Auschwitz. I now said that at his trial a Jewish physician-inmate had told the court how the SS men were waited on and "cherished" in their quarters by beautiful young Jewish girls, "like Pashas". To this Captain A. replied: "Well they had had a heavy night's work! They needed some recreation!" (*This was doubtless a naïve commentary on how the TKV teams consoled themselves.*) I asked more questions on how the men managed to do such work and carry on? Captain A. said they were "all good comrades", and felt united as being in the same boat together. No, they could not refuse orders or mutiny—unthinkable for the SS. By themselves they would grouse and criticize what was being done, especially after a drink or two. Drink was always available. But what was the use of griping when nothing could be done—"and above all Hoess must not get to hear about it".

Since his personality was not so hard to decipher, I decided to concentrate in this case on the aftermath effects, and on Captain A.'s retrospective evaluation of his former leaders and their teachings. It was clear that he had a certain reflex loyalty, e.g. "One must not speak ill of the dead" (on *his* side). Fairly relaxed now, he confided to me rather timidly that Himmler had really never been popular—an ill-tempered little petty tyrant. "Now Eicke—that was something quite different—he was 'Papa' to us all. Ah! he died a hero's death at the head of his troops on the Russian front." (*This is also true. Eicke became the commander of a fighting "Death's Head" SS division. His place as Inspector of KZs was taken by a man called Gluecks.*) Other figures were now mere names. A. had achieved a pretty massive degree of forgetting of detail, and his feeling for regret and reparation was blunted. (*This was not a man one would hope to influence—least of all in a day's session.*) The picture he painted of his side of the fence in the KZ service was mainly one of emotional apathy, made possible by a comradeship of the damned, with much alcohol and such sexual orgies as could be organized behind high-minded commandant Hoess's back. Frank grousing among comrades was also in evidence.

No, he could not say he had ever suffered from bad nerves or nightmares. He had always been a good scout and comrade. His worst period was in 1945, when after Hitler's collapse he had to go into hiding. Here he confirmed what was stated in the preliminary notes. He kept right away from his family and his native Franconia, and got himself a common law wife. He was always moving around from farm to farm. During the whole period before his arrest he was always on the alert, waiting for the detectives to catch up with him. This was especially sharpened when he read that the Federal Government had set up a central office for tracing war criminals, after the Allies had given up this function. "Naturally", he knew that such an office was the work of that (now frankly named) Jewish conspiracy of revenge which meets monthly in New York (*shades of the Elders of Zion*) to work out instructions for the evidence to be offered for an ever-growing list of prosecutions of the likes of him. He now hints, rather surprisingly, that he had already been tried "in the East", i.e. by the Soviet occupying power, "where, as everyone knows, the Communists give minute instructions to all prosecution witnessess". (*It seemed that as the Soviets did not identify A. as Auschwitz staff his sentence was light.*)

It now transpired that Capt. A. had really throughout our long interview aimed at enlisting my sympathy for his own and his SS comrades' predicament. A "professor from England" might be an influential person, but he could see now that I had no great powers to help him. He had no use for long-term research into the causes of violence—he would not live to see the betterment. All he wanted was to rehabilitate his reputation in the eyes of his sons upon whom "the conspiracy" would also visit its wrath. "I would not let them join a political party, nor the new German army—no, only a church or the Salvation Army or something like that." *The assumption was that one had to belong to an organized body or group to be somebody.*

Had he known what he knows now he would never have joined the Party which he only did from economic desperation. He meant by this both that his leaders did not win and that they abandoned their poor underlings to take the punishment. Had he known that the revenge of the conspiracy of the "witnesses" would go so deep and last so long, he would have given himself up in 1945. Then he would have been simply shot with all his other good comrades "who now lie peacefully in a cemetery near Landsberg, with little wooden crosses". (*This is a reference to the courts-martial on captured TKV and KZ staffs by the U.S. forces around 1945-6. Landsberg gaol, where Hitler and associates had been in 1923-24, was the prison where these SS men were held and executed by the Americans.*) No! What Captain A. wants is a "man with a long arm and power", be he German or foreign, who would at last stop this disgraceful persecution of the faithful and dutiful, to stop the pillorying of the likes of him by the newspapers. He could see I was not that kind of power figure. . . . Yet it was clear that A. was also getting some support for his ego from feeling that he was a most "notoriously abused" war criminal. The last hour or so of my conversation showed me that he was living entirely in an inner dialogue with his imaginary attackers. His activity in prison was (workshops, etc., apart) the ceaseless collecting of every scrap of information concerning his case, always hoping that new material would provide the basis for an appeal, as well as longing for a magical deliverer "with a long arm" who would see that he is not made to suffer so unjustly any more. Once, he said with pathos, he had belonged to the Evangelical Church, but the Nazis had made him resign from it, because "you couldn't believe in Christ who was a Jew, while attacking his race".

I left this man with the feeling that he was in complete despair, which he had, after all his early defensiveness, uncovered for me. The deputy prison governor told me, as we were exchanging parting comments on Captain A., that it was true that his court proceedings had dragged on a long time, because his had been among the first batch to come to trial under Federal auspices, and the judiciary and attorneys were still groping on unprecedented procedural territory and therefore had had "far too many" witnesses, not yet having learnt how to cut down the proofs to essentials.

Comments Here was another demographically typical Nazi strong-arm man, from Julius Streicher's own country. It was probably his class feeling as a small town tradesman's son that had turned this poorly endowed, economically and emotionally deprived, unemployed fellow towards the Nazis rather than the working-class movement. His case once more recalls Wangh's statement about the dynamic link between real hunger and the regression to more infantile privation (Chapter Two). There does not seem to have been a time when A. did not feel underprivileged and discriminated against; always picked for the bad jobs while the fine gentry "had it good". His identifications were not at all with officers—he remained in his way always a "ranker", one of the ones who are pushed around. In this way he could have been an Eicke-like pal to his non-commissioned men, shielding them and seeing to it that, behind Hoess's back, they all indulged themselves. The longing for a good father to deliver him from inimical forces all round him runs like a red thread through his whole life story. Again the split in this fundamental dimension of personality is clear. There are no really good fathers. They all disappear and let their orphan boys take the rap. Possibly A.'s actual father, as a "war-hero", but certainly Eicke as his "Papa" in his new life, were something like models for him— and Eicke, at least, was no upholder of a mind of one's own, even though he communicated a rough, gangster-like right to grouse and cheat the authorities. Discipline and obedience are something apart from this—almost coercion like that of driven cattle with head down, not in the least eager or starry-eyed.

Underlying this is a pervading hatred centred on the Jews almost as a ground-swell; but anti-Semitism, just like his readily restored persecuted feeling against his own SS generals, is an aspect of a general grudge against "Them" in general, all who are unjust towards the little men, now also including the Federal judges, and the Allied victors. The structure was illuminated by the change of his transference feelings for me; one of "Them" against whom he had to have a warder to protect him—I became a possible rescuing figure in whom he became relatively confiding, and then—the let-down feeling—no deliverer after all—he was on his own again—I was useless to him. The most horrifying experience, however, was to discover the raging pitiful hurt orphan under the shrill denial of guilt in this great bully, with his plea for justice and strong arms to save him. What a Godsend Hitler's party and the SS must have been for this hate-filled man, not only with the promise of a job but supporting his self-hatred as a "policeman" against the contemptibly helpless and defenceless like A. himself had felt.

In this mediation between gang solidarity and good fellowship of a pseudo-soldierly kind and the sanctioning of violence by the gang leader, the tough, leather-faced anti-establishment figure of Papa Eicke seems to have been the decisive influence for this whole generation of TKV personnel. The veneer of patriotism and ideology was very thin, albeit perhaps crucial as the sanction. His paranoid attitude had remained quite unaffected: however many Jews he had "helped to shove" into the gas chambers, still the great and powerful conspiracy of them plotted his ruination—a haunting fantasy image of a host of *witnesses*, of secret power. I think it is clear that restitution making, humane repentance or remorse were totally absent. A.'s grudging concession that he had once belonged to the gentler society of his Evangelical Church was weakened by his contemptuous, uncomprehending reference to it as just a safer sort of mob, but incompatible with the more manly, one-of-the-boys comradeship of Stop-at-Nothings, where he was fed and clothed and accepted if he kept to its ethos. Even in our society this man would have been a potential gangster—strong arm type.

Like his Franconian compatriot, Streicher, he was possessed by his xenophobic, anti-Semitic resentment. But while in Streicher's *idée fixe* about the Jews, even at his trial at Nuremberg, there was a highly "pleasureable" pornographic element for him and his "Stürmer" readers,[1] A.'s image of the Jews was one of scheming, powerful hate and retribution—a terrifying mirror of his inner world—that would pursue and harm even his sons—whom he had abandoned as he himself had been in unconscious fantasy cruelly deserted by the loss of his parents. This was, incidentally, his only spontaneous reference to his children. I was not allowed to know much about him as a private person.

This powerful paranoid motivation in warding off the enemy must have accepted his sanctioned violence as a KZ killer almost as a prescription for mental health. To be ordered to annihilate the embodiments of one's fantasied bad objects, and even encouraged to try harder, could have obviated the effort of mental repression and splitting that might have made A. a clinical victim of full-blown psychosis in more civilized settings. This is, I would guess, why he never attempted to ask for a transfer to some other service. His objection was to being driven by hard taskmasters, not to the work which was unpleasant, as a slaughter-house or a steel-foundry might be. As a heavy manual worker doing night shifts he felt he deserved good treats, such as plenty of alcohol, or Jewish beauties, for doing his best for his bosses who were in effect no more human to him than his victims. He scarcely realized that most of them had already been executed or were being sought by the law of Germany. No, they were just the bad fathers who had abandoned him and *his* kind, and they should be where he stood.

It was evident that A.'s hold on reality was precarious. He must have been almost entirely dominated by his own narcissistic need to defend his ego in a totally hostile world, and he chose the way most consonant with his inner world: to serve these bad masters in the dogged gang spirit of the underprivileged, and to show where he could that he too could have power of life and death and get his own back. With the exception of some perfunctory mention that he once had a family, this dynamic was, it seems, the only relationship with others of which he was capable. Such love as he had was for dead, idealized Eicke, and for the "comrades". There was not even a capacity for real rebellion.

In *The Authoritarian Personality*,[2] William R. Morrow, reporting a study of American prison inmates from the point of view of their standing on the High F test scales, has this to say:

> The general run of criminals are *not* to be thought of as genuine rebels who act according to some principle, however dissident, and whose conflict with authority is accompanied by some consideration for the weak or oppressed. On the contrary, they would appear to be full of hate and fear towards underdogs. Themselves disfranchised . . . they are yet unable to identify with other groups.

In the American setting of the study, this showed strongly as a rejection of Negroes as having "untamed instincts", being lazy, ignorant etc. Similarly, Jews, as a "powerful" out-group were condemned as "acquisitive", seeking power, whereas the subjects felt victimized by the Jewish out-group's power. The study tends to show that the ordinary convicted criminal, in at least the U.S.A., is more likely to be an ethnocentric, xenophobic man of Right-Wing stamp and fascist leanings than a tolerant "democrat" siding with the oppressed. X and Z, in Winnicott's language (see Chapter One), have in common their defensive paranoid hostility to projection symbols of both the weak and despised *and* the threateningly dominant. It is not difficult to imagine in which direction their aggressive drives are more likely to receive active expression, nor how relieving it must be to surrender their frail sense of ego-control to the anonymity of a like-minded group or gang and their rudimentary guilt feelings to the group's leaders. We gain some insight into what is meant by the psychoanalytic concept of "internalization of a bad object", how it torments its owner unceasingly and impels the constant search to identify it in various powerful persecutory figures that carry an unmistakable quality of a merciless authority.

Summary score on variables   There is a high degree of love privation and, throughout pre-SS life, of severe economic insecurity. Clearly sought Father-figures with whom identified uncritically. Powerful ambivalence turns all except dead father-figures into bad or useless. Strong affiliation to organizations as substitute maternal security providers. Tenderness taboo was very high. Sadism (*a*) Cult of manliness strong, expressed as gang solidarity and minimal concern for women or children. Projection massive and based on the most primitive paranoid internal world peopled with depriving, threatening objects whom he sees in his victims (not I hate Jews, the Jews hate *me* = us). Thus his activity becomes a direct expression of his inner image of authority— of what fathers are like and therefore require their sons to do.

Depression and hardly knowing why people are getting at him now is only in part a function of childhood religious teaching. It is that his few good objects, like Papa Eicke, have been taken from him, that he no longer can belong to a gang in which killing "enemies" was approved, in tune with his best-loved parent figures. The good fellows who were shot and buried at Landsberg were what he mourned, not the dehumanized herds he shoved into the gas chambers. It was hard to imagine that he could ever have been different. His life only began when he joined the adolescent Nazi gangs. No wonder he still wanted some powerful daddy to come and tell the world he was a good chap.

LICENSED MASS MURDER

I have seldom, if ever, experienced such pain at the depth of degradation of, or non-arrival at, a human level as with this man. This may be
the nature of fiends: that their inner world is so empty of loving
figures and experiences that they, needing to love, must needs love
those like themselves—the fellowship of the damned who hate lucky
sissies and softies who can love and create. It was therefore obvious
why the SS appealed to him as his right milieu, and why the prospect
of police and KZ duties was not merely an economic incentive but a
satisfying field. Nearly all the motivations listed in Tables VII, VIII, and
IX were applicable to him, except that he was not from one of the
occupied or ethnic boundary territories. Nor was he a "law and order"
punctilious "soldier" in the Prussian sense, but rather a smouldering
rebel whose Father-figures had to be clearly on his side before he
gave them full loyalty instead of ambivalent, grudging conformity.

I do not think any further summing up of his defences against guilt
or misgiving is needed. They are abundantly clear from the preceding
account.

2. The Unworried Killer

The third case study is that of a close collaborator with S2, but who
had been arrested and tried for his crimes at a different time and place
from the latter. Unlike Captain A., this man was a smiling, forthcoming
and helpful subject. Butter would not melt in his mouth. He spoke in
an ingratiating soft Saxon accent, and his quite sensitive features seemed
to belie the heinous cruelties and capacity for killing for which he
was sentenced by a Munich Court in 1960 to "fourteen life sentences"
for 14 proven murders during his tenure of a block leader's post at the
same KZ as S2.

BS, as I shall call him, had written out for me a neat, four-page long
curriculum vitae which was in ill-sustained "gothic" handwriting, a script
reintroduced as "good German" by the Nazis. This, supplemented by
the official legal dossier, will form the basis for introducing the case.

Curriculum Vitae (April 1967) The tone and feel of this document is
that of a schoolboy's essay, a mixture of self-pity, obsequiousness and
omissions of all details of his KZ service, while, for example, giving
me the names and locations of all the firms he had worked for both
before and after his professional SS service until his arrest in 1957. There
are many crude spelling mistakes, but his former employers are all

called by the formal "Herr" in front of their status title, e.g. "Master Coachbuilder". (All the towns or villages in which he had worked before joining the SS were within a few miles of each other.)

BS was born in 1907 in a village in Saxony as the fourth of five children (stressing "eheliche" = in wedlock) of a "machinist" and his wife (maiden name given). His childhood passed in another village, where he attended school at primary level. When BS was 7 his father was called up for the Landsturm (territorial army) in which he served until 1918, and survived (no combat). "All the war years were for us children a hard time, there was no such thing as school vacations, only work to make life sustenance bearable, barely time for school home-work." "My confirmation suit (BS was a Protestant) I had to earn myself in my last year of school, as my mother could not manage this, so I went into the quarries in my last school year and hewed paving stones for road building, until I had my suit complete, that was my summer vacation." For three years (1922-25) he served his apprentice-ship with the "Herr" coachbuilder in a small Saxon town, attending trade school concurrently, at the end of which he passed his qualifying test as a craftsman (Geselle). He now left *his* master and worked, "with few interruptions until 1933—with strange masters". (*In all this part of his paper there is a clear indication of self-pity at his hard fate—not unusual in German youths who talk of "going into strange parts" (die Fremde) even when it is the next village.*) In 1931 he joined the Nazi party and at the same time the general SS. His last job, with a "Herr Wagnermeister" came to an end in 1933 owing to lack of work, and BS was unemployed. The local SS unit now asked him "wouldn't he like (Lust hätte) to be recruited for the formation of a Waffen SS or later into the police; in my then situation I accepted at once and so on 22.11.33 I was transferred to the Special Commando Sachsen (Saxony)—political 'Bereitschaft'★ Dresden, from my Home Unit 48, this was voluntary (freiwillig)." "Was there Service!" (Dienst War!) "Infantry training and guard duties in the city at all the higher headquarters of the SS and SA." In 1935 the whole unit was moved to Sachsenburg and embodied in SS Death's Head battalion (Sturmbann) "Saxony" under command of Hauptsturmbannführer Simon. In 1936 he was transferred from the unit to the commandant's staff at Sachsenburg, and seven months later (1937) he (with two others, named) was further posted to the

★ See Chapter Three. This was the alternative name for the guard troops also called *Verfügungstruppe*.

concentration camp as block leader, where he was "active" (tätig) until September '42 as block and "commando" leader. *This is all BS has to say about this most crucial point of his career, and he turns with evident relief to a more reputable phase in his SS career.*

"Already in 1941 I had volunteered for front-line service", he now writes, despite a motor cycle accident which had left him with a "half-stiff leg". BS has been categorized unfit for military service, but in 1942 he was posted to a Waffen SS armoured division ("Prinz Eugen"), quartered in Belgrade, as a sergeant-major (Hauptscharführer), as infantry instructor and platoon leader. This unit had just been formed and was committed to action against partisans in Serbia in 1943. "Later I applied in 1944 to SS Division Viking (he misspells it "Wicking") to the anti-tank section Germania, where I stayed until the capitulation. Action seen: Hungary, Lake Balaton ... Poland, Russia—and lastly again in Styria where we experienced the capitulation." The whole Viking Division was taken prisoner by the Americans. (*This was of course spring 1945. BS now describes his captivity with the same sense of bitter fate as his childhood.*) "We came only at the end of September to Dachau in formation; until then the division had to provision and shelter itself in the open. Either in small tents, in so far as tenting was available, or otherwise one just had to build leaf huts to be protected from rain. Except for the leaders, the greater part of the men were underfed and louse-infested. Only in Camp Dachau (*this was the erstwhile KZ*) did we receive ample and good rations."

By June 1946 he was released from U.S. captivity and enrolled as carpenter in a "signal-depot" which must have been an American military installation. Here he worked for 2 years and then obtained private jobs which he details. The interest in this part of his curriculum is that he seemed able to keep jobs easily; improving himself, and staying up to 6 years with one firm, until December 1957—always in Bavaria. He continues: "In January 1957 I was summoned to the criminal branch of Munich police, there I was asked whether I had ever been in Camp S which I at once confirmed (bejahte). I was then told that I had been sought for some time because of murder at that camp. I was then questioned on this matter on the basis of statements by witnesses, and was then allowed to go, for I said to myself all this can be cleared up (dies muss ja alles zu klären sein). The officials, too, said to me not much will come of this (da wird nicht viel herauskommen), and so I was still at liberty until 3.12.57 and followed my regular occupation.

Because of this the thought of fleeing never came to me, although I would have had opportunity and money for it." This was the formal end of his paper, but in Roman script BS wrote "Please turn". There followed the best part of a large page of "Remarks".

"After my release from American captivity on 26.6.46 until my arrest on 3.12.57 I reported under my real name to the police in Munich as required (vorschriftsmässig).

"I have had to omit in this life story several details in order to write down as briefly as possible according to the best of knowledge and conscience (nach best. Wissen u. Gewissen).

"Also at that time, '46, we were not released by the Americans to the Eastern zone, reason; because the Russian (sic) has reimprisoned all from the SS and has declared the American release certificate as not valid.

"I have not had any previous conviction (Vorstrafe) but this was in the examination-in-chief interpreted by (*name of judge*) that BS has known how to evade the grip of the police; this is only brought against the little man to give more force to my sentence (um meinem Urteil noch den nötigen nachtruck★ zu geben). Had I had previous convictions, then these would have been held against me. One can do as one will to conduct oneself in public life, that is democracy?" (Signed).

The resentment and sense of "can't win" of the underdog suddenly broke surface in what had been a very formal and controlled model soldier's document. I have purposely left some of his German mistakes and also translated some of his sentences clumsily, as he wrote them.

Legal Summary and Judgment (May 1960) The court dossier confirmed the general outline of BS's life story as given by him to me seven years later. I cite the legal record for details of his KZ activities and other evidence illuminating the unpleasant side of this now quiet, well-behaved man's character.

It was stated that in 1937 he was promoted from the equivalent of corporal to junior sergeant when he became a "block leader" in charge of the "isolation block", which the judge said represented a still worse punishment section in what was already the desperate predicament of all KZ inmates. BS himself, in the dock, had summed up his functions in that post as "looking after the right things" (nach dem Rechten sehen). In 1939, in addition to the motorcycle accident, he had been hospitalized for venereal disease. Later in that year he married—not the woman who had given him V.D.

★ Sic.

The court evidence of BS's career from 1942 read as his own statement. But it was brought out that during his service with the motorized Waffen-SS unit in Serbia he was twice wounded, and that in 1943, still with the same unit, he had had a clash with a superior officer which resulted in 18 months' detention in a military punishment camp and demotion. (*This could have been why he left the Prinz Eugen division and was later posted to the Viking division in the real front line.*) The U.S. army released BS with others of the captured division because his KZ service was not known to them. The judge commented that BS abandoned his wife and child in Saxony, and lived with another woman in Munich in order to avoid his home town where his record would have been known. By this woman he had three children.

The interest for our present purposes centres on the judge's recital, in his summing-up, of the attested crimes and offences BS had committed. There was damning evidence of 14 individual murders which the defence had not succeeded in mitigating into the lesser crimes of "grievous bodily harm" or "manslaughter", with the implications of absence of intent to kill. Nor did the judge allow BS's plea that the witnesses "were only out for revenge". He described the prisoner as "zealously and blindly obeying the slogans (Parolen) of those times, his brutal disposition, given the opportunity to be acted out, turned him into a murderer". Witnesses (camp survivors) had described BS as a "wild beast who could have torn his own child to pieces". There was a long description of his ingenuity in devising fiendish tortures, as well as of crudest brutality. We read again of the hosepipe—now used mostly to drench victims he was "punishing" in the winter cold and letting them freeze to death, or else playing the powerful water jet on peoples' neck and heart, causing heart failure. Other methods included the "sport" of making the victims do a "bear dance", i.e. having to turn round and round a pole until they collapsed from giddiness, when they fell they were trampled to death with hob nailed boots, shot or severely beaten up. The slow torture by "pack-drill", knees-bend, etc., he ordered an interned opera singer to accompany by arias.

BS had been heard to say to a group of inmates in his block "I'll make your dying tasty" (Euch werde ich das Sterben schmackhaft machen). His favourite indoor method was to crowd his victims into a broom-cupboard—or, it seems, preferably into the water closet and there, standing tight like sardines, let them suffocate. At times he would be apparently friendly and "humane", only suddenly to deliver a vicious, often fatal, solar-plexus blow at his unsuspecting victim. The dead he threw, or had thrown, into cesspits, in which he occasionally was also said to have let the still living drown.

His immediate superior, my *Case S2*, whom BS's defence had brought as a favourable witness, in fact testified that "if a prisoner had to be liquidated I took BS with me because he was a big tough fellow and he killed with equanimity (Ruhe)...."

During the trial, BS was described as showing no remorse, as denying every charge monotonously with the words "all invented"—by the malicious witnesses who were only testifying against him for "business" gain (cf. Captain A. above). He also claimed that he had to keep order among 8000–9000 prisoners, "who had killed not a few block leaders". He expressed himself furious that not he, a German soldier, was believed, but these Jewish witnesses who were making a business out of avenging themselves on one who had overlooked their crimes. "Today I regret that I was so lenient." At the close of the evidence BS declared he had not changed—adding contemptuously "these were, after all, only political prisoners and Jews" (Es waren ja nur politische Häftlinge und Juden). The presiding judge's judgment made the points that BS had volunteered for the SS special commando in the hope of economic advantage; that this was no automaton but an intentional killer who invented his own methods of torture not ordered by anybody. The state authority did not help—though the prisoners were in its power it did nothing to protect them. The judge also brought into his judgement the findings of a psychiatrist who had examined BS. These had shown that BS had done badly in school and was deficient in capacity to feel pity or guilt and that he had a cruel nature. In BS the judge saw a combination of dullness (Stumpfheit) and ambition. "An inferiority complex was coupled to a great power drive that found its ascendancy over others in making them suffer."

The Interview (April 1967) A whole day, at the same Bavarian prison as *Captain A.* (above).

This is a spare, well-preserved man of 59, with a face almost "refined" and sensitive by comparison with the two previous men described. In the press photographs he had a Ronald Colman moustache which gave him a sinister look surprisingly absent on meeting him 7 years later. His manner is just as predicted from his biographical essay—polite, smiling and deferential. He combines this with a good deal of suspicion and manoeuvring to find out what the "Herr Professor" would be after. I explain the object of my talk with him, i.e. that, knowing him to have been a KZ staff member and what deeds he had been convicted of, I was interested in his life and how he came to be in this predicament—his *whole* life, long before he became a Nazi. Visibly relieved, he begins by denying all the charges and launches into a tirade though in restrained and controlled manner, which repeats his stand at the trial. These are the wicked inventions of the "witnesses" who were out to revenge themselves on the men whose hard duty it had been to protect their new Reich against the international scheming of its enemies and who had been too lenient towards these implacable foes. I interrupt him when I have learnt enough to appraise his smouldering unaltered Nazi viewpoint and massive defensiveness. I repeat that I would really like to know how he came to feel like this and how things were when he was quite young.

BS now tells me of his parents, describing them as a lax but sincere Protestant family. He explains his father's job as the mechanic looking after a small rural industrial motor-driven workshop, but adds that the father would not have liked to be called a "working man", which was to this family a proletarian status. Yes, father was the kind who voted for the Social Democrats in the old days. But he was very respectable, a strict and just man. He would warn his children not to repeat a given misdemeanour—only if repeated would he give a beating for it. BS was 7 years old when the father was called up in 1914 into the *Landsturm* (*cf. Captain A.*—H. V. D.), and he could never feel very close to his father of whom he saw little. BS always felt much closer to his mother, who had more understanding and represented security. "She taught us our prayers." He describes, in what I have learnt to recognize as a recurrent stereotype, the "hard time" the family had because of father's military service—the image of the poor overworked worrying mother pinching and scraping. Despite the fact that father returned unscathed to his home and old job in the village, this picture of penury and hard luck was continued. BS said: "Father could now never buy his house or become independent", even though he was never out of work. (*The impression, not verifiable because BS stuck to being very "respectful" towards his father's memory, was of a rather ineffective, uncaring head of the family who was never out of work but never saved or improved himself.*) The mother sounded like the more energetic, managing and thrifty parent. We now hear again of BS's "having to work instead of play", in a "strange place" for his apprenticeship, although, it turned out, he lived at home during all this time! *One quickly got a picture of an incredibly narrow, blinkered and parochial background, pinched and economically static, with a bleak, pleasure-denying driving Protestant ethos, earning one's money for the "best" confirmation suit. When Nazi recruitment reached this area it must have seemed—and did—a terrifically exciting thing to such young backwoodsmen as BS, whose movements "in strange parts" had been, as verified by the map, in a radius of some 12 kilometres.* He was sheepish and reticent about any question on early sex experience.

He was still a craftsman in the waggoner's workshop when at 24, together with all the lads in his village, he joined the Party and his "home troop" of the SS. He hardly knew what it was about, but the uniform was smart, and one felt quite a special chap. They talked there of the need to save the country from the Jews and the communists. And in 1933 his master had to sack him because there was no work. "You felt you were no longer an honest man as you ignominiously queued up at the labour exchange to have your card stamped. (*"Stempeln gehen"—to go to be stamped—was a cliché for being unemployed.*) I now listened to an almost *verbatim* repetition of what he had written: of how he gladly seized the chance offered to volunteer for "auxiliary police" training with the Verfügungstruppe at Dresden. His commander, Lt. Colonel Simon, was a wonderful man—"strict but just" (*the very words used about BS's father*). "It was all purely military later at Sachsenburg": infantry drill and tactical exercises.... Yes, they also had courses to attend on blood and race and heredity, and they were taken round to see various "mental institutions", so that he knew how important it was that inferior material must not be allowed to get into power. "There were maps on which clever professors in civilian dress showed us what the world would be like if Germany lost and world communism were to triumph—and, Herr Professor, the world looks just like that now!" It had all come to pass as they foretold. (*It became clear to me that BS had joined, not only, as the judge at his trial had said, for a job, but also for a sense of being somebody—for affiliation and excitement. The doctrine—a confused mush somewhere, had come only after he became involved.*) He stressed his pride to belong, to take a personal oath to Hitler and thus to become an elect, special world saviour, a hundred per cent reliable and ready to obey. "And how they drilled us (schliffen) till we howled with rage—over obstacle courses, crawling through pipes; pack drills and long route marches in the heat, with taps all turned off so that we could not drink. Yet no one would dream of asking for a transfer, such was the comradeship. One got so that one lost all criticism; one just lived in this life; one was simply as SS man. One lost the thin thread to the parents. There was no other thought than *Kadavergehorsam*."

Only after that came the KZ service. At first BS's unit had "simply to guard a camp for interned habitual criminals". Hoping to get some comment on Eicke, etc. from him, I asked if he could still recall any of the KZ authorities. He makes as if to rack his brain, but says he remembers none. He talks instead of a "head 'flu" (Kopfgrippe) he was ill with in 1936. "His memory ever since has been rather poor—he gets into states when he cannot think." Going off to sleep he often wakes suddenly with a feeling that something has hit him on the back of the head. I probe this a little in order to discover the nature of this convenient head symptom. It is not an intelligible organic symptom; it is unconnected with recoverable dreams or nightmares. None the less he says he "takes hours to calm down after such an experience and before going off to sleep again". The present prison doctor had said: "It is only your nerves". BS claims that this symptom was the reason why he was considered unfit for continuing service in the smart para-military Verfügungstruppe and posted to KZ duties as block leader.

I debated with myself whether an interpretation of his resistance to telling details of his KZ life would have the desired effect, and decided that this 30-year-old hysterical symptom, acknowledged as constituting a "real" dis-ability by his former SS medical selectors, was proof against a single verbal attack by which I might lose contact with BS.

He showed me that he knew I knew that he had done terrible things by what followed. He talked, directly after this allusion to his impaired memory, of the cast-iron strictness of camp staff regulations for keeping order and discipline, and how tied to Himmler's and Eicke's edicts he and such as he were. Yet in the next few sentences he told me that as block leader he was the absolute master in his block: "Nobody could give orders on how I was to administer the place—I was in charge of 500 inmates." And he hinted that "everybody" knew what the attitude to these enemies of society was. It was more than one's life was worth to be kind to these people. Spies among the "trusties" were everywhere, these people were in and out of the commandant's office and reported everything that went on ... and you know if one is married. . . ." BS now spontaneously takes up various "horror stories" that were given in evidence at his trial: how these depraved people had tried to be cheeky and he had knocked them in a rage, he had to show who was boss, under the ever-present eyes of the camp informers who would report him if he wasn't severe, and how they were only too ready to gloat over his downfall for leniency and laxity. And now these same people whom he had spared were at the trial testifying against him. He turned with relief to telling me how glad he had been in 1941 to be allowed to volunteer for a Waffen SS unit as man-power became short. (*This part of his story will not be enlarged on here as it is not strictly relevant, and had been sufficiently recorded in his written account.*)

Gradually, he said, during the campaign against the Tito partisans, and despite his trouble with a company officer which seemed to be part of the difficulty of realizing that he was no longer a powerful boss but had really to obey a commander, he came to see what a horror his KZ life had been. However, the turning-point, as with S2, came for him when his division was captured by the Americans in Austria and they had to experience hunger, cold and wet. Then, he said, he knew what privation and cold really meant, and so he realized what had been done to the KZ inmates. When I point out that this is a very different attitude to his defiant stand in the dock, he says he has now had time to think and he exclaims: "never again if I had a second chance". I noted at the time that I wondered if this man really meant it, or was playing for my sympathy, as the others had done. "There is nothing left"—his wife plans to divorce him as a "lifer" and convicted criminal —he is quite alone, his people are all in the Eastern Zone, and he had lost touch with them all. "Such is the lot (das Los) of the little man." He becomes indignant now over the unhelpfulness of his defence law-yers: "They only wanted my money". His barrister scarcely intervened during the examination of himself or witnesses. And after the trial he told BS that he too had lost relatives in KZs. Another attorney turned out to be a Roman Catholic. BS would not have employed him if he had known this to begin with! That's what the small man has to face who only obeyed orders under pressure. There was no money to search all the documents. The big fellows who could spend the money on their defence had got away with a few years' gaol because they had good connections and could see that the record was put straight. "People tell me to forget—but I can't." This turns out not to be his deeds but the sense of injustice of what has been done to him—which is all he has left to brood on. We take leave in a depressed mood.

Comments Demographically this was another typical candidate for the Nazi party. Lax Protestant and a rural artisan's son from an under-privileged, war-impoverished and inadequate paternal background, his family none the less had pretensions to some sort of middle-class, anti-proletarian status. There seems to have been some degree of anti-paternal identification ("father a SPD voter"), and much peer group pressure to join the Party and the SS, on the quite sub-rational grounds of "everybody is doing it" and swank. The Party ideology was quite secondary and induced late by authoritative indoctrination. This man had never seen a Jew or a communist where he lived. He was of barely average intelligence, village education but good manual achievement as a craftsman. The assessment of BS in terms of my High F scale fails to score the "standard" patriarchal home influence. But it became clear to me that he had, instead, through the experience of an inadequate and largely missing father developed a need to compensate for this deficit in terms of the cultural model by the submission to his respected masters, on the basis of a deep sense of weakness and powerlessness. Clinically he was such a deceptively "nice" man because he had so little dynamism—only a shallow, compliant passivity. He could only have become a "wild beast" under strong outer influence. We have to rate him very high on anti-social sadism in view of his record, but it was clearly a compensatory sadism only exercised against prescribed targets and faded as soon as the outer pressure ceased. We score BS high also on "Cult of Manliness" for the obvious enjoyment of belonging to the gang of the black élite and the barrack-square life. Being treated almost as he later treated some of his victims—the pack drill and other time-honoured "recruit-bashing" procedures—seems to have satisfied the not adequately met craving for obedience and a high degree of underlying libidinal satisfaction in being submitted to this form of "manly" assault. This monotonously recurring theme in thousands of Germans—the pleasurable sado-masochistic experience of being "made into a man" by being insulted, driven and coerced in the name of some higher purpose—is once again in evidence.

It is a tenable view that, if the human capacity to introject and to split ambivalent feelings towards objects be granted, to experience gratification in such an assault by authority represents a perversion of instinctual needs and aims. The hate already engendered in a child by experiences of bleakness and privation, such as form BS's background, is vividly reactivated by the square-bashing and other cruelties, with the added libidinal element of Papa Eicke's techniques turning this into a distorted expression of paternal love. The subsequent official blessing on being himself such a "Papa" to the inmates allows the re-acting out of all this stored hate on these hapless victims. "I will make your dying tasty" could be the direct literal result of this assimilated experience. A child that has had a spanking from a parent will often be seen spanking its dolls in later play.

To this simple, limited man, the most elementary rationalizations from his upbringing sufficed to make his murderous activity quite acceptable and "ego-syntonic". There had to be order and quiet, these "Jews and prisoners" were after all nothing but foreign bodies that had to be eliminated in accordance with the good professors' teachings. After all, *he* had himself had to conform and stifle his rebellion. He was a model boy who was earning his superiors' praise in this way and showing the weak and subversive who was master. There seems to have been so little guilt and revulsion during his tenure of the KZ block leader's post that he was indeed "the unworried killer" on whom his senior colleague S2 could rely without misgivings whenever a "job" had to be done.

The dullness or emotional blunting to which a psychiatrist's report had referred at BS's trial is not easy to evaluate. Was this equanimity, so prized by S2, a primary characteristic—the "thick skin" of a rustic primitive—or was it a reactive trait? The observed data from my contact with him favour an intermediate diagnosis. Without elaborate neuro-psychiatric tests, accuracy in defining "sensitivity" is not possible, but I did not think this man more blunted or bovine than an average countryman. Nor can I accept a brain-damage effect of his "head flu" allegedly dulling his memory and perhaps perceptions. The evidence points to his having *learnt* to repress his real feelings at the so-called Oedipal phase of his development. Here he could have grown his thick, manly shell, gritting his teeth and "accepting the hard fate of the poor little man who must break stones rather than play, serve strange masters" and so on. It is a capacity I have experienced in even more marked form in the culturally favoured "impassivity" of the Russian peasant, but also as a recurring feature in my war-time German interview subjects. The latter referred to it with pride as "stur" (roughly "dogged"), underneath which self-pity at their hard lot was never difficult to discern. The quasi-physiological alibi of the "head-flu" functioned for BS as a convenient denial and forgetting mechanism in his interview with me as a defence against insight and recall. In his KZ phase the positive gratification of reliability, 100 per cent loyalty and living up to the gang norms set by, for example, S2, were sufficient to make him the "blind zealot" he was called by the judge. We may call this recourse to his "head flu" an hysterical mechanism. One of the constant findings in hysteria is the subconscious, masochistic self-pity and reliance on a bodily symptom to express it, while the emotional attitude is one called "*la beélle diniffrence*" by the older French neurologists. This was, I think, a large part of his imperturbability. It was seen *in excelsis* in Rudolf Hess's almost total amnesias, developed under our eyes, when things became too unpleasant. For BS the mechanism seems to have sufficed to mute his doubts, though between the lines he let me know that the transfer to a Waffen SS unit was a relief. But he neither drank nor smoked to excess in the KZ. Nor were there the possibilities of Auschwitz orgies with girl-inmates. His was a camp in Germany, under the vigilant eyes of prim Himmler.

During the later part of his interview BS really conceded the "unpleasant experiences" of his KZ service. These he had reconstellated as the battle with depraved enemies who were dangerous ("not a few block leaders had been murdered"), and therefore had to be absolutely cowed (Eicke's doctrine again). Once out of the milieu, he even evinced a capacity for review and for regaining some autonomy—if only in seeing that if one starts on a slippery slope one gets sucked into the vortex. That was his "never again", his complaint of the injustice to the little man.

Summary I would score BS low on paranoid trends. He was no committed ideologue—he took the doctrine of his authorities because it saved conflict and provided a good excuse for keeping his frustration rage off his in-group, who had really administered all the hurts he had ever had. The fiction that his victims all merited extra punishment (because in his "isolation" block) helped further in this direction. Nor did I think that his capacity for tenderness was exceptionally low. The evidence was in the way he spoke of his mother, who was not simply dismissed as "prima". In fact, the quality of affiliation, of needing to be safely attached and to belong, were as evident as in S2. In his own way BS loyally "stood four square" by his SS oath, and had to protest his unwavering faith in Court. Even the judge had remarked that this was not a generally explosive or aggressive character, since he had left the KZ service and had lived peaceably in the post-war community doing his old coach-builder's job and keeping a lot of children. If one was to sum up BS's personality in current psycho-dynamic terms, I would describe it as characterized by ego-weakness. Dependent and joyless, his values were those of a helpless little person propelled by hard necessity to do as he was told and to welcome the moral corset of placing himself under such coercion. "His not to reason why." Lacking a strong internal model for identification with which to make choices or protest on moral grounds he took his behaviour cues from whosoever was over him. Whom should he love or pity, but his SS mentors who made him feel somebody and promoted him? His essential inadequacy in object-relations and ego-function showed up when he went to a real fighting unit, too high in rank for such a role—hence getting into trouble and being punished and demoted. Before and after SS service he had always been a quiet, narrow craftsman.

This case reminds me of the Chaplin film "The Great Dictator". The great comedian appears as Hitler and as a frightened, dumb soldier. I took it as part of Charles Chaplin's purpose, by playing both parts, to show what ruthless power drives slumber in the oppressed, hounded "little man's" depths, as already hinted in Chapter Two. Now the tyrant and the victim are combined in the same person. BS had had his brief and terrible glory as a master of life and death in the Death's Head troops. There was even some poignant truth in his plaint how unjust the world had been to him—in giving him no adequate inner strength to withstand the systematic "carrot and stick" techniques of Himmler's training for murder.

BS was one of those "ordinary" inconspicuous men who bear out Hannah Arendt's dictum about "the banality of evil". This average man could have lived his life in quieter days unnoticed, a respectable craftsman and probably harming nobody. But for the times in which he lived, and the way his weaknesses made him respond to the blandishments of group power and his own self-aggrandisement, his regression to living out his insecurely repressed hate would most likely have been confined to petty occasions. He seemed, at any rate, to have readily mastered his sadism when the sanction for it fell away, and returned to his deferential, bland façade.

His motivations for joining the SS (via nominal Party membership) seemed to be chiefly social affiliation, wanting to cut a dashing figure and throw his weight about. The next step, into the political para-military formations, was determined by unemployment and the scent of power—this was already 1933; but the lure of "manly" training and playing at soldiers was evidently also a deep need in this mother-dominated man. Then followed the systematic hardening we have followed in the preceding men—always in the same training and con-ditioning school and by the same methods. To keep him the unworried equable killer does not seem to have depended so much on conscious overcoming of aversion as on his always shallow, hysterical and self-centred affect to which he could add the typical hysterical mechanism of splitting or emotional dissociation (with his "head-flu" as a further, later alibi). His need to show off that he was not weaker than the next man and stood out by his unthinking, blinkered zeal in the job, without hesitation or weakness (safely split off) and being Iron George's pet accomplice was evidently enough, knowing his Führer would approve and even praise. Being blinkered and of poor intelligence, this SS ethos held during his trial, though it had shown cracks when he went to a real combat SS unit, and also during his U.S. captivity. We have traced in some detail how, since his sentence, BS had managed to reform his pre-SS personality, which however retained his deep feeling of the self-pitying, hapless underdog and the corresponding strong social resentment to which the SS and the Nazi party had so strongly appealed.

CHAPTER SEVEN

TWO MEDICAL HUMANITARIANS

My next two case studies have in common a perversion of medical techniques in the service of SS policies that implemented in brutal and wholesale ways the Nazi doctrine of "survival of the strongest" and served as justification for killing those the Party wanted eliminated as useless, dangerous or merely inferior. Of the exponents and executants of these inhuman purposes I propose to cite first a medically qualified public health doctor, and secondly a sketchily trained sergeant (Scharführer) in charge of the prisoners' sick bay or hospital ward in a KZ. Both were members of the SS. Both in their different spheres illustrate the effects of Nazi dehumanization and degradation of medicine in the service of organized murder, with echoes of the "Euthanasia" programme briefly touched on in Chapter Three.

I. The Mental Hygienist

Doctor *MO*, as I shall call him, was interviewed in a prison in West Berlin in 1969. Aged 65, he had been serving his multiple life sentence there since his conviction in 1961 of active participation in the murder of 26 mentally defective German adults in a small Upper Silesian town in 1945. The murders took place when the locality was becoming a likely combat area with advancing Soviet troops. MO was further sentenced to loss of all civil rights and to being struck off the Federal Republic's medical register. His consent to being interviewed was—as in most cases—a result of the wish to put his "human predicament" to a foreign colleague whom he might impress with his scientific integrity.

No written *curriculum vitae* was felt to be necessary as this was an educated and highly verbal man. He is married with five children.

Summary of Official Evidence and Court Judgment MO was born in a village in Brandenburg in 1904. He was the son of a schoolmaster, the third of seven children. He obtained a place in a gymnasium, whence it took him till age 20 (1924) to pass his Abitur (school-leaving and university entrance examination). He studied "philosophy" and medicine at Berlin, and after interneeships in various hospitals he joined the state medical service in 1934 (when Hitler was, of course, already in power). He was appointed as the medical officer of public health of a county town (Kreisstadt) in Upper Silesia, the scene of his crime. In this town's purlieus there was a small hospital for mental defectives run by a Catholic community. The medical care of the 100 or so inmates was a part of his public health responsibilities. The patients were mainly harmless "dull and backward", with a few cases of severe mental subnormality, in an area itself rural and "backward". In 1944, MO was made battalion medical officer to the local defence militia (Volksturm). In the court evidence it was stated that after the events about to be detailed MO made his way with retreating elements of the armed forces to Czechoslovakia, where he was taken prisoner by the Soviet forces. Identified as a member of the general SS, he was sentenced to 25 years' detention by the Soviets and deported via a series of camps to one beyond the Urals. Here he functioned for a time as a camp doctor but was later transferred to physical labour. In 1953 the Soviets repatriated him with other "late returners", via Berlin. In 1954 the Berlin municipality appointed MO to a modest assistant public health post in a working-class district. Here the Federal Nazi crimes investigation caught up with him in 1956, and he was arrested and tried in the city's High court.

It was stated that MO married in 1930 while still a student and that his five children were born between 1931 and 1942. He joined the Nazi party in 1933 and the SA "medical service" two months later. In 1934 he transferred to the SS, joining a medical unit called "Sanitäts-sturm Ost" (medical company East). By 1938 he was his district's administrator for "racial policy" (one of Himmler's official SS agencies); in charge of the welfare of large families. He was also described as a lecturer on the "biology of inheritance" (Erbbiologie). The evidence then details the location, lay-out and working of the "St Joseph's" mixed geriatric and mental defectives' home, which I omit here. Of the inmates most were of higher grade, well-behaved and socialized, not only able to do some work but also, e.g., to help put out a fire in the building. This evidence was assembled to show that this was not a mass of mindless, useless imbeciles but a group of trusting, simple, child-like persons. By March 1945, the Catholic priest in charge became worried and approached the Nazi mayor with his misgivings about the fate of his flock with the approach of Russian forces, and his knowledge of the Nazis' views on "euthanasia". He could get no change out of the burgomaster. It was shown that MO had made some earlier efforts to get these patients transferred to a larger institution further away from the front line, but the later batches had been refused admission owing to great overcrowding with evacuees. We next read that in March/April 1945 three men—MO, the urban district administrator and the district peasants' leader (all Nazi functionaries)—had held meetings, at which, without discussing humane alternatives, they had by a tacit consensus indicated, mainly by gestures, that liquidation of the stranded remaining population of the Home was the right course. No one had argued, no one objected. Though some inmates had been got away in trucks, there was still, according to the witnesses, plenty of transport available, had the triumvirate chosen to use it. Instead it was standing by to evacuate the Nazi functionaries with their wives, children, "girl friends" and ample belongings; the cars having been kept in readiness, filled up with petrol, for a long time.

The evidence now showed that at the point when the decision to kill the patients had been taken, MO had advocated poisoning, instead of shooting, as "safer" or "surer" (sicherer). He had the patients paraded and administered tablets—not once (because ineffective) but twice—by mouth. The third attempt was by injection, represented to the victims as a "protective inoculation". Even after this only four out of 26 patients involved died. On the following day the three killers decided to shoot the survivors after all. Witnesses described terrible scenes of flight and pursuit of the by now thoroughly panic-stricken and desperate patients, locked in the building, with the three pursuers, including MO, shooting wildly and inaccurately at them, trying to get them into a cellar. The triumvirate had, it emerged, tried to order the town police to carry out the shooting, but in vain, as the police had not only refused but had themselves fled from the town. Witnesses stated that the trio had been heard to call the policemen "Scheisskerle" (shits) for thus "letting them down". The evidence of a medical colleague's wife stated that in the evening MO had said to her husband: "Today we've done a lot of work—we have done all those idiots in."

The defence had argued that an earlier Hamburg court had let a group of similar "euthanasia" killers off. In that case 56 physically grossly deformed children had been killed, parents' prior agreement having been obtained by the doctors by a devious trick. The parents had been warned that a dangerous, possibly lethal treatment was proposed as a last resort to help; should they not agree, then the "monsters" (hydrocephalic imbeciles, severe spastics etc.) would have to be discharged back to the parents' care. This technical assent, plus the plea of acting on "Führer's personal orders" had sufficed to get the accused off. During the trial MO had pleaded not only "lack of transport" but also his principled agreement. "I was in favour of killing worthless life (nicht lebenswertes Leben)." Challenged with the Hippocratic oath he denied ever having sworn to preserve life.

An illuminating deposition was brought to light in the official documentation. Among the inmates of the mental defective group of St Joseph's was a depressed, rather simple but not defective country girl, Miss R., whom the community had sheltered when nobody else would because she had had an illegitimate baby by a German soldier. The Nazi triumvirate were determined to include her in their "mercy killing". Several times they had to spare her because of pleading by the priest, nuns and other people who knew how devotedly she had helped in the Home. In the end, and with growing panic over the Russians' approach, they gave the final decision to shoot Miss R. "who after all was nothing but an immoral woman".

This last story throws a vivid light on the double-faced hypocritical and priggish "morality" of Himmler's Black order, which his henchmen could at need always invoke as justifying their righteous defence of the "purity" of the body politic.

The Interview (July 1969, a whole day) The prison governor shakes hands with the prisoner as he is brought in and, being thus formally introduced, I have to observe the social custom too. We are left in the governor's comfortable office, with MO quite at ease with a "colleague", and rather conceited. This is a cultured, well-preserved man with a slightly epicene 18th-century face that would look right under a powdered wig, a long nose and a somewhat cynical, almost condescending expression. He says he understands from a fellow-interviewee what I am after, and at once tells me how unjust the Berlin sentence on himself had been. Medical personnel administering *euthanasia* had not been convicted in the Federal Republic—why, it was practised in the Third Reich even during the war "in peace and good order". From his manner I gather he approved of the policy, but he refused to commit himself to my question. I now say: "In any case your action was scarcely euthanasia." He agrees, and begins to justify himself:

"I am sentenced for life on the sole crime of killing 26 mentally defective patients in a town only a few kilometres behind the front line in Upper Silesia in March-April 1945!"—as if the response of any right-thinking person must be how unreal and over-fussy the law was, considering the emergency then existing for Germany. "Although of course we knew that the war was lost, we had not ceased to defend ourselves". He felt identified with the quasi-military role of an army medical officer aiding the civil power in a front-line town to clear things for the armed forces. I merely say "the judgement stated you had not used the transport available to evacuate these patients", avoiding "why". Well, he replies, the Wehrmacht had supplied the transport and had taken responsibility for getting most of the patients out, but the army had gone, without finishing the operation. And the hospital at K., further back, had protested they could take no more. *The deeper reason now emerges.* "The military town commandant had seen these defectives wandering about (as apparently they always had been allowed to do), and had warned us that this was a military zone—'what if Gen. Schoerner (the last, fanatically Nazi, Army Group Commander on the Eastern German front) saw these people—then I'd get it in the neck!' " So the town commandant had asked the district leader (Kreisleiter) to *do* something. MO adds: "Contrary to the evidence in Court I was not at the first meeting." The decision was to kill these patients, and to order the police to do the shooting. Now I ask MO "Why?" He replies with some surprise: "But one cannot have civilians in the zone of military operations!" When I say "so it was done for military tidiness and good order", he shrugs his shoulders to show any fool should know that was obvious. MO continues: "But the police refused to shoot these people—so now I was pulled in because a doctor has to be present to certify death in such cases." (*This argument is a good example of a device frequently met with amongst the SS: MO was using a quasi-legal fiction to justify his involvement in this wanton and despicable mass murder.*) I say: "But if the police refused, why was that not the end of the matter for you?" MO becomes even more disconcerted at my failure to grasp where his duty lay: "But can't you see, Herr Professor, that if I had not intervened the whole thing would have been a bloody mess—the Kreisleiter would have done it! So of course I had to urge a more humane way—poison." So MO in his official capacity goes to the little hospital's pharmacy. "But of course the pharmacist had evacuated it already." All the lethal poisons—the opiates, etc.—had gone. But MO found a white powder lying around: "I don't any longer remember what it was," he interposes, "I hoped it would work if taken in sufficiently large doses." (*Between us we could not deduce the likely chemical, as from what follows.*) "Well it didn't go right at all"—none died on the first dosage by mouth, and even on the second day when he doubled the dose these poor people were just nauseated or vomited. With this result on the third morning, MO had found some ampoules of what he believed was called "Novalgin" (on which I commented it sounded like a compound for pain alleviation); he hoped that intravenous injections of this would do the trick. I had to ask: "Why could you not let them be and take their chance?" "No", replied MO, still clinging to his sense of his calling, "I had to stand between them and the Kreisleiter! You see they had no initiative—they did not resist us—they did not flee as they could have done!" Two or three of the patients died soon after his injections—but even MO could not be sure whether it was from the effects of the injection or from long malnutrition and stress. "So then we shot", he said laconically. "I had to certify death and indicate those still alive who should receive the mercy shot (Gnadenschuss). . . . That's all." "My Kreisleiter—or was it the Kreis-administrator?—an old soldier returned to civil work because of war wounds—did the shooting." I ask: "What did you experience at this time?" MO replies: "Strangely enough I cannot remember, but my sanitary orderly (Sanitäter) testified in court that Dr MO sat on a chair on the first floor, slumped into himself (in sich zusammengesunken), while the shooting went on in the cellar." "You see my memory is gone after 8 years in Russian captivity. Twice I suffered from dystrophy (a general medical term indicative of the effect of malnutrition especially on nervous and muscular tissues—H. V. D.). That is said to have a damaging effect on memory." I remark: "What a predicament you got yourself into." MO continues: "I could have washed my hands of it, then the 26 would have been shot—as in the end they were—I wanted to prevent the bloodshed, be more humane."

It is to be noted once again how in this man, too, the defensive manoeuvre of feeling sorry for oneself was used to shift guilt away from the fate of those much more "dystrophic" victims. Two other characteristic points occur: The first is the "reassuring" remark that the Kreisleiter was, after all, an old soldier with war wounds, which somehow made him a decent authority and excused the decision. The second was the remarkable German squeamishness about "blood" which I had found in my war-time morale studies—part of the general tendency to "depersonalize" killing by distance and "tidy" weapons, discussed earlier. The development of the gas chambers from the mass shootings is implicit in this tender concern for the susceptibilities of the killers themselves.

MO now becomes aggressively defensive. He throws at me one of the witnesses at some other trial—the mother of a child that "had had to be shot", who had said: "It would have been much nicer if the child had been put to sleep." I now remark that it might have been better for everyone if those harmless 26 people had been left where they were to take their chance with the Russians—but no, for the sake of the town commandant's dread of the general, they had to die! MO now triumphantly produces the standard Nazi rejoinder I had often heard before: "KZ were the inventions of the British in the Boer war!" I say: "Granted—but one stupid military brutality of 70 years ago does not excuse another; and I had not been speaking of KZs but of your action against a batch of very harmless fellow Germans. In any case this is just the kind of brutality our research aims to study and understand." I continue: "This kind of killing seems to me to emanate from a wish for omnipotence—the claim to be arbiters on who may survive and who must die—good SS doctrine, is it not?" MO is now thoughtful: "I was never in favour of such a policy", he says, "only of sterilization of inheritable disease carriers. This I remain"; and he goes on to quote a distinguished German geneticist, a pupil of Galton and Huxley, whom the Nazis persecuted! "It must be understood that sterilization should be done in due order and under legal safeguards—not the wild things the SS did with the Gypsies—that was wild and illegal and had nothing to do with genetic handicaps." To prove further what an objective and right-thinking doctor he really was he now describes his course for his public health qualification which included *proper* eugenics, with the dropping of more celebrated names of his erstwhile teachers. No—euthanasia was *never* discussed in the SS—it was never a public topic—it was practised secretly. "I was *only* in the general SS—nobody there had any views on euthanasia—these things were decided, as was Auschwitz—in secret—we never heard *officially*." I interpose: "And unofficially?"—MO hastily replies: "Yes, unofficially—rumours—but it was so unpleasant one preferred not to think of it, one used a half-unconscious repression (Verdrängung)." MO now informs me he had read Dahrendorf's *Society and Democracy in*

Germany—the indictment of his generation for their closed minds. He generally lets me see that he is not unversed in the area of my interest nor hides his head in the sand. He discourses on the pressure of primitive emotions in the over-civilized nations and arrives at their comparison with the Russians.

This, as I noted elsewhere, was a constant preoccupation of many Nazis— the highly ambivalently charged attraction—repulsion for the pristine, primitive and hence very potent image of the Russian "barbarian"—so fresh and strong.

MO, with intimate experience of the Soviets' handling of prisoners, first comments scathingly on their breaking of the Geneva Convention on prisoners of war, and their deceptive international façade, and then goes on to tell me, with sentimental warmth, stories of how the good-hearted simple Russian soldier had redeemed this bad image by his kindness and inborn delicacy of feeling for the unfortunates he had to guard during the convoys to Siberia. This glimpse of his *völkisch* affection for the goodness of the simple man was soon obscured by MO's serious indignation with conditions in the Soviet prison camps. First that his officer's rank and his professional status were not respected! Secondly—a side glance at the contemptible deterioration of his German brother-officers' ("even of high rank") moral decline—"why, out of their craving for tobacco they did not even scruple to steal from their own comrades!" As for himself—he *sold* his tobacco ration for extra food (presumably bartering with Soviet camp staff or other inmates). I say: "It seems that at least on tobacco you are a fanatic", and MO laughs.

MO now spontaneously turns to his early life. Frugality and abstemiousness were natural in his upbringing. "How fortunate we were in that our father was a village schoolmaster in Mark Brandenburg. It meant a natural life for us seven children. There was no money, but none of us ever envied those who were better-off. Our parents brought us up to be content. At 10 I got into a higher school in the neighbouring town—lived with an aunt on a minimum. "What one hasn't one doesn't want." And then, through his diligence and good school record, came the transfer to a famous Berlin boarding-school endowed by the Hohenzollerns, where for the last three years of schooling the authorities had offered him a free place and bursary. "I owe this to my father—yes he was strict." In reply to my prompting to describe him further, MO said: he was not a German nationalist but voted democrat. Though a middle-of-the-road man politically, father believed in Discipline and Order (Zucht und Ordnung)—Obedience there had to be! "No it did not feel as strictness because one knew nothing else." From here MO jumps straight to praising the greatness of Prussia and its virtues. "It starved itself into greatness" (grossgehungert). In reply to my question whether this was an aspect of Protestant abstemiousness, MO vehemently denies that a real Prussian is frugal from religious principle. Asceticism is a conflict over something one really wants but casts a nasty sidelong glance at God to pretend one doesn't. . . . No, Prussian frugality comes from living in the "sand-pit of the Holy Roman Empire" as the area had been called owing to its poor soil. "If it is not there one simply does not have it." Scratching a living out of the earth means constant endeavour—perhaps like the Scots must be. Again disclaiming that this Prussian capacity for discipline and self-denial has any connexion with Weber's "Protestant ethic", he prefers to see these virtues as folk-traits of "good blood", rather than attributable to the Christian God. "Always we have been hard up, ready to postpone and never to sponge."

A lull comes, and I ask MO what inclined him to join the Nazi Party. He responds with a string of clichés I had often heard. He can remember the hardships and sorrows of the First War—then Weimar— a few good years under Stresemann—then the 1929 crash in the U.S. and its repercussion on Germany—that terrible deterioration of life and political climate—the party strife. The Nazis promised unification of the nation and "so one joined". The first year (of Hitler's regime— H. V. D.) went very smoothly, but already in 1934 the first doubts came. The first year had been marked by Discipline and Order (Zucht und Ordnung—*the same words he used of his father*). "But after that people were put against the wall without legal trial. I always said to myself: so long as certain men of honour stay in the government, I am content. Thus, the Minister of Justice, Dr Guertner, who was not a Nazi, pronounced that things were all right (die Sache in Ordnung war) when these illegal arrests and shootings occurred, and one was reassured. And again, Count Schwerin von Krosigk—a man with a big family (Kinderreich), and Evangelical; he stayed in the Cabinet. And Herr von Papen—also no Nazi—so attractive (sympathisch) and a gentleman—so long as such men remained at their post that was the test (So lange er mitmacht muss es in Ordnung sein)."

I now say: "And the SS?" MO replies that he joined the Party in March—as a "March violet" (a reference to the joking analogy made between the heroes who fell in March 1848 and the band-waggon Nazis who only joined in March 1933 when Hitler had won the election). Then came the "takeover" with its big growth of the Party and the SA. "One had to show one was willing to do something for the saviours of our people—voluntarily *for* the people. I became medical officer to a SA group. This was not nice—nothing but first aid drill. Even worse were the social evenings: these common, vulgar fellows—no level at all (Kein Niveau!). Swinish jokes—rooms blue, full of smoke—that was not for me!" So he thought that as he was switching from his hospital post at proletarian Pankow (now the "capital" of East Germany—H. V. D.), to another hospital in Berlin's West End, he would transfer to the SS. That was much better—quite a different spirit (Geist). "I don't want anyone to think I did it because of the Roehm business—no I was still in the SA when that happened." The SS social evenings featured lectures with "substantial content". His decision to become a public health doctor came out of this. He became fired with the vision of eugenics—breeding good big families—taking care to improve the stock and the nurture. I now hear more "science" of genetics and positive mate selection, covered with respectable names, but really standard Nazi doctrine of "Blood and Soil".

At this point MO was taken to his lunch and on return was rather pleased with the food. He extols the virtue of simple, healthy fare and thence launches into a homily on the self-indulgent habits of the Americans—"those over-civilized peasants!", who compare so badly with the healthy, natural Russians, frugal and tough. I hear quite an outburst of hate against the U.S. "Woodrow Wilson was a dreamer! His creation, the League of Nations, was nowhere more repudiated than by the Americans themselves." "And Versailles! It was the Americans who gave the *coup de grâce* (Todesstoss) to Germany, because they had lent the Allies so much money that they could not allow them to lose the war." I remark that, interestingly, he appears to hate Versailles and the Americans more than the Nazis' usual target, the Jews. MO replies: "Yes—the Jews came much later. Few Germans were rabid Jew haters even in 1938 (Crystal night)—a very small minority. It was Hitler's own rabid anti-Semitism, due to his early experiences in Vienna, which caused the later developments—it became his *idée fixe*. Not even the SS were rabid, not fanatical, more obedient once the word had gone out." I say: "This obedience as an SS was fateful for you." "Yes," MO says, "catastrophic." His wife had fled to the now

Eastern Zone with the five young children. He was away in U.S.S.R. captivity for 8 years—and she was the "wife of an SS war criminal". After those eight years he was in better shape than his family in the Russian Zone.

"I was landed in West Berlin with a batch of other repatriated prisoners of war. We were received with great speeches by the chief burgomaster and city fathers—returned heroes—nothing but fine words and all lies! We were promised jobs and recompense—and what did I get—only a small job as assistant (Referent), when I had been a chief medical officer for a county town! A young man with two children was appointed before me!" MO now really gets worked up. "The mendacity of the Berlin authorities! 'So that is daddy's Western freedom', say my children already infected by the East!" I say: "Did you then expect the Berlin health department to sack others for your sake?" to which there was no reply. Instead MO continued to vent his resentment against mankind in general by a disquisition on its steady degeneration since the coming of technology—yes even the (as yet good) Russians will come to it—and the newly developing nations too. "It is the *empty heart*. Prometheus was rightly chained up in Ancient Greece!" He goes on once more to quote Dahrendorf—being the prison librarian he gets all the new books—yes and Mitscherlich's *Inability to Mourn* (not yet translated into English—H. V. D.) in review —"it is true the Germans are like that. Those smug bourgeois should beat their own breasts instead of projecting all their nastiness on to the Nazi and SS scapegoats!" And he had read Toynbee and cites a long bit about the Germans being no different from the English, and it "could happen to Toynbee too" (by which we both understand that MO means the break-through of murderousness). I manage to interpose: "That is why my team is studying this problem." Now he becomes still more attacking and plays Enoch Powell's "racism" as his trump card. I say: "Mr Powell wanted essentially to send as many immigrants as possible back home"—to which MO, sharp as a rapier, replies: "Ah—that's just what we heard—that's all we were told— send the Jews back to Poland! No, Herr Professor—you are too late with your work! Technology has conquered Man, and Man has lost his soul and culture." I ask: "You have no faith in Mankind—not even in the young who are protesting about this?" "No", he raps out. "Look at the brutality of these students—brutal and inhuman to their fellow-men! And ours (German students—H. V. D.) who have it best behave the worst—I could spit at them! Contrast them with the Czech students: so dignified and protesting *with* their country against tyranny. They behave well and risk their all. And our whippersnappers (Rotz-nasen)—what do they risk except a cold douche from a firehose and a chill!" MO continues his tirade against humanity by inveighing against "all that moon nonsense"; "the more technology the emptier life becomes! Spengler had said it all." At one time there had been fresh centres from which new cultures could germinate and grow—Egypt, Babylonia, China, India, Mexico, Persia, Greece and Rome, Western Europe ... "all have perished". There are no fresh germinal areas left unspoilt by the others—now even the new China is copying the West. As he goes on he becomes more and more triumphant and gloating in his apocalyptic attitude. Finally I point out how cheerful MO has become after expressing all this angry gloom. It is time—his warder comes to collect him. Courteously he apologises for his outburst. I say I had come in order to get an expression of his views on life. We part. At no point did I feel any warmth or positive bond with this man.

Commentary Perhaps the reader will agree that my chapter heading as it relates to this man is not simply sarcastic. It was meant more in the vein of the irony that MO, in his humane calling and his broad philosophical concern with preserving or improving old "natural" qualities of his culture and enriching family life, should have ended in this predicament—a convicted mass murderer; at the behest—not even on any direct orders—of his Party machine at a low local level, when even Himmler's police rejected this gruesome and unnecessary action. In MO there is exemplified the tragic confusion of strands of motivations between duty and deep hate, of obedience to incompatible systems of affiliation and loyalty. Of these the least potent is the medical, Hippocratic code, displaced by his identification with the race-hygienic and totalitarian-manipulative assumptions of the Party and the SS, idealized in the name of the greatest good for the ruling in-group. With due apologies to the great achievements of public health and social medicine, I think that these impersonal aspects of medicine are spheres where the depersonalization and dehumanization of the tasks is always easier than in the clinic where individual human beings rather than "categories" are the centre of one's efforts. To social medicine compulsory inoculations or slum clearance are good ends, while to her physician the lawful eviction of poor old Mrs Jones from her condemned little home is a personal tragedy. It is not surprising that in the setting of the emergent Third Reich a person with MO's values could here find a congenial field for externalizing his high authoritarian character traits scarcely softened by any human warmth.

MO is an uneasy mixture between "only a little man" (not in the inner counsels of the SS) and a claim to be a member of an élite. The "we" of the triumvirate in his town were the arbiters over the life and death of subordinate human beings, felt themselves important collaborators in military decisions, conscious of their high responsibility to the army. The background for MO's aspirations and arrogance, as I see it, is the "local boy makes good" story of the village schoolmaster's big family. MO gets to the fine school in the metropolis, graduates and proceeds to ally himself with the "fine gentlemen" of the band-waggon phase of the SS's sudden expansion. He despises the swinish vulgarians with whom he has nothing in common, just as the teacher, the doctor and a few other village dignitaries doubtless felt and had been revered as the leaders or élite of the local community. MO's identification with this paternal authority posture, representing Discipline and Order is easily deducible from his own career choice in public health fusing the father image of the fertile family man with the SS ideology of big family hygiene for the master race.

None the less we can perceive an unconscious split underlying this idealization. I see this, first, in the over-vigorous denial that MO, or anyone, could be capable of resenting economic hardship and privation, or be guilty of envy of wealth and ease. Father's strictness with his seven children saw to it that frugality was valued as the good, fortunate life that had made Prussians great. To this are later added Nazi elements of contempt for "American" self-indulgence and corrupting technology, and Rousseau-esque extolling of the "good backwoodsman" with his golden heart, in MO's case extended to the Russians. It is a moot point whether his emphasis that the father was not a "nationalist" man of the Right was meant as a sop to me or as an expression of mild regret. His pride and positive identification certainly go to the traditional rural community based on strict discipline and "no nonsense", and to the life he had enjoyed in the countryside with a privileged "gang" of siblings, of whom he gave no individual details. His mother was not even mentioned.

So far, then, I score MO high on an idealized, typically authoritarian identification with a strict, ordering father image which became his own inner model for professional action and consent to the "serious" blood-and-soil, ethnocentric health doctrines of the party and SS, to which rather than to any armerw, more personal human concern, his first loyalty was given. Though as a professional man MO had no previous overt history of a high cult of manliness, his stress on his military status, as the medical officer to the local defence battalion during the later part of the war, evinced his latent aspiration to soldier-liness—of being in the front line, and having therefore now to "take hard decisions without hesitation or weakness". Instead of resisting the town commandant and the Kreisleiter in the name of handicapped human beings, hisessen tially inhuman, "man-of-iron" denial of this worthless material's right to protection and safety—or even to survival—can now be justified as part of high military necessity. MO, despite the differences from his humbler, cruder fellow-killers described in previous chapters, is now seen as exactly the same sort of brutally sadistic and conformingly obedient SS functionary as if he had been drilled by the Death's Head instructor—only less efficient and not inured by routine. All the mental characteristics are there. The justification by higher state necessity and military obedience; the dread of the C.-in-C.'s wrath if the theatre of operations was not clear and tidy as demanded by orders; the agreement with high SS policy on the elimination of worth-less human beings as part of the German war for survival; hence that the SS man's—even SS doctor's—first loyalty was to follow this doc-trine; to "stand firm" in the faith even though the cause was already hopeless. The close connection between his hate against weakness and dependence and the taboo on tenderness was clearly shown in his court statement: "I am for the killing of worthless life." Much as he tried to prevaricate and modify this attitude in his interview—protesting that he was really only a humanitarian and eugenist in sympathy with "lawful" quiet mercy killing and with sterilization—the unfolding of his philosophy showed MO to be a convinced "liquidator" when he had his chance. His SS role as one of the three unflinching men of destiny prevailed over mercy and concern in the disposal of those inconvenient 26 defectives. The hollowness of his fiction, that he only wanted to save them from "bloodshed", was pitifully exposed by his botching unconcern for how effective—or even appropriate—his ethic-ally superior poisons were. This professionally disgraceful performance, inflicting even more terror and prolongation of his victims' suffering, showed his essentially destructive amorality. It was based on his need to go one better than his "old soldier" Nazi associates in proving his

100 per cent SS loyalty and ruthlessness. It contained the other SS fiction—that of legality and of denial of sadistic motive—in his insistence that a physician had always to certify death, if possible, from some respectable cause. Poisoning was not so revealingly noisy as shooting if questions were to be asked, less messy, less obvious to any witnesses. It was a miniature performance under panic conditions of what Himmler's whole organization had stood for in its planned "secret" mass-murder, under the self-deceiving cover of purification and elimination of problematic and inconvenient human beings. MO rose to the occasion when the 26 patients, already genetically condemned by his creed, proved a nuisance and threatened to provoke the Nazi general's anger—but also to interfere with the "leaders' " own smooth get-away. That night he could be the true SS soldier and tell a colleague of "all the work done". It was calculated murder of devalued beings who proved inconvenient to one's plans, no different in principle from Eichmann's alleged increasing hurry and panic lest the job would be left unfinished if the Allies won too soon.

We must try, on the data obtained, to construct an adequate theory of how and why this doctor, with his protestations of a "happy and healthy" background, succumbed to this monstrous acting-out of murderous sadism, so determined as not even to be sobered by the failure of his amateurish techniques. Once more this would appear to be a case of escalation of inner disruption under the pressure of group "contagion". The inner disposition can be shown to have the herein recurrently recorded internalized experience of severity, bleak frugality and moral coercion which had to be reconstellated in the subject's mind as a loving favour, with the splitting off or repression of the frustration-generated hate into a quite severe internal persecuting bad object. At this distance from his "forgotten" but idealized childhood it is guesswork how much of it was due to having to accept so many younger siblings, or to swallow so much envy of better-off schoolmates at the upper-crust grammar school in which he was a penurious scholarship boy; or the social climate of school and university with its middle-class fear of the "lower orders". At one level the result of such repression showed itself in his reactive need to deny envy and greed, to despise moral failure or weakness. We recall his self-righteous pharisaical condemnation of his "swinish" SA comrades with their obscene jokes, and of the poor girl who was "only an immoral woman" and therefore need not be spared. This is gross psychological projection.

At another level we see the emergence of the "poor, humiliated victim" side of this relation to the persecuting internal object in the accounts of MO's own hardships—quite unrelated to his own masterful attitudes—when the Russians do not honour his status; or when his starvation in Siberia produces "dystrophy", or when Berlin city hall does not give him the job he thinks he should have as the returning hero-victim. So much for his freedom from envy, greed and need for being indulged. Projection is also grossly at work in the way he can insightlessly redirect Dahrendorf's analysis of the German citizen's lack of concern on to the "smug bourgeois" who uses the poor SS as a scapegoat. MO does not realize how in this contempt for the self-righteous, unconcerned German he is expressing his unconscious hate against the very respectability and Prussian severity in which he was so proud to have been cradled. It is typical hate against the painfully assimilated, anti-love (anti-libidinal) model of the obedient, striving manly boy, down on softness and self-indulgent weakness.

Freud, in his *Civilization and its Discontents*,[1] had long ago analysed the connection between unconscious hate of civilization, of its restraint on enjoying love and warmth and of the limitations on the free exercise of aggression which "Discipline and Order" had imposed on men. MO was an example of such discontent and hate. Again projecting this chilling experience on his environment, he talked with perhaps greatest sincerity about the way in which culture and technology had produced an *inner emptiness* in man. There really was no hope that mankind would find a new way of regenerating itself. Men are irredeemably bad, but how nice if they could have remained primitive, potent and "fresh" like his Russians. This Spenglerian gloom has been aptly named in German "*Kulturpessimismus*" which Freud not only described but to some extent shared. Frau v. Baeyer-Katte, an insightful observer of her society, has recorded her observations on the development and sources of Nazi attitudes in men's minds.[2] She cites several examples of people whose personal resentment at the excessive renunciations, or else at the deterioration in the status and cultural influence of their middle-class between the wars, had made them hostile to civilization, expecting, and half-wishing for, its downfall and chaos. They then became easily vulnerable to Nazi language and ideas with their promise of renewal, of sweeping away the old, rotten bourgeois dead-end world and replacing it with a clean, affirmative, "back to sources" world. Such was MO's hostility to America and the West and to their tool, the Weimar regime, all of which had to be written off as doomed, materialistic and corrupt.

Dr. v. Baeyer-Katte points out how these "Kultur pessimists", who flocked into the Nazi party, could put their faith in Hitler's airy, semi-prophetic promise of a Reich "that would last a thousand years" and not care what form it might take, so long as it reaffirmed a simple, healthy "back to nature" unity of "all that was sound and creative" and condemned all that was alien, unhealthy and degenerate. The paranoid element in this "Blood and Soil" doctrine should be obvious from all that has been said earlier. Essentially born of the passivity and "helplessness" of such characters, this despairing trust in the magic transformation by a great leader was a minifestation of deeply destructive feelings against dangerous "otherness", i.e. the non-conformity of individualism. It was a neurotic attitude of intolerable inner contradiction between the compulsion to submit to the "rotten old" authority (church, law, conscience) and the desire to break out, rebel, smash everything. It was the latter which was now projected on to what was alien, Voltaire's "écrasez l'infâme".★ Norman Cohn has shown how similar to such ideas were the periodic "millennialist" movements of mediaeval central Europe.[3] Incubated among the downtrodden poor and hungry, smarting under tyrannies of various kinds, these movements had in common a conviction that "the Last Days were at hand", that Satan under one guise or another had, or was about to take, power and possessed all the existing leaders and institutions, spiritual and secular. Against these the movement would rise, in a crusade of the elect under a leader with prophetic charisma who proclaimed that the time was at hand to purge the world of all corruption and prepare for the millennium, in which naturally the elect would rule in glory, peace and plenty. The majority of these movements found plenty of authority in Holy Writ to prove that theirs was the divine mission to slaughter the enemies of God as his chosen angels of wrath.

I have made this brief excursion into themes to which I hope to recur in the final chapter, to help me, and perhaps the reader, to clarify the dangerous fantasy-systems active in this undistinguished doctor, to whom the SS and its great cleansing mission came as a sheltering as well as releasing organization. The escalation towards violence, that found its most extreme model in the TKVs of the concentration camps

★ Voltaire's words were meant for the Church.

and the Einsatzgruppen (those completely radicalized "ideal" practitioners of "cleansing"), finally broke surface in MO who, under the influence of front line panic and of "Old Soldiers" as his guarantors, could at last show he was one with them and "had a go".

2. THE MERCY KILLER

GM, as I shall call him, was interviewed by me in a prison in Hesse in 1967. Here he was serving multiple life sentences imposed by the court at Fulda in December 1960 for many proven murders and homicides committed during his service as the sick-bay "charge nurse" at a KZ in Austria during 1944, with the rank of SS sergeant.

*Curriculum Vitae** Written in a clumsy hand and poor style in 1959 as a deposition during GM's investigation by the prosecution.

Born 1903 at M. (a small town) in Sudetenland, while this was still part of the Austro-Hungarian Empire. Here he went to the primary school and then three years to a "Bürgerschule". Apprenticed as a mechanic (Schlosser), but could not finish "because his father was called up into the Austrian army" in World War I. (*This is an unlikely reason*) GM next stated that for two years he served as a probationer lay-brother in a Catholic mission near Vienna, but left because he felt no vocation. He returned home (by this time in the new Republic of Czechoslovakia), and got a job in the "timber industry" (Sawmill—H. V. D.). He was next called up for military service in the Czech army, as his family had become Czech citizens. He served in an engineer (sapper) regiment, where owing to being bilingual he rose to the rank of corporal. On his release he returned to work in the sawmill and in 1928 married a local girl by whom he had two daughters, born in 1929 and 1936. In 1937 he became a municipal street or road worker (Strassenwärter) until January 1940. After the German troops entered the Sudetenland (following "Munich", late 1938—H. V. D.), he writes: "I came into the general SS" (*the wording conveys a sense of passivity, rather than of his own choosing*), and in January 1940 he was "drafted" (eingezogen) into the Waffen-SS. He next lists his service locations: first an SS depot at Gotenhafen (Nazi name for Gydnia near Danzig on the Baltic—H. V. D.), thence to the female KZ Ravensbrück, and from there to the Austrian camp and its various out-stations. (*The main camp was a specially severe "punishment camp",*

* Summarized.

while the subsidiary ones housed slave labour). He does not specify at all what he did there, but continues at once that then he was in Austria at the end of the war when he succeeded in crossing the frontier into Czechoslovakia, "in order to get home". Here he was apprehended by the Czechs, but escaped back to Austria. He was again arrested by the U.S. army and returned in a convoy to Karlsruhe in Germany. From this collecting centre he managed to disappear, and at Karlsruhe the employment office assigned him as agricultural labourer to a farmer. He soon met a war widow who "got him better work" as he "did not have it good with the farmer". "Later I lived with her" (wohnte ich bei ihr). "I heard my family was no longer alive", so he married the widow in a registry office. He went back to his old occupation of road work. In 1954 one of his daughters traced him. So he "had to have his marriage declared invalid" and parted from the bigamous wife and returned to his family in 1954, now domiciled at Fulda. Here he stayed at first with his mother and later with his (real) wife. In 1955 he was arrested at Fulda, his bigamy having drawn the attention of the law to himself.

Summary of Court Proceedings and Judgment   GM's father was a pure Czech. His mother was an ethnic German, who died in 1960. The father was a prison warder in the Austrian town jail of M. until called up into the army. He was killed on the Russian front in 1917 (when GM was 13-14 years old). GM had two brothers, one of them a monk, the other a "well respected" (angesehen) merchant in his homeland. The evidence showed that GM and his brothers were brought up "as Germans by their German mother". The interruption of GM's apprenticeship was due to unemployment (not to his father's death—H. V. D.). It was his mother, a severely religious and devout woman, who sent GM to the monastic mission near Vienna as she wished him to become a member of the Brotherhood. Here GM never advanced beyond attending to the central heating and similar menial tasks. It emerged, in addition to the details of his marriage, military service, work in the sawmill, etc., that GM obtained employment with a private security company to which the town assigned the outside patrolling of its prison "perimeter". GM had applied to become an inside warder (like his father had been), but the Czech selectors had refused to employ him because GM had declined to declare himself as a Czech, opting to be part of the Sudeten-German minority. The evidence stated that

GM joined the Nazi party and SS when Germany occupied the Sudetenland, "although he had evinced no previous political interests". His wife's brother was the local party leader (Ortsgruppenleiter), and "the accused had hoped for an improvement in his economic position".

The official documents showed that in 1940 an SS medical officer (named) initiated action to have GM declared unfit for the Waffen SS, as too unstable mentally ("labil"). Home leave from Gdynia followed, but in 1941 he was called up to be posted to the TKV training unit at Oranienburg* (one of Eicke's original training depots). It appears that here GM was discovered to have had some first-aid instruction as a member of the home town voluntary fire brigade. He was now assigned without further nursing or medical auxiliary training to the SS medical branch and given a course of instruction in the techniques of "euthanasia" by injections of air (which causes fatal embolism of the blood vessels) and of benzine. After being thus recruited for "special treatment methods" GM was allowed no further home leave. His misdeeds relate chiefly to a period when he was not in the punishment camp but in a "working" KZ for slave labour.

The bulk of the official record of the trial and the judge's summing up was made up of evidence of GM's "monarchic rule" once he had become the charge nurse of the hospital barrack at the Austrian KZ in 1944—"where he maltreated prisoners in a shocking manner, killing by injections, by throttling or by starvation". "He never showed compassion because he did not consider the prisoners human." The prosecutor described him as "animated by quite exceptional malice and scarcely credible bestiality". Witnesses had described him as always more brutal when the commandant was present. "He kow-towed towards his superiors and kicked those under him." Having, in the prosecutor's words, served as a "decent" ("brav") road man and (*this is new*—H. V. D.) verger in his parish church, "he might have continued a straight life had he not *volunteered* (my italics—H. V. D.) for the SS —including the TKV". He had been known as a modest, pious young man. At Ravensbrück (the female camp, his first posting—H. V. D.), he was said still to have been outraged ("entrüstet") when he saw other SS men maltreat inmates, but his boss had said "he'll get used to it". So, the prosecutor continued, he took his direction from evil example, wanting to impress the commandant at his Austrian KZ with his zeal. At the trial he talked of people he had strangled "as of no further

* See Chapters Three and Five.

use" (zu nichts mehr zu gebrauchen), i.e. he admitted strangling. "There were too many useless mouths" (in coarse German "zu viele unnötige Fresser"). This complete dehumanization was extended to all his prisoners, who were "simply numbers"—among them French lawyers, a Greek doctor who after the war became royal physician. GM had said of all such persons "those aren't people—they have to be handled quite differently". This meant merciless beating of people who were sick or had to be admitted into the over-filled hospital barrack. A particularly cruel incident occured when 15 young Slovak Resistance fighters were brought to his camp by the Gestapo. All were wounded. GM had them thrown naked into a bare room without windows, their wounds not dressed, and starving. Here he beat them daily until successively they died. He had admitted in court that he had helped a batch of inmates by giving them ropes with which to hang themselves. Eleven had done so, but in three cases he admitted "he had helped a bit" (nachgeholfen), by hanging them on bedposts. A young Russian trying to escape had been run down by a pursuit car, and his leg was broken. When sent into the sick bay, GM had thrown him into a cellar among the already dead where the Russian expired.

Some of GM's atrocities, verified in the court, were such that I hesitate to record them here. Essentially they showed that his greatest venom went to persons who suffered from diarrhoea and were incontinent. His favourite site for beatings were mens' buttocks, but there was much evidence to show that his habitual method of killing was by manual throttling; though he would also use his jack boots to trample prisoners, whom he had floored, to death.

Something like a systematic pattern, typical of the inner contradiction in SS "higher policy" emerged from this trial. On the one hand GM's was supposed to be a camp for inmates capable of work in neighbouring defence industrial plants, who were to be "spared". On the other hand the camp leadership was stated to have "made a good business" out of hiring these slave labourers to industry at 5-6 Reichsmark a day, while only allowing them budgeted rations of one-tenth that value. With this starvation regime a man lasted 150-200 days before collapsing from inanition. That was the moment for sending him to hospital which was, according to the evidence, including GM's own, expected "to do what was necessary" to dispose of these "useless" enemies of the state. This appeared to be the main function of the "sick ward". A picture of GM's reign as the de facto overlord of this "Place without Hope" (Ort ohne Hoffnung), as witnesses called it, illustrates both the depths of degradation to which SS medicine had sunk and the face-saving of its image which was part of this incredible picture.

GM was depicted as strutting about his domain as the indubitable ruler, in white gown with a stethoscope *and* a rubber-truncheon. Under his direction worked a number of qualified foreign medical prisoners. His attitude to persons sent for hospitalization was to question their need for it. Men with bandages had these brutally torn off "to see if they were really wounded". A Jew begging to be admitted out of despair was so severely beaten up by GM there and then that he died in the entrance lobby. A French prisoner-physician testified that GM's one acquired skill, the killing by "injection", was daily practice. Yet at other times GM would requisition medicaments from the pharmacy, proposed by his medical "slaves", but rarely administer these. Castor oil was his treatment for all abdominal conditions. He would then forbid such patients to go to the toilet, but beat or kill them if they soiled themselves. Described as sullen and morose, there was an occasion witnessed by all the surviving medical prisoners, when after someone had complained of going without a drug GM took all the remaining supplies of medicaments and poured them into a bucket, saying: "In future no patient will lack anything!" (a pun in German: "wird keinem Kranken mehr etwas fehlen") and actually *laughed*. Jews were the principal objects of his hate. He admitted to starving those "patients" he did not like—then they became "useless". A Hungarian physician survivor described in court how GM had made him draw up the official daily returns of deaths. The doctor was forced to enter fancy diagnoses and even append faked temperature charts that fitted. The monstrous last column entry was "The body had to be cremated for reasons of hygiene".

GM's bearing during the trial was a mixture of denial and self-exoneration with progressive concessions that the charges were true. He made his statements with "fluttering eyelids but in a calm voice full of Bohemian "Gemütlichkeit". He had admitted a series of murders at the time of his arrest but disputed these later in court. He conceded five cases of strangling but with the emphasis on "*only* five". As the evidence piled up, he would at first say: "Much as I regret to have got into this witches' cauldron (Hexenkessel), I cannot do other than stick to my original statement." The number of killings admitted rose from 5 to 10, then 18. "Yes, in KZ X. I was in most cases compelled to kill, and I regret this deeply today."

Then, in May 1959, during the proceedings, he declared that since 1945 he had not had a calm conscience any more: "I want to come clean (reinen Tisch machen) and stand straight for what I have done." The number of deaths for which he accepted responsibility now reached 200. He could, however, never be brought to use the word "töten" (to kill). Newspaper reports described GM as "always remaining the dutiful little man who could not at all understand what an unjust world wanted of him". At times he would suddenly show his impulsive irascibility. He or his defending counsel used the pleas that he killed on orders to liquidate, but never reached the numbers desired by his superior officers, under the duress that had he not obeyed he would have been made to suffer. This was discounted by the judge because the camp was meant to keep prisoners alive and fit for work. Alternately, in other contexts, he pleaded, especially in the injection cases of sick persons admitted to his care, that he had acted from compassion (Mitleid) to save them needless prolongation of suffering. This was also disallowed by the court, since he killed those he had first starved into collapse. Though he admitted starving people he pleaded that "there was a dearth of supplies", and to the last he denied evil motives and played down the numbers advanced by the prosecution. The court was fair—it deferred some charges on lack of definite evidence. These related both to fatal injections and more bizarre methods. GM followed the judge's summing up with an expressionless face, and stood motionless to attention during the pronouncement of the sentence.

The mixture of "manly facing" of the charges and obstinate denial and minimal concessions would seem to be a general feature of these SS killers' attitudes at trial. As for the first, there is the general SS indoctrination of courageous "standing foursquare" by one's deeds as the worthy stance of the élite brotherhood, which would be justified by history. The contesting would seem to have been a position recommended to these accused by the association of former SS men who came to function as a kind of legal aid and welfare society tolerated in the Federal Republic with its humane and liberal policy on the freedom of association and of the person.

GM had been examined by medical and psychological methods. The prison report stated (May 1959) that he had some impairment of hearing; some sub-cortical insufficiency (a euphemism for his defective emotional control which even the SS had found—H. V. D.), a raised blood pressure and some bronchitis with wheezing. His body configuration was described as showing "feminism"—i.e. an untypical fat distribution and pubic hair for a male (a condition not infrequent in middle-aged men of thick-set, "pyknic" build). He was excused exercise and work in a dusty atmosphere. GM's excitability had led to his being placed in a single cell, but later in 1959 the prison medical staff found him a "suicidal risk" and he was ordered back into a shared cell with special suicide precautions. His personality was described as sullen, unresponsive and difficult to see through (undurchsichtig).

The Interview (April 1967, GM now aged 64). A thick-set, pale and pasty-faced man, with knitted bushy eyebrows over penetrating dark eyes and a toad-like slit of a mouth. The whole effect is most repulsive, like that of an Edgar Wallace villain. Nothing of the Nordic soldier about him. I explain my wish to hear his life story and how he came to be here. We are comfortably seated in the Governor's study and have all day. GM at once plunges into an animated denial that he was ever "a Nazi". He says he *had* to become a Nazi in 1939 (after Hitler's occupation of the Sudeten area—H. V. D.) because he was "pressured" (hineingedrängt). Understanding how he wished to make public his self-exoneration to a foreign scholar when his trial had not done so, I said his life, after all, started long before that time.

It was impossible to get a description of his first ten years. GM's father emerged as a remote, possibly uninterested but mild figure, whereas the mother was seen as controlling, severe and almost fanatically religious, "pressuring" her sons into strict Catholic observance. GM mentioned his brothers (see above), and then his father's call-up into the Austrian army and his death on the Russian front, at a time "when there were no widows' pensions". "We all had to work." He did not want to be a mechanic, he had wanted to become a gardener, but he "could not choose". To my question he replied he did not recall any "great feeling" when news of his father's death was given to the family. GM jumped straight to his own call-up into the Czechoslovak army (*without mentioning his years as a novice in the religious brotherhood*). I had, once again, the by now familiar recital of the hardships of his adolescence—"not like modern times"—full of bitter self-pity and resentment.

GM served in a Czech pioneer regiment (the equivalent of the Royal Engineers in the British army—H. V. D.) with a complement of some 70 per cent of German speakers. He, as a bilingual, was used as an intermediary and interpreter between the Czech officers and these men. GM said these ethnic Germans reviled him (bemeckerten) for speaking

Czech, as if he was a traitor. He felt he belonged to neither party properly. He was sent to an NCO school, and added: "I have to live where I can earn my living." He had therefore thought of a 12-year regular army enlistment for security, but turned it down "because they did not give enough guarantee of certain post-service employment", and his service in the Czech army might even be prejudicial to him in the irredentist Sudeten area. At the end of his period of conscripted service he therefore got a job in a sawmill in his home town, but changed to becoming a security guard with a Czech firm when a vacancy offered although he did not like it—"my certain living mattered more than sentiment". This post included the patrolling of the outer walls of the prison in which his father had been an inside warder. The organization seemed to be analogous to a non-governmental "veterans' corps" used on contract.

This corps had an inspector (who was a Czech), with a daughter, four years younger than GM, who already had two illegitimate children. GM kept being invited to their home and "could see what the inspector was after". GM was repelled by this girl and her reputation, too clearly for his boss who now hinted that he liked to see his corps men married. So GM went and courted a German girl whom he could trust because she "had all the female virtues and was not a fashion doll (Modepuppe)", and soon after married her. Within three months he got the sack from his job with the security guards and was back on casual gang labour (Hilfsarbeiter) on the roads.

By now there was plenty of Nazi propaganda about in the Sudetenland, but GM was emphatic that he was one to hold back and "wait and see which way the cat would jump", though his own brother-in-law was the party leader in the town. Nobody in Czechoslovakia opposed this propaganda—the Czechs seemed helpless, so it got to be more and more of a movement. After the Germans walked in in 1939, GM said, the local dignitaries such as the doctor, the school headmaster, the postmaster, etc., still sat as always at the same table at the inn; only now they were joined by two new gentlemen in black uniforms canvassing for membership of the SS among the local young men. Though 4 out of 5 of the clients were Czechs—they all paid up and joined, at least as "supporting members". Once GM had joined he was given a regular job with the road service—(Strassenwärter). He had a German "master" (Meister—foreman in this context) put over him who had the gold Nazi party badge and was a great propagandist. It was this foreman who "pushed" GM and several others into the full SS. "We hardly knew what it meant. There were five of us Germans, three of them old, all the rest were Czechs. We were passed in as fit and signed on. Only then I realized I was half a soldier again, when they started on the drill with us". . . . "Yes it was the little men who had to carry the can" (mussten dann hinhalten), he said in a complaining voice.

GM now recounts how he was drafted to an SS reserve depot at Gdynia in 1940 where he was assigned to the "active SS". He developed stomach trouble by the following July and an SS medical board of two doctors pronounced him as unfit for the Waffen SS. (*It will be recalled that the diagnosis was of emotional instability in the documents.*) So then he was made a clerk in the medical department—"nothing else" (*this to deny that he was taught how to give lethal injections*)—and later given 8 weeks' home leave. After this he was recalled and posted to Oranienburg which was the central depot and headquarters for the entire Waffen SS. (*He mentions no course of instruction or that his was a voluntary transfer to the TKV.*) GM continued that from here he was assigned to the female KZ at Ravensbrück. This he disliked intensely because, he said, "I am not a fool for women (Kein Frauennarr)". He was repelled by the thousands of female inmates "who had had no sexual intercourse for years, and who ogled you and kept calling after you". "I became very troubled by this and asked for a transfer; so they put me into the camp sick bay with a male and two female doctors in charge." (*He did not specify his duties, except that this was the SS staff hospital.*) After some time in this post he was transferred to the Austrian complex of KZs, where also he was initially in the camp staff sick quarters at the central or HQ compound. Only then, towards 1944 was he put "in charge" of the ancillary "work camp" hospital barrack for the inmates.

Here, said GM, was "everything"; Jews, "Red" Spaniards, Frenchmen, Poles, Hungarians, Slovenes and Russians. There were also common criminals, "politicals" and "anti-socials" who were in preventive custody. He had some prisoner-physicians who did the medical work, but he was in charge. "Someone had to see to it that there was order!" "There were always people there who were dying—some from malnutrition, some from despair." Wasn't it kinder to put these doomed sufferers out of their misery? Why, he could remember two "fine old French gentlemen" of the upper class who were terribly weak and desperate, because they were to be moved from the work camp to another KZ. So he gave them "the injection" because he wanted to spare them that dreadful journey which they could not have stood. Yes, he suddenly added, he wanted to anaesthetize them! "Yes when it is time for me to meet my Maker, then before that Higher Justice it will be seen that I was not a bad man." I say at this point that GM could not deny that in those camps where he served somebody caused a lot of prisoners' deaths, and that he must have known his superiors wanted enemies of the regime eliminated. GM avoids a reply to this remark, but instead says I should bear in mind that there was a lot of "self-sabotage" among the inmates, a cover name which included both self-induced sickness (in other words malingering), and mutual denunciations of each other. *In this, of course, GM employs one of the frequent defence rationalizations of the TKVs: these contemptible subhumans were so dishonourable that they did not deserve pity—as indeed his next remark displayed the other favourite (see my last schedule in Chapter Four under "denial").* GM's face now assumed a very unpleasant sadistic expression as he continued: "And these prisoners always broke the rules which brought punitive measures into action against them." What was a man to do in face of this threatening chaos and anarchy? Everything was short—staff to supervise them, space, food, medical supplies. Nobody cared what happened in the camp—*he* had the responsibility—a Scharführer (SS sergeant)! The only German medical officer, nominally responsible, was an air force doctor from a nearby station who looked in once a day and asked "anything special to report?" When GM gave him the list he merely said: "Very well—you get on with it", and drove away again.

The camp commandant, an SS lieutenant (Obersturmführer), was always drunk. GM relates how this man boxed his ears when something displeased him. And how could GM retaliate? He wasn't going to risk being shot for a man like that! But he did once telephone the medical officer to report the commandant's behaviour towards himself, and got the unhelpful reply: "Why don't you hit him back?" At once, however, GM displaces his resentment to his foreign prisoner-doctors' iniquities. They were so unfair and deceitful! His hospital barrack for prisoners was so cramped—a ward for 50 people usually had to house several hundred, lying four to a bunk. Yet here was, for example, a Polish doctor sending him a Pole with nothing wrong with him: the Greek doctor had said so! Yes, no wonder he did lose his temper with these rascals who tried to cheat him for the benefit of their nationals, to get them off work! When he, GM, could do nothing for them! Yes, he did lose his temper and hit these malingerers out of exasperation, he won't deny it—but *never* to hurt them, no never! When supplies were so short and he could get none by ordinary channels, he once went to the SS senior medical officer to see if that way he might get some needed drugs. That man produced a stick and said: "This is the best medicine for those people."

I now said that GM had answered my earlier question: he did know that his superiors wanted the inmates maltreated and destroyed. To this he shrugged his shoulders and said: "I had a wife and two daughters —so I had no choice but to obey." Now, he continued, he was totally disenchanted. Had he known what it would lead him to when he joined the SS he would not have fallen for it. He had learnt how bad all human beings round him were. "Take those kapos" (the common criminal "trusties"—see Chapters Three and Five). Often he saw these people pull the caps off prisoners' heads and throw them beyond the boundary fence. When the prisoner ran to retrieve his cap the sentry would shoot him for crossing the line as "trying to escape". GM said: "I had signed a document that any contravention of superior orders meant death for me." So here were these "illegal" shootings, and the only thing to do was not to take any notice. *He* would not have acted without orders to kill, even going as far as he dared to defy such commands. His limit of opposition to orders, he believes, came in the case of those 15 Slovak Resistance fighters who were brought into the camp by the Gestapo operating against such internal partisans. GM said: "I tried to make the Slovaks comfortable, but when the Gestapo officer saw this, he told me at gunpoint that if those men were still alive by the next day his gun would be pointed at me." Well, so GM spirited them away into a disused room where the authorities might not find them. But again he had to face his commandant with the enquiry: "Well, have you despatched those Slovaks?"— "No, this is your last chance!" What was he to do—so he gave them ropes telling them they were doomed, let them hang themselves. Impatient and explosive (jähzornig) he may have been but never a murderer. As an English Christian I must know, he said, that there was a law higher and even more strict, and how deeply this religious law was in him. At this point GM vouchsafes me the information that he had spent two years trying to become a religious brother; was it thinkable that such a man as he could go against these principles? I replied that it was unfortunately thinkable, for I knew of many Nazis and SS men, brought up in the Catholic faith, who had given it up and in their SS faith had committed the kind of deeds we had been talking about. At this point the prison routine of supper asserted its claims and the interview with GM ended.

Commentary The reader will recognize a certain recurring pattern in the self-presentations or personalities of these interviewed men. This typicality relates especially to the manner of pleading their humanity and essential goodness in self-justification. This is always to stress the aspect of the "little man" who has to do the nasty jobs and stand the punishment; hence the *passivity* of being helplessly sucked into the vortex by forces he dared not safely resist. This is an aspect of being the "good", obedient, soldierly subordinate, true to his vow of loyalty, and standing foursquare before the judgment of history or Divine Law, however wrongfully traduced he has been by all the revered authorities now turned cruel and merciless. There is also, recurrently, the cloak of forgetfulness, of virtual denial or, if that is impossible, of side-stepping the direct affirmation that it was indeed he who did these things. Somehow he was involved, but not really, there were plenty of others, and how could he avoid sometimes having to give the appearance of being as bad as they, had he not his own safety to think of, a required norm of group behaviour to copy?

Coming to a closer scrutiny of GM's performance on my variables, I have first to state that, notwithstanding Captain A. (Chapter Six), this was the most generally repugnant character I met. He was devoid even of the defensive anxiety and, one may say, the appeal of despair that gave me my moment of horrified compassion with Captain A. GM's was a reptilian, cold personality oozing callousness and self-interest. He was the under-endowed, impulsive, unstable brother in his family, who before the SS never got beyond a road-labourer, always out for security and a better, softer living. What moral values he had were never assimilated but remained, as it were, the externally imposed precepts of his mother: his early activity in the Church, and his rigid anti-libidinal attitude towards women and sex. Here he had a very obvious and deep taboo from an unresolved, unconsciously resented, tie to his mother. His wife was chosen on that model, and the only other person we hear of is another widow who rescues and houses him. We recall his horror of "sexual" women. One can see

GM being a passive son of a strict and forceful mother. He takes everything and gives no love or gratitude; on the contrary, resents it. In this case the "Oedipus" solution of early years seems inverted. The historical father was a shadowy, ambivalent figure in GM's mind, and his place was taken by the mother. We may even speculate whether the cold, calculating son had not unconsciously adopted an impassive, stubborn resistance against being a soft weakling in his mother's hands, but longed to have a father authority instead, not subject to a woman. It is impossible to assert such an identification without data GM could not give me, of the image of his parents' roles in his early years. It certainly seems he was not permitted to have a good relation to the father. He wanted to be a prison warder and a soldier like father, but the German mother wanted him to be a German and a monk. GM never identified firmly with anything but always waited to see how the cat would jump. He was even reviled for having a Czech father. We see his conformity to what German authoritative figures tell him to do, not least because they can hurt and sack him. He is powerless and contemptible. The SS was the line of least resistance, and promised security. There is no hint that he had any ideological or national fervour. But the German Father-figures had power, to join them was to erase the humiliating weakness of being half a Czech sub-man himself, and so he would be a good mother's son. Like my other interviewees S2, Captain A. and BS, GM felt underprivileged and hard-done-by economically. To this was added the feeling of being the backward son who was neither a religious nor a commercial credit to his mother. The chief quality one was aware of was GM's brooding, nasty diffuse resentment at being an underdog. Even the Waffen SS wrote him down as a reject only fit for a sanitary orderly. This was an example of the type of TKV recruit earlier described as "the dregs of the population", of whose bad qualities and wanton cruelty even Hoess, the commandant of Auschwitz, had complained with despair as letting down his vision of the clean, committed killer-saint doing the Fatherland's hard bidding in the soldierly manner.

Even for GM this high-minded model became his alibi or mandate. Once given excessive authority, and anxious to please his "masters", all his pent-up resentment and underdog fury could vent themselves on people he even recognized as better than himself but who were now in his power. At this point the thin veneer of the "nice quiet" young man who had been a church helper and had learnt a bit of first aid for the fire brigade (the submissive face of the sado-masochistic character) cracked to reveal his internal pressure to be a hard boss and prison warder, to get even, to show who was master. He could now identify with his German detractors of the Czech army days and, in projecting his weak, despicable alien self to his foreign victims, turn the persecution he had suffered against them. We can conclude, that in repressing the hate fraction of his ambivalent Oedipal object-relation, GM became both the conformist and the secret resentful rebel against such coercion. I scored GM high on projectiveness, on tenderness taboo and on sadism. His "father-identification" was equivocal. It *seemed* as if his dichotomy was not so much between love and hate as between strength and weakness, the emotions being hate (grudging respect) versus contempt. The former goes to "German"—the mother *qua* father object; the latter to "Czech" or "alien", to the oppressed, despised father whose absence the unconscious interprets as betrayal—hence easily to racist ideology—and to himself.

The typical social variables of insecurity, economic privation, broken home (fatherless) and "ethnic frontier" mentality are all here. But perhaps more clearly than in some others the personal intra-psychic factors impelling GM towards his callous, cold and secretly gloating cruelties stand out. His predilection for (*a*) throttling; (*b*) inducing and/or savagely punishing diarrhoea; (*c*) starving those he hated most; (*d*) his strange ambivalence about giving and witholding "medicines" and (*e*) the falling in with turning "good" or medical injections into poisonous, destroying injections forms a pattern to some extent intelligible, thanks to psychoanalytic research into early psychic mechanisms. I must try to display this somewhat technical matter, as it goes to the roots of aspects of infantile omnipotence and unconscious primitive object-relations highly relevant to our theme.

GM shared with several of the other interviewed men a strong sense of insecurity and privation of good things; and also a defective sense of personal identity. There was a double bind: having to be ashamed of the Czech half of himself, but also suffering social disadvantage and economic discrimination for *not* being a Czech, all imposed by his exacting, fanatical Catholic and German-opting mother. His manifest inferiority feelings coupled with real privation in the war years (1914-1920) must have touched him, as the son least able to rescue this impoverished, declassed (for was father not an official?) war-widow, more severely than his successful brothers. All this would favour, as

Wangh has also argued[4] a regressive reactivation of infantile longing for the supply of good food and love of which he felt deprived. With this primitive "greed" was coupled typical resentment against the originators of the frustration that had to be internalized as "bad, anti-libidinal objects". Both classical psychoanalysis and Fairbairn's more recent theoretical formulations agree that the phenomena comprised in the term "anal sadism" tend to be important channels for discharge of this bad internal object relation, felt in fantasy as evil body contents and hence to be ejected. Excrement becomes the symbol of all the badness and hate taken inside as oral privation, just as at the stage of toilet-training the acquisition of muscular control over the anus and so over the faeces can become the setting for rebellion against the depriving, punishing authority figure, internalized as well as outside. Witholding a stool as an act of defiance or passive resistance is a well-known nursery manifestation of it. But also to be dirty and faecally uncontrolled is both disgraceful and weak; and it can become a more "explosive" act of hate, defiance and rejection in the earliest war against authority. To the reality of such unconscious equation of faeces with weapons of attack the daily practice of psychoanalysts can testify. In my own practice there have been not a few patients who, frustrated and enraged with me or with outside persons have developed immediate diarrhoea or vomiting or both. So far, then, GM's hate-laden inner world can be seen to contain this primitive theme.

Two further aspects of it need to be commented on. First, the two-faced significance of the bad internal matter that has to be ejected. It is not only the internalized image of the rejecting frustrating figure which is thus being expelled—that is one face. The other face consists of the subject's own feelings of reciprocal but impotent hate and destruction felt against that figure—in fact the bad destructive side of oneself. The second aspect is closely related to the first. The psychic process of incorporation or internalization of a hated object is itself perceived in the unconscious infant mind as a highly emotionally charged ambivalent act. It destroys by making the object disappear—whether this be through greedy "love" or through hate. Once inside however, the introject continues to haunt the subject. In analysis this dangerous and disturbing experience of "something bad inside" is encountered not only as, for example, a fear of a devouring illness such as cancer. More significantly for the psychology of GM, it manifests at deeper level as direct fantasies of good, filling milk having turned into *poison*, or into *bad faeces* or both. What should have been loving, feeding, strength giving, has turned into a useless, dangerous object which one hates and that hates the self. Again the dual signification appears—the tormenting object that threatens is bound to the ego's own hate and fear of this bad object. The resulting paranoid-depressive complex affects the whole self-perception of a person so conditioned. These are the original sources of feelings of uselessness, inferiority and powerlessness. But for reasons already outlined, this powerful, threatening inner persecutor has to be abjectly obeyed and submitted to. Among the symbolic ways in which the powerless subject can deal with this internal enemy, psychoanalysis has described the development of omnipotence fantasies—in part compensatory for the sense of impotence fantasies which are woven around the already mentioned newly found muscular powers of the anus. Thus Fenichel:[5] ". . . elimination objectively is as 'destructive' as incorporation; the object of the first anal-sadistic action is the faeces themselves, their 'pinching-off' being perceived as a kind of sadistic act; later on, persons are treated as the faeces were previously treated. Second, the fact of 'social power' involved in the mastery of sphincters: in training for cleanliness, the child finds opportunity effectively to express opposition against grown-ups."

Here, as I see it, may lie the gratification derived from sadistic squeezing—"having power over"—the internal objects symbolized by these rejected, poisonous body contents. We have now to complete the hypothetical dynamics of GM's cruelties and favourite methods of practising them by what we have already learnt of the prevalence of paranoid projection as the High F way of dealing with inner tensions, and have confirmed out of his own statements. GM's story is a living illustration of Wangh's generalization on the predicament of this man's generation and its vulnerabilities to Nazi infection. I quote:

It is also likely that many of the (German—H. V. D.) mothers, brought up under the dictum "Kinder, Kirche, Küche"* were inadequate for the role which their husbands' prolonged absence assigned to them and that they were more punitive towards their sons than they would otherwise have been. The passive-masochistic longings which this fostered (in the sons—H. V. D.) reinforced in later life the tendency to submit, preferably to a man because of the greater castration anxiety aroused by submission to a woman.

* Alliteratively: "Kids, Kirk, Kitchen".

We have heard about GM's tenderness taboo and antifeminine attitudes. Wangh continues:

> Prolonged absence of a parent is always regarded by the children as a rejection. His futile longing, mixed with causality-supplying masochistic fantasy, produces feelings of unworthiness and humiliation. He then frequently *projects* (my italics—H. V. D.) the derivatives of those feelings on to someone else. The young generation of which we speak here, orphaned temporarily or permanently during childhood, did just that. It rid itself of its own suicidal depression by displacing self-humiliation and self-contempt on to the Jews and other supposedly inferior peoples, thereby ultimately converting suicide into genocide.
>
> Children brought up under such stress have a low tension tolerance. Their weakened egos are prone to seek relief through action. The need for impulsive action and the need for organized re-enactment combined will follow inexorably along the path of childhood patterns. . . .[6]

While psychologically we know that "suicidal depression" is the effect of the continuing unconscious defence against the hate and rejection felt by the subject against the internalized bad object that creates the inner tension (in such cases very appropriately termed "the raging super-ego"), it is also widely held that the paranoid defence against this intolerable depressive feeling of being "bad" oneself is an even more primitive and hate-laden phase. We recall that GM was a quiet, submissive son, serving in church, letting his mother manage him; marrying a girl after her image. At the female KZ he felt revolted by maltreatment—of women, as if this came too close to his own internal conflict. But in the main, when he experienced the "organized re-enactment" of his own paranoid defences against his inner inferiority and weakness, he proceeded to act these out in striking conformity to the anal-sadistic model I sketched from object-relations theory. All that he had harboured of the hate of the bad object was now turned against the at last available projection scapegoats, his victims. He could squeeze these worthless faecal objects to death. He could, by becoming the punishing authority figure himself vent *its* rage (not his own—we heard *he* was never murderous) on those dirty, incontinent vermin, "useless mouths to feed", who contravened rules, tried to get more pity or food or medicines than they deserved. He had now himself regressed to act out the dreaded omnipotent figure who could turn the "good milk" of healing drugs into the poison he had had to hold in himself for 36 years.

Among the attractions of joining the SS for GM were not only the promise of a job and of belonging, but also those of acquiring a manly authority instead of a mother; of being relieved of his uncertain, humiliating dual nationality; of being identified with authority and "keeping order". Above all, however, it more than satisfied, as he was put into the KZ service, his need for expressing, acting-out with full sanctions, and guilt free, his infantile anal sadism. At last he could be at the handing-out end of his bad internal object. And most of the rationalizations listed in Schedule 4 of Chapter Four likewise seemed to fit GM's needs, both at conscious and unconscious levels. The reader need only turn to those tables which, composed by Leites 15 years before I interviewed GM, could have been written on the strength of my findings in him. The chief variation was the deflection of this man to a quasi-medical role in which his preoccupations with faeces and digestion (not forgetting his own digestive stress under the rigours of SS discipline) found an "ideal" field. He remained convinced he had only done his duty and killed what ought not to live or what it was humane to dispatch. Only when the law of the new German authority, more closely resembling the ethical principles on which he was reared, had caught up with him he developed—or reverted to?—a glimmer of depressive unease. He was troubled by guilt during the remand period and was watched for possible suicide in the prison. The bad object had to be re-internalized.

CHAPTER EIGHT

FREE ENTERPRISE—TWO PRIVATEERS

My next two case studies are on former members of the Nazi security police organization in occupied Poland, with some incidental connections with the KZ service. They represent the somewhat less structured elements of the SS–Gestapo units that had been created with the public façade of establishing order and internal security in the rear of the operational troops of the Wehrmacht. Their real, secret task was that of rounding up and concentrating Polish and Ukrainian "opponents" or Resistance fighters (real and imaginary), but more especially Jews. These were the units which were given the cover name of *Einsatzgruppen* (special task groups) during the phase of movement, and later became the executive arm of the so-called Higher SS and Police leaders attached to the civil governors or administrators of the occupied territories.

As such they had a great deal of direct contact with the civil population, very lax discipline and much freedom of movement in the cities in which they were based. It will become apparent that this role in the context of Nazi policy gave scope for the exercise of arbitrary power and cruelty to quite minor figures, and facilitated shady and corrupt dealings for self-enrichment by blackmail and extortion from the subject populations whom they cowed by terror.

Here I remind the reader of what I said in Chapter Three about Hitler's population policy in his East. As if foreshadowing the long-term plan, Heydrich, chief of the SS/Gestapo Security Service (SD), at a conference in September 1939 ordered the heads of *Einsatzgruppen* in Poland to free the East German provinces (some Polish by the 1919 treaty) of Jews and to concentrate all these and the Polish rural Jewish populations "in a few cities which should be railway junctions". This was the beginning of the so-called ghettoes, of which the Warsaw one was to be the most publicized scene of later horrors. The Gestapo made ghettoes in other major Polish cities too—in a sense also concentration camps and "guarded" by Heydrich's SS police detachments. It is in two such units that the men about to be described had served.

FREE ENTERPRISE—TWO PRIVATEERS

1. The Jews' Best Friend

BT, a former senior sergeant in the SS, was interviewed in a West-phalian prison in 1967. Here he was serving a total of 22 life sentences on conviction of as many proven personal murders, as well as of complicity in at least 4000 cases whom he had selected for transportation to Auschwitz death camp. He was tried in the high court of a Rhine-land city and sentenced in April 1964.

Curriculum Vitae This was a well-written document, skillfully self-exonerating and intended to prove his essential harmlessness.

BT was born in 1900 in a small Silesian town as the eldest son of a small independent leasehold farmer (whom he called "*Landwirt*" meaning agriculturalist, rather than "*Bauer*" or peasant, indicating a claim to higher class status). He went to local primary school until 14 when he was confirmed in the Protestant Church. He helped his father on the farm and hoped to make his entry into a forestry school, but failed because he had not done the necessary book-work. He was called up for military service in 1917-18 in a reserve artillery regiment, but only saw training and home service. By Christmas 1918 (a month after the Armistice) he was demobilized and back home, once more working for his father. BT married the daughter of a neighbouring farmer in 1927. She was seven years younger, and by her he had four children. He adds that his eldest son was killed in action in Russia in 1945. He also records six grandchildren.

BT gives some indication of his personality when he writes that "in 1928 it pleased the dear Lord God to gather my dear mother unto himself", and that his father became ill from pining for her. So in 1928 BT took over the homestead and ran it for a few years. In 1934 he had an eye accident with haemorrhage into the vitreous. In 1932 the farm workers of his area elected him to the local authority council on the social Democratic party ticket. "But in 1933 (after Hitler's accession—H. V. D.) I was to be arrested, so I laid down my mandate (legte ich mein Mandat nieder)." He continues "Thus I evaded arrest, I then joined the General SS reserve and got my seat back." BT says "this was done at the insistence of his sponsors" so that he could continue to represent them on the council. "It was only a nominal membership in which I simply paid a subscription." Somewhat contradictorily, BT now writes of how he made attempts to join the police force (*we recall that the SS and SA flocked into this voluntarily*—H. V. D.) but the eye injury made him medically ineligible.

In 1936 (when Hitler reintroduced conscription—H. V. D.) BT was called up for military service in a pioneer (engineer) regiment. (*It is interesting that his sight seems to have been no bar.*) This unit was employed to construct defence works on the river Oder, "camouflaged by trees". Released, he became a civilian construction worker for the German Air Force, building an airfield, until 1939. "When this job was completed they seized on my membership of the SS reserve (*he is careful to use this more innocuous qualification*) and transferred me in 1940 to the Waffen SS."

In view of what follows, this was evidently Himmler's already promulgated euphemism for the TKV, eagerly seized on by BT, just as he tries to depict the whole process of his SS service as enforced.

BT now states that he was sent to Buchenwald, near Weimar, for "weapons training", and was promoted to SS corporal (Unterscharführer). With training completed, "they" posted him to duty in the KZ of Buchenwald; but he protested, and as the result was transferred to an SS unit in Weimar which had guard duties at the Gauleiter's headquarters. Then came a second posting order, to Poland, for duty as a block leader at a "labour camp". He again protested that he did not want to go. This time, he claims, not only was his leave cancelled but he was ominously asked by his superior officer whether he did not have a wife and children—and whether he wanted to be put in a KZ himself? It was in this way, BT writes, that he came to give in and was sent to the ghetto at T. in Poland, "where all the crimes of which I am accused were supposed to have been committed."

BT's paper skates lightly over his party allegiance and progress and depicts his entire SS career as if it were a compulsory service, under military orders.

As in nearly all these self-descriptions, BT has nothing to say on the whole period of his service in the Polish ghetto and labour camp. He simply concludes his *curriculum* by stating that his wife lives in the city in which he was sentenced, that his sons work in the local steel mills, and that he had been a "rural worker" until his arrest.

Abstract of Court Evidence and Summing up (1964) The indictment showed that BT was first attached to the unit administering the ghetto at T. around 1941. This was in 1943 followed by his promotion to Oberscharführer and being put in charge of a new part of the Jewish ghetto, "created specially for BT" with the designation of a "Commissary leader of the compulsory labour camp".

This coincided with a change in higher policy—the dissolution of the ghettoes by sending the inmates either direct to extermination, or keeping the ablest-bodied for forced labour—in this case in the same town.

The indictment stated that in this labour camp BT had unfettered power over life and death, and no detailed instructions from any one above him. The prosecutor said that "all degrees of arbitrariness were permissible". He divided BT's activities into three phases: (1) In the first it was the policy to get maximum output from able-bodied Jewish prisoners. During this stage BT was said in evidence to have "simulated the greatest benevolence" towards his victims. Witnesses said: "BT was like a father to us until we had nothing more to give. When our valuables came to an end then his benevolence did too." Thus, it emerged, BT had the reputation in the ghetto and its associated camp that he was affable, and adept by means of this humane charm at extracting money and valuables out of the local Jews. It was all done in a sort of official but kindly way in the best confidence trickster manner. He got his victims to declare what they owned, by way of property, etc., inferring that if they were straight and handed over he would see to it that nothing bad would happen to them, that they would be well looked after—it was an unfortunate government regulation he had to carry out, and so on. "Then, when a man had parted with everything—he would be shot just the same". At times, richer Jewish prisoners were led to believe that if they paid enough BT would even help them to escape abroad. In defence (repeated also to his warders during remand custody), BT motivated this behaviour with some pride as a patriotic duty—namely to squeeze all he could out of the Jews for the benefit of German wealth in conformity with the official Nazi policy of expropriation and confiscation.

Phase 2 came when Hitler's "Final Solution" policy was implemented in the ghetto. An SS officer called Goeth arrived and took charge in BT's camp. Convoys of Jews began to be sent to Auschwitz and other extermination camps. Now BT's role was that of a selector of the batches of victims, while still carrying on with his earlier programme of extortion and double dealing on fresh arrivals nominally as slave labour. Phase 3 was his continuing charge over the residual camp, with the remaining ghetto inmates under his control for dismantling and other disposal duties. During these two phases BT was shown by the evidence to have been a brutal and pitiless persecutor. He had not only shot people himself or ordered them to be shot on his own initiative for the usual trumped-up "infringements of good order", when "no more use", but he was also a user of the whip on his victims. During the heart-rending scenes when the ghetto was being emptied en route for the death camps, BT was seen to go up to a woman who refused to be parted from her baby and trample the child with his heels or, in another case, bash a child against the wall and then shoot it in front of the mother. The more helpless and exhausted a prisoner, the more savage was BT's kicking. In his defence he asserted he was "much too lazy to kick a child". He admitted only one shooting.

BT was also untiring in hunting down any Jews who tried to conceal themselves or their valuables from the SS. Those discovered were the ones he shot with his pistol after maltreatment. Concealment of sources of wealth seems to have excited his sadism especially. There was evidence of how BT had brutally kicked and then shot one such Jew (named in court) on whom he found concealed a pair of children's shoes, because Mr K. would not disclose where he had obtained them. In 1943, BT had a bonfire made of 56 Jewish bodies "to celebrate the Feast of the Atonement".

In his summing up the judge had expressly affirmed that BT's killing and brutality had at no time been in response to orders, nor under duress as he claimed in his plea, but voluntarily and arbitrarily at his own whim.

The German press accounts reported that BT heard his sentence silently and shaking his head.

The Prison record over the years since his arrest mentions a spinal fracture in 1956, a rectal fistula in 1958 (pre-arrest), but no later or current bodily disease. Mentally he is described as "unremarkable", loquacious, "devoted to wife and children", "makes a polite, peaceable impression", no trouble. "Is up for murdering Jews in ghetto during war. Admits one shooting, but defends himself vigorously. ? How far credible."

The Interview A cheerful-looking, bland, "very ordinary" and well-preserved man, with greying hair, who is certainly loquacious, and from the first lays on an oily charm and winning smiles, is courtesy and deference itself. Invited by me to tell me his story, he makes a "spontaneous" statement which is almost an exact replica of his written self-description. There is a certain sly disingenuousness in his "frank" admission that he was always a "Mitläufer" (meaning not so much a fellow-traveller, as one who "hunts with the hounds and runs with the hare"), one who went "whichever way the wind was blowing". Well, why not switch parties if he could thereby avoid arrest and keep his job and his place on the council, "especially if one had children"? Yes, he was always a bit of a timid, chicken-hearted opportunist. He did the least harm he could—why he even refused to serve in a KZ the first time. "I would not touch it—that was Buchenwald, when it contained nearly all Germans." But the second time, when it was already war, he could not refuse, he wasn't brave enough to suffer. Of course he was not innocent. But he was not guilty of the crimes of which he had been accused just because he was in the ghetto unit—no, he could not have killed. He expands on the theme of what he *did* do: getting all those Jews to declare their possessions and then to take them over. "But I assure you, Herr Professor, I handed over every pfennig, every trinket, and got receipts for them from the administration; it was all done for Germany in her need of that wealth. I did not keep a single pfennig for myself." And again, how could he have been a real killer—if he had been he would have had more promotion! "I was no hero, just the victim of the system that demanded such services." And then, as if to deflect the talk to happier themes, BT switches to his childhood.

Father started as a farm worker. In 1907 he took over the holding (Hof). "Our life was secure." He had been the foreman, then there had been the flooding of the river. . . . . But it was a good simple life without privation. Father had been a former regular soldier, an old monarchist Right Wing Social Democrat voter. "It was a case of church every Sunday for all of us, and prayers aloud at home every day for the children until I was 12 or 13." I interpose: "So it was quite a strict home." Not at all, replies BT, "We were allowed our own will, I was free to choose what I wanted to do, and even freedom to idle. That's how it came that I did not pass into the forester's school. It was a lovely Christian home, with the mother so full of loving kindness, teaching us to be gentle and humble like our Lord. . . ." (*Not all the turns of smug religious phrases could be noted by me, but there were plenty.*) So, unlike other lads, BT grew not to like fighting or roughness. He could not bear to shoot animals as they do in the country—and worst of all was it to see the sufferings of these poor God's creatures that had been wounded, instead of killed cleanly, by bad shots. That was how he was, gentle and content in a family who were always secure and settled. There was no unemployment nor any want even after the First War.

BT continued in praise of his family's Protestant ethic by describing the prudent good husbanding of resources, not to waste. From here he goes on to reproach himself for leaving his wife like he has, and to discuss the allowances and pension she gets from the state, or what she would have had had he not been convicted; the security of his sons, their wages, pensions expectations—all showing his keen interest in money matters. Yes, in the service he had often been praised for his head for figures, for his good business sense and efficient management of his labour camp. He was no great he-man, only a little unpolitical man who could however pride himself on his high sense of order and methodical efficiency. He said he was never anti-Jewish. He had the best possible relationship with the Jewish leaders ("elders") in his camp. His only wish was to keep his Jewish industrial workers well fed and fully employed. No, he exclaimed, if he hated anyone, it was those false witnesses at the trial who had framed him, mostly by mistaken identity, saddling him with other peoples' crimes. *He* knew who the real perpetrators were! These men were all going free. He now mentions a series of names—chiefly of SS higher echelons at general's level— "who have not even been tried".

BT's hatred and accusation now turns to the camp informers (*ignoring the fact that he was in charge of it all*), the snoopers who brought false charges against people who were in consequence killed. These snoopers were often Jewish, non-German or Volks-German (i.e. Polish citizens of German descent—H. V. D.) interpreters, who were traitors to their own people, rabid in their vindictiveness and zealous to be noticed and promoted. Among them were the murderers of his two Jewish camp elders whom he had *saved*. They were "killed by their own people", lest they survived to give evidence on the things that had gone on in the camp. BT then said: "And of course the last 80 people I saved from that camp would have been splendid witnesses in my defence—so of course they too had to be liquidated." *This was the nearest to an insane statement BT made to me: the restructuring of reality in terms of an infantile, totally egocentric fantasy according to which external objects and events all revolve round the self and carry the feeling of malignant purpose directed at hurting or persecuting him. The bad self is firmly projected into these people who were the "real killers".*

I asked BT whether he was not really in charge and could have prevented "those things". He replied that he "stayed aloof" from what went on in the camp. Of course he was aware of brutalities and executions; but "I just did not see anything".

In fact, in the interview BT used the by now familiar defence manoeuvre of helplessness in the face of overwhelming evil known to be the real policy of his country—so best to ignore it—the mechanism of splitting and projection.

He went on that this could be done by drinking a lot of vodka. That was the way in which all the Gestapo-men managed to do their duty. He thought this was terrible—he a lifelong abstainer and non-smoker—but at that time he downed vodka without turning a hair. Using my routine question in this situation, I asked: "Somebody must have done the killing in the camp of which you were in charge?" The reply from BT came with venom: "I was an honest SS man—not like those swine from the Gestapo, who were the real villains and executioners!" When I remarked that under Himmler the Gestapo and the original SS were joined and their personnel assimilated in the occupation security units, BT evaded the point by saying that he rejected Himmler, who recruited that riff-raff into the SS; he was neither a soldier nor a gentleman, but a mean and inhuman fellow without feeling for his men. BT contrasted him with Goering, who was both—and treated his men accordingly. The happiest time BT had had was when he was working for the air force on that aerodrome—he wished he'd never left it.

From beginning to end this man remained self-possessed, pretty cheerful and talkative. I could not discover why he had chosen to volunteer to see me. He said it would be interesting. He had frequent visits from his wife and sons, who lived within easy distance, and they brought him small luxuries. It was indeed difficult to imagine this quite relaxed friendly elderly family man having a record such as the court had incontrovertibly proved to be his. He was collected by his warder from the interview at the end of our long session and expressed his thanks for a pleasant encounter.

Commentary BT was in most ways quite untypical for one's expectations about an SS man. His was an anti-hero stance—the little timid man who gets by where the swaggering warrior fails. Remarkable also was BT's spontaneous comment on his "non-authoritarian" childhood, almost as if he knew the psychologist's hypotheses. Of my hypothesized variables, some were lacking, others not immediately obvious. The positive findings were the rural "lower middle class" identification, and the idealization of his childhood as teaching him lofty values and making him such a good, happy if lazy boy (in fact smugness!). Among personality traits there were similarities with the preceding man—GM, albeit less obvious. There was the same feeling of passivity and sense of a THEY who pushed one around, with a similar defence that all round one were bad people who somehow involved one, on whom responsibility could be fastened. There was also a similar picture of earnest, prayerful exhortation by religious parents with a sense of having failed them by not doing well enough to please them—in BT's case the failure to make the technical forestry school. To this well-marked authoritarian submissiveness there was added the self-confessed trimming of his sails to the wind, to avoid trouble, to fall soft, swim with the stream. Writers like Frau v. Baeyer-Katte and Dahrendorf indict this as one of the most serious German defects, facilitating the ascendancy of totalitarian tyranny.

In this latter characteristic we may see the chief motive for BT's rapid change of front from Social Democratic rural coucillor to the SS by which he ensured his security. There was no evidence that he had any political fanaticism beyond a diffuse ethnocentric feeling that he preferred not to be cruel to Germans but did not mind maltreating foreign submen if this meant keeping out of trouble himself, and indeed currying favour with the authorities who already had it in for him on the score of the old Social Democrat record and his stand against KZ work at Buchenwald.

One of the most striking attributes of BT was his extraordinary interest in property and financial security. Not only was he, for a chronic prison inmate, keenly alive to all present provisions and entitlements of Federal German citizens but he was so proud of his achievements in extracting the last possessions from his Jewish victims, with an unctuous sense of righteousness and patriotism that would do credit to a keen Revenue or Excise official.

All this, however, does not amount to a hypothesis to explain BT's murderousness. My inference is that in this case the man dared not defy the TKV again, having once got in, but simply descended into the prevailing ethos. The expropriation of his victims' property was highly congenial—one could almost feel his cupidity and enjoyment of robbing—whether or not he retained any of the loot, which was more than likely. I have already commented on BT's notions that "people who could have given evidence for him had to be eliminated". This is a frequent belief with gangsters, robbers and secret service personnel. *He* was a good friend of his Jewish protégés—but what about the rest of the ghetto SS—would not the vengeance of the "trusties" and secret informers come on his head if he was reported to be soft? He knew what the hierarchy of the SS wanted once the "Final Solution" orders from on high had to be implemented. One strong motive seems to have been, as always, to cover himself and swim with the stream: how could a timid little man, with his sense of order and need to please, stand out?

A second, in BT's case, less transparent latent motive can only be inferred from the hints that behind his smug, gentle exterior and wish to please lay a deeply repressed early sadistic strain. His touching account of how as a child he hated witnessing local huntsmen, including his father, shoot and wound "poor innocent little animals", on the surface looks like what I termed "social" reaction-formation against murderous aggression in my Table I (see Chapter Four): "gentleness, submissiveness; horror and condemnation of sadism", etc. In psychopathology this reaction would be widely held to originate in the depressive phase not fully overcome. The repudiation of aggression is a retreat from one's bad internal object relation: from the menacing object that had to be taken in, and from one's own feelings of hate against it. There has remained a secret haunting by, and preoccupation with, the cruel, killing figure that can harm and destroy "little creatures". This spontaneous report by BT to me was clearly in the context of describing his childhood—his father's and father's friends' shooting expeditions. It discloses the existence and the attempted rejection of the bad aspects of the inner paternal figures, with himself as a threatened little creature. His idealization of parents as so good and indulgent that runs like a leitmotif through his, as through hundreds of my other interview records with Germans, thus conceals by psychological denial the deep fear of the angry aspects of the authority figure. Excessive dependence and obsequiousness are, as frequently inferred in these pages, due to the pressure to propitiate, hiding the owner's "bad" feelings towards, the aggressor. But this is the very situation in which there is the maximum unconscious identification with the aggressor, because he is inside one and one feels what he feels. In joining the KZ service BT's moral defence gave one last response—he declined to become his own bad internal object against other Germans—the inmates of Buchenwald in 1939-40. The training and indoctrination, which we know was given to the TKV recruits, acted as the precipitating or traumatic event for BT—as indeed for the majority of these craven conformist characters: now the external authority matched his own unconscious identifications with the bad inner objects. This, so to speak, turned his object-relations inside out. We heard that by the time he had, during his quiet, post-war life and his imprisonment, returned to his more usual personality, his defences by gentle, smug, "Christian" attitudes had been reconstituted. But during his role as a wielder of authority he could act out the bad object, especially, one gathered, by shooting and by venom against children. BT's hates were expressed to me more consistently than in some of the other subjects, towards Himmler, Gestapo officers, etc., as the people who shot and maimed "little creatures". These had been—as the threatening, killing image of the father had originally been—the authorities on whom he was dependent and who must not be provoked for fear of their retaliation. By identifying with them he denied his conscious ego-image of his "good Social Democrat Christian" father, and merged with the bad objects' hate. What now enabled him to play the role of "master of life and death" in his ghetto labour camp was the emergence of the hithero repressed part of his ego related to the killing father with a gun he had had to come to terms with. The sanctions offered by SS doctrine (freeing the Fatherland and dispossessing its enemies from what they had stolen, etc.) was all that was needed to make this part of him function without much guilt, using chiefly alcohol as the solvent for his none-too-severe conscience, but mainly living in a state of temporary paranoid regression in dread of official retaliation in which he could use his victims as scapegoats or projected targets for the hate that he could not turn on his real internal aggressors. BT also took refuge in the bureaucratic ritual of "faithful acquisition of property", a known secondary sublimation of the interest in "body contents" (cf. GM in preceding chapter). When all the good things the victims owned had been extracted they ceased to have value and became expendable. We can only deduce that this *greed* for first sucking them dry and then killing them could have been motivated by very deep oral sadism against the breast, from the deepest earliest levels of the paranoid phase, borne out by his acts of destroying babies in front of their poor mothers—"taking all they had".

BT's case seems illustrative of the evil done by the Nazi and SS leaders in reactivating latent murderous fantasies related to early phases, against which his defences by gentleness, smug harmlessness, etc. had covered him, but which had failed under the threat of being re-enacted by the regime against himself. It seemed as if his choice was: "either I kill or they will kill me".

2. THE POLES' BEST FRIEND

KW, a senior sergeant in the Gestapo when he committed his crimes, was interviewed in the same Westphalian prison as BT, in 1967. He came from a small town in the area, and the high court of that area tried him in 1965, after arrest in 1961. His sentence was for "9 times life" in respect of nine fully proven killings of Jewish victims in the Warsaw ghetto.

Curriculum Vitae Written for me, this showed that he was born in 1914, the only son of an "independent master painter", and had two older sisters. His father was absent on military service until 1920, having been captured by the Russians. He returned home with severe ill health resulting from poison gas and consequent heart/lung trouble. The father could not resume his independent craft enterprise which was leased out, and took a small sedentary "government" job of the doorman kind. Soon after this one of KW's sisters had a severe accident to her spine, and was paralysed from the waist down, leading a wheel-chair life. The father died in 1926 (when KW was still only 12). In the still more straitened circumstances the mother had to take lodgers to help pay for the sister's medical care until the girl died in 1934. KW attended primary school and was then apprenticed as a motor mechanic (Autoschlosser). He worked until age 19 in a relative's garage, but from 1933 he was mostly unemployed except for brief spells of casual labour. In 1935 he decided to volunteer for military service in Hitler's newly enlarged army on a 12-year engagement. But he developed stomach trouble ("Magenleiden") and soon was discharged as unfit. He now took various casual jobs not specified. (*No mention of his joining first the Hitler youth and then the Nazi party in 1936.*) In 1938 the Wehrmacht re-enlisted him, but he was soon again invalided out. Then in 1939, he says, he applied to join the motorized traffic police of Hannover. "I was not accepted but received the message that I should report to the Gestapo at Bielefeld." He was next posted to the SIPO (short for *Sicherheitspolizei* or security police) in Warsaw. He says that here he "only did clerical work", and that his job gave him contact with the "Polish underground", with which he collaborated from 1940 "in order to mitigate the cruel persecution and annihilation of the Polish and Jewish population". He further says: "as I was unmarried at that time I could pursue this dangerous path". He writes that in this secret role he saved the lives of 32 Gypsies, "as could be testified by their 'King', and many other persons". In 1942, he claims, his own authorities were suspecting him of traitorous dealings with the Resistance.

KW ends his self-description by a bitter, vague reference to a physician "who made it his business to deliver me to the Allies", and by saying that he "never went back to Warsaw after sick leave in 1944, except as a civilian". *I noted at the time that I could not fathom the connexion between these last two statements. The slant of KW's piece for me clearly purported to present him as an old friend of the Allied cause in the heart of the Gestapo.*

Abstract of Court Evidence and Summing Up Evidence showed that KW had been on the establishment of the "Jewish Section" (Judenreferat) of the SIPO, itself under the HSSPF (short for Higher SS and police leader) at Warsaw. Here he was stated to have "carried out independent ('selbständige') acts of cruelty and murder 'out of lust for killing (Mordlust) and suchlike base motives' on two cases and of two further cases 'perfidiously'. His victims were always Jewish". The official indictment showed that he joined the Nazi party at 18 and chose the NSKK (the National Socialist Motor Corps) as his activity. Here he "assimilated the Party's Jewish programme", and he was known in his home town as a "committed Nazi"* and Jew-hater. At this time, even before Hitler came to power, there was evidence that he would stand in front of shops owned by Jews threatening people who patronized them and taking photographs of these clients. The widow of a Jew, who had been a German officer and lost a leg in the First War, testified that KW had deeply and coarsely insulted her husband in public.

The official depositions confirmed that KW had tried to join the motorized Hannover police, was refused and then accepted the job with the Bielefeld Gestapo, and was given the "assimilated SS rank of Oberscharführer." Contemporary documents showed that this was a voluntary enlistment, as was his transfer to the Warsaw post; also that the SD (the SS secret security service) had marked him "unfit for major

* "Ein schwerer Nazi".

independent responsibility and barely fit for office duties". Witnesses
of his behaviour in Warsaw described him as going about the ghetto
always carrying a pistol and a whip. Frequently he was seen riding in a
rickshaw pulled by a Jew. He was known by the people there as "The
Shooter" (der Schiesser), "Angel of Death"—and also as "The Pervert"
(der Perverse). Rumour, related in court as such, had it that KW raped
young Jewish girls and then shot them. KW had also been witnessed
approaching a Jewish woman and young child, bashing the child to the
ground, shooting it and then killing the mother. Jews in Warsaw
greatly feared him and scattered or hid at his approach, and he went
about like a scourge, hitting, shooting or just intimidating people at
his whim, to no predictable pattern; always alone. A different angle
on KW's behaviour in Warsaw was the wealth of evidence of his
activities on the black market, principally in cigars, for which his home
town is famed. In this aspect of his life KW was often dressed in
civilian clothes, and stayed in the leading hotels of the Polish capital
regardless of expense. Here he was the open-handed friend and patron
of prosperous hoteliers, smart bar-keepers and flashy black-market
operators among the Poles and, he claimed, some Jews whom he
evidently supplied with cigars and, in view of his known association
with the Gestapo, persuaded to treat him as their special guest. It seems
to have been this section of the "Polish underground" with which KW
was in such amicable touch. He cut a figure as a dashing, debonair *bon
vivant*—on bribes from people in dread of him. Witnesses described
KW as a "power-drunk, trigger-happy sybarite". The indictment
showed that KW's pseudo-Intelligence activity was not even author-
ized by the Gestapo, though he was said to have acted "in the spirit,
but against the orders and regulations, of the "Final Solution" organization ("Endlösungsapparat").

In his defence, KW had gone to great lengths to provide himself
with cunning and false *alibis*, which it took the investigating magistrates
and later the court some trouble to disentangle and pierce. Some of
these came from his erstwhile Polish contacts. On arrest in 1961 he was
described as truculent and inscrutable. A fellow prisoner-during the long
period of remand in custody described KW as a mean, scheming fellow
who was always complaining. At one point, in 1963, KW staged
a bogus hunger strike. He managed to persuade this cell-mate (also
under investigation) to supply him with part of his prison rations
secreted in the cell. When this protest failed, KW made a demonstrative

suicidal gesture by slashing one of his wrists with a razor blade, after which he was kept under constant observation.

Unwisely for his later loud and angry protestations of innocence and charges of false imprisonment, mistaken identity, etc., in court, KW had given way to his need for boasting and bravado during this stay in custody. He had in bantering and humerous vein confided to the cell-mate how he had shot a girl in Warsaw because he wanted to annoy one of his fellow SS-Gestapo men by this practical joke, knowing she was the colleague's mistress. When the cell-mate now asked KW how many people he reckoned he had "done-in", KW, still in high spirits, replied: "Would you remember how many girls you've slept with?" This cell-mate had turned "king's evidence" and told this conversation in court having confessed to feeling badly about breaking the unwritten code of gaol-bird honour. Some of the witnesses KW cited as proving alibis or in support of his humanity and friendship for Poles and Jews failed to support him.

A third angle on KW which emerged in court was that whenever it suited him he would fall back on his old "stomach trouble" to get home sick leave. By 1944 (when Warsaw was being threatened by the Soviet army—H. V. D.), KW took sick leave and stayed home on false medical certificates, and made his living on the black market in cigars and liquor in Germany. In this way he came to be interned as a known SS man by the British forces in whose Zone he lived.

Medical Notes in Prison KW is, in comparison to others in his position a troublesome inmate. Nervous, tense, he had frequent duodenal symptoms. Latterly some evidence of possible gall stones and a prostatitis which are under investigation. Still considered a suicidal risk. Persistent pleas of inability to do his stint of work "because too nervous". By comparison with early arrogance (KW served his remand at the same prison) he is now keen to get out and has promised to behave well. Had been a constantly demanding, litigious "barrack-lawyer".

The Interview KW almost "breezes in" with a "so glad to meet you" stage-welcome. A tall fair Nordic with good looks; the panache of a man about town, even in his prison garb, not out of place in the Ritz bar. Avidly accepts a cigarette. He has, clearly, planned his address to me. As most of the others, he goes over the points of his defence he had put forward at his trial, deeply hurt that these were rejected. I state my usual request to talk about his whole life as I am interested in him, not only his trial. KW now gives a coherent spontaneous account of his background, reiterating most of the data in his *curriculum* recently written for me: being the youngest of three; his father's captivity and return, a broken ill man who died when KW was 12. He does enjoy enlarging on the theme of how happy and free from strict discipline his home was. With a knowing, cute wink he says: "You can imagine that as the baby son I was much spoilt by my parents, as far as their reduced circumstances permitted. Whatever they could they gave me. I was my mother's pet." KW added that it must be stressed how upright and honest were his parents and the values he received. "Always be decent and straightforward was my motto." He mused on how modest were the indulgences of the children of his day. Fifty pfennigs to go to the fair seemed like a dream—not like these present-day youths who have so much money and "must have everything". Here, KW seemed to impress on me, was a decent honest boy brought up in the old-fashioned way, grateful to his good, simple, impoverished parents for all their care and love, and especially to his wonderful mother who had managed so self-denyingly after she was widowed.

KW now went on to describe the little town in which he grew up (one familiar to many members of the British Control Commission— H. V. D.!). By the time he was adolescent, all the "lads" were in the Hitler youth. Having been fastidiously brought up, he did not care for the rough crowd that went on to join the brown-shirted SA (cf Dr MO). These gangsters, he said with a wrinkled nose, were "lower class types" who liked nothing better than getting into street fights. This he did not fancy at all. So he joined the NSKK where "one met a different class of young man"—people with their own sports cars, much closer to his own passion for automobiles. "Our sort were under some pressure to join the SS", and they tried to persuade him, too, because it was the élite young crowd in town. "But I did not want to, because these people were too up-stage for me." I gleaned from all this that he wanted to stress how well he knew his limitations of education and that his taste was technical rather than political. He said his ambition always was to join the road police on motor-bikes with their smart white accoutrements. This, he added, was when he was discharged from the army on account of his stomach trouble. (*He could not enlarge on this disability on which he had no insight. To the army psychiatrist it suggests a familiar pattern of stress dyspepsia as a let-out from being under discipline or similar emotionally unacceptable conditions.*)

KW now skilfully depicted his "drift" into the Gestapo and so into the Warsaw ghetto detachment as a series of mischances or wrong decisions "when he could so easily have chosen something else and then he would not now be in prison". From traffic police to SIPO at Bielefeld, offered by the (by now SS-integrated—H. V. D.) authorities seemed only a little difference for a motor driver. And then it was his obliging easy-goingness which made him consent to go to Warsaw in exchange for one of his pals who had just got married and could thus have KW's job at home. From here the story becomes one of ingenious whitewashing, denial and injured innocence. Why, with his medical history he could as easily have become an employee of the town or the local judiciary. He was, even in Warsaw, only a little clerk in the Judenreferat (Jewish section, see above—H. V. D.). Like BT he allowed me to see he was no hero or party fanatic. He was only glad he had never been made into a *Beamter* (official) but had always remained only an *Angestellter* (employee). Warsaw was good in this way, he said, because this status allowed him to engage in business on the side. So he made quite a lot of money by "importing" cigars into Poland. "I used my stomach trouble quite a lot to get sick leave to get home and come back with more cigars." He so describes his life that one could almost forget he was not a full-time trade representative—"that's what really interested him". And his Gestapo chief of course knew all about this and did not object—they were good friends. Life in Warsaw was pleasant, he had countless good Polish and Jewish friends there. In hushed tones KW now lets me into a secret he had to guard carefully: the girl he married was in fact half-Jewish. (*What he omits to tell me, but I knew from his dossier though not from his own curriculum, is that he only married in 1948, had one child and that his wife divorced him on learning his story in 1965.*)

"Of course one had to be very circumspect in the Gestapo—we were allowed to have dealings with the Jews—and yet!" he said. But could it be imagined that a decent, friendly chap like himself was really guilty of the atrocities with which he had been charged? No, these things were not done by "us decent real policemen of the Gestapo". It was a case of mistaken identity in his own case. I asked: "Then who were the real perpetrators of what you have been convicted of doing?" He replied: "That was a totally different organization—the SS, their SD. These people had it in for me as well! These sleuths had discovered that I did not like living in police barracks but had lived in a Jewish hotel* in Warsaw. They had tried to frame me by bringing a charge of improper dealings with the enemy against me before the SS and police judicial authorities (*it will be recalled that the whole SS were accountable only to their own legal department*), but my chief saw to that." (*No doubt on the plea of KW's patriotic zeal and secret duties!*) Warming to his subject, he now confides to me that the SD had got wind of his contacts with the Polish Resistance. These SS men were the brutalized, inhuman men who loved killing; among them there were the "150 per centers" with their cadaver obedience who only knew duty and orders; and also the promotion seekers. These were the bad men. Had he been one of them he would not have remained a "poor little sergeant". Every postman in Germany had the War Service Cross—so why was it he was not decorated? It was because these swine—the SD of the SS— were on his trail. KW now comes back to the centrepiece of his written *curriculum*—the gratitude of many Poles, Jews and Gypsies who owed their life to him. But no—not even his old friends Gomulka or Cyran- kiewicz† had come forward in his defence. These were the people who knew he had clean hands. And here he is now, wrongfully sentenced on the lying evidence of perjured people—the only man out of his unit of 400. "All the others are going about as free men"—and some of these had even testified against him.

By now—towards the end of our session—KW's debonair urbanity had given way to an intense state of petulant anxiety and tension. He tells me, as I rise, just before his warder arrives to collect him, how alone and unhappy he is, too nervous to read or occupy himself—and how not only his digestion but now also his bladder makes him feel he has something really fatal inside him. He suddenly looks a broken, old, terrified man.

In a brief review with the director of the prison, I am informed that a cancer of the prostate gland is indeed suspected. His behaviour remains, as noted in the earlier reports, demanding, complaining and unco-operative. He is said not to miss a single trick or loophole in the prison regulations on which he can discredit his cell-mates or his warders—a pitiable trouble-maker and irritant to the staff.

I also learnt that the British occupying power arrested him in a

---

* This is KW's statement; The hotel may have originally belonged to Jews. We also know that, from Goering downwards, some Nazi bosses protected a few "special" Jews if they were useful to them.

† Communist statesmen of present Poland.

general early round-up of former SS, but had no specific evidence and he was released, to follow his post-war occupation of a truck-driver, until the Federal war-crimes investigations caught up with him.

Commentary This man, as the reader may agree, represents a different sort of murderous personality from the group previously described. The apt label of a "power-drunk, trigger-happy sybarite" allies him more with the swashbucklers among the Nazi leaders—with Goering rather than with prim, fanatical Himmler. In a sense KW was right to claim his difference from the "150 per cent fanatics" with their blinkered cadaver obedience justifying themselves by their loyalty and zeal, inhuman and dedicated, like the "civil servants" he despised. He is to us a more "ordinary" egocentric, narcissistic criminal, a rebel against authority, who used the Gestapo-SS cover and its double standards for his own ends. Its sanctioning of violence made it easy for him to enjoy unlimited and unpunished power of life and death over unresisting victims, whether with his gun or with his blackmail of frightened hotel-keepers and black-marketeers. The only evidence of an "ideological" component in KW's motivations was his anti-Semitism—even as a young lout—and this too seems to have been at the primitive level of a Notting Hill tough.* He used his anonymous Nazi-gang affiliation entirely to threaten and browbeat timid burghers, to cut a figure and throw his weight about in much the same way as the bike-riding Hell's Angels, Rockers and similar anarchic adolescent gangs in contemporary Britain.

It will be remembered that KW told me he did not really like "getting into fights"; he avoided the real SA Party troops who expected to be hurt by their opponents—the organized Left Wing militants. KW was not that kind—not like S2 or Captain A, or some of the "Old fighters" I cited in Chapter Four. For him the exercise of power had to be free of risk of retaliation and contain an element of self-display. He wanted the *fun* of it—including the smart white trimmings of a traffic cop, or the powerful roaring bike or car. Undisciplined and cowardly, he seems mainly to have followed his narcissistic wish for glamour when he volunteered for the "new" Wehrmacht. Its realities of Prussian drill and privation soon resulted in his psychosomatic dyspepsia which got him his discharge—and which he was to use with typical neurotic purposiveness ever after. (Here the comparison with Goering as a

* This refers to the so-called race-riots in the so named district of London when undisciplined gangs of white youths beat up Negroes there a few years ago.

young man breaks down—the marshal could use his *panache* to become a celebrated fighter pilot in World War I). KW's capacity for affiliation and submission to a group only stretched to his need to swagger in a fine uniform, "to be somebody" a little higher and nearer to an élite in the new Germany than the impoverished unemployed youths of his time. Essentially he was quite clearly a "loner" who resented regimentation. This applies as much to his wish to have money with which to "lash-out", irrespective of how it was obtained, as to his free-lance Jew-killing to show his power and extra-legal standing, covered by the SS doctrine of zeal. The more commonplace attraction towards joining one of the mushrooming uniformed services of the Third Reich was the trouble-free maintenance—pay, lodging and food, with which Hitler won many chronically hungry and unemployed youths to his banners.

We must now try and look a little more closely at KW's personality and history. Demographically he was another "classical" recruit for the Nazis. The small town independent *"petit-bourgeois"* origins, the economic and status privations and consequent acutely felt yearning for abundance and for "being somebody" fitted. KW voiced them as disdain for "rough lads" and in his declaration how respectably his parents had brought him up. All the points made by Wangh[1] were here to be seen once again. What was more clearly stated than by the rest of my subjects, was the history of direct maternal influence, leaving on KW an imprint of a self-willed, irresistibly cute mother's boy with a corresponding conviction that he was "special" and had to have what he wanted. This trait is frequently observed in criminals, and is a manifestation of an infantile "omnipotent dependence". It is often coupled with a great need to show off and be lavish spenders in order to enhance their narcissistic image in their own and other peoples' eyes. This narcissism stems from the incorporation of, and identification with, the spoiling, gratifying mother whom one can exploit unconditionally and whose admiration merges with one's own feeling about oneself. For such a person "the world is my oyster" to break open and suck out. When the fantasy system, on which this primitive relation to sources of satisfaction depends, is thwarted, the thin veneer of narcissistic charm cracks to reveal the underlying paranoid insecurity, envy and impetuous greed (see Chapter One). When the objects from which (or whom) gratification and loving sustenance is exacted make demands on the ego in turn, they become *bad*. KW demonstrates this well, not only in his relation to the army which he could not "digest", but also in his rejection of all loyalty. He is the typical double-agent, "con-man" with a deep split towards the world. Like BT described in this chapter, he beguiles only to threaten, shows friendliness only to exploit. It is not inconsistent with this primitive paranoid ("oral") level of object-relations that KW might have been a rapist-murderer. His conversation with his cell-mate shows how closely murder and sleeping with girls were associated in his mind, and how he could coolly and "for fun" pay out a fellow-SS man by shooting his mistress. That is—human beings are only felt as counters to be used to satisfy his greed, hate and thirst for getting even or feeling on top.

From his early history it is likely that such a link between the extreme cruelty towards women, periodically ending in their brutal murder, had its roots in his family constellation. There is the evidence that he became for his mother, with an initially absent and later severely damaged husband, the centrepiece for her loving devotion—but presumably à l'Allemand, in which the spoiling was apt to be punctuated by attempts to take the ineffectual father's place, and in any case to extol the "manliness" of her little son who so obviously was the "cock of the walk". That this treatment resulted in severe Oedipal guilt conflicts need not be doubted. The fantasies of triumphing over his useless damaged father were too severe a load. The Fatherland's enemies, who had in reality captured and injured his father, were for him ready-made scapegoats, originating in the paranoid "Stab in the Back" legend out of which Nazi doctrines of revenge and manic reassertions of unimpaired virility and power grew. KW could by accepting this creed dispose of his individual parricidal fear and guilt about the damage to his "poor useless" father. These enemies—crystallised into the Jews who were responsible for "capitalist wars"—not he, the little Oedipus, had done this deed. He can now avenge the crime and kill and intimidate and exploit them, as these guilty traitors to the Fatherland deserved. This also frees him for guilt-free enjoyment of the self-indulgent life: vicarious parricide as the pre-condition of potency.

A second and more specific theme can be seen in KW's predicament of being the favoured male vis à vis his sisters and mother. Here he acquired his attitude of unquestioned superior male rights and powers to demand what he wanted of them—it was his experience of his actual mother and it fitted the old German devaluation of women. It also emerged, however, that unlike "modern youths who want everything" (as he said), KW had to be content with very small indulgences. Greed and envy of more privileged and better-off people, a predicament of a big group of "de-classed", hungry German lower middle—and working—class youths, could not be directly felt as caused by his mother's cheese-paring, but had also to be displaced into a latent motive of forcing women to give him all he wanted without argument. At this point we note another split in KW. It is the familiar one arising from Oedipal demands. The forbidden libidinal demands on the mother have to be repressed, so that the mother figure can be preserved as "good" and non-sexual. The repressed libidinal element can only express itself in displacement to devalued, exogamous, "foreign" women with whom uninhibited sexual aggressiveness is possible. This so-called "libido split" between "sacred" and "profane" love accounts for a great deal of sado-masochistic perversion in psychiatric and forensic cases of rape and torture, in fact or fantasy, of females by mother-tied and otherwise impotent men. In my original High F schedule of variables I included this trait of "libido-split", but it did not turn out to be statistically significant in discriminating High from Low F. But in KW the evidence of his behaviour in Warsaw fits the psychopathology of impulsive recurrent murder on a sexual background. There is also little doubt that KW's attitude to his authorities was a displacement to "service or state" of his "mother cathexis" (as in Table I). They could be treated as mother was treated—take all you can, defy and circumvent their silly regulations, do as you like because you are a special privileged boy, above the restrictions. How well omnipotent SS and Gestapo claims to being a law unto themselves fitted KW's fantasy.

Into this image of the privileged exploiter there intruded the further guilt and anxiety over the injury (and later death) of KW's sister, during his first 7-10 years of life. This also can be interpreted as contributing to his special double feeling or split in which he is both the aggressor against young women who deprive him of treats by costing so much—and should therefore be killed—and avenger of the poor girl, in retaliation for whose maiming and death many more other young girls shall suffer the same fate. This was also "sound Nazi doctrine" as shown in all the Gestapo killings of 100 hostages for every German life exacted in Czechoslovakia, Poland, etc. Given KW's poor ego-development with little capacity to feel depressive anxiety for his attacked good objects, most of his emotional transactions remained at the level of undifferentiated identification with the aggressor, when he feels threatened or—more importantly in KW's case—frustrated in being the one-and-only, in getting what he wants NOW. When this has been said, I felt that in KW there was at least some element of the "human" rascal, a zest for having a high old time. He would probably have been a delinquent of some kind in almost any social system. It is the terrible responsibility of the Nazi and SS ideology to have positively rewarded the regression to, and breakthrough of, direct acting-out of the most primitive paranoid-level internal object-relations of such predisposed individuals.

We are on more banal ground in noting this over-protected and fearful man's self-protective over-compensation to appear manly and "one of the boys" during adolescence by adopting the Nazi stance and gradually being drawn further into the need to *appear* a smart, ruthless stop-at-nothing, a sort of bogus Iron George. This escalation, as I have repeatedly suggested, was necessary to compete with the norm setters from Eicke's stable, forcing the TKV's and their Gestapo brethren constantly to "live up" to more and more extreme examples.

I would summarize KW's impulsions towards becoming a killer as being generated from an almost entirely individual intrapsychic system, with only the façade and social facilitation provided by the, none the less, highly congenial Nazi ideology, in which these same intrapsychic elements of a criminal gangster-conspiracy must be admitted to have formed an important facet. From among the spectrum of motivations I drew up in Section 4 of Chapter Four, KW did not show any evidence of being driven by eager submissiveness or hero-worship. His motives came from both overt and unconscious aggression and hate: avenging past wrongs done to him—mostly economic; proving his omnipotence and phallic manliness; and indeed indulging his sadistic pleasure in doing just what he felt like, with a strong pleasurable sexual component. At the same time, like all bullies, he saw his victims as weak and despicable, and almost certainly these projections of his own cowardice and "nervousness" on to his abject victims were major mechanisms sustaining this free-lance murderer. By way of "consolation" to himself he therefore liked to feel how grand and respected he was around the Warsaw high-spots, the inn-keepers bowing and scraping and rewarding him, and how good a friend to the Poles, with whom (as an essentially rebel-character) he felt some sympathy and whom he patronized. Even his government's enemies were split into good and bad; the "white" Poles and the "black" Polish Jews. KW had, in terms of recent fiction, a typical adolescent James Bond fantasy—the mysterious, debonair secret agent handy with a gun and a sumptuous lady-killer.

That he is, in psychiatric terms, a hysterical psychopath, is of less interest than the workings of his conscience, as seen in the official accounts of his behaviour and in his bearing with me, The qualities of remorse or feelings of conscious guilt are totally absent. KW had not matured to a capacity to tolerate the anxieties of the depressed phase. He turns everything he might feel along these lines into brazen denial, projects them into others—all authorities are bad: his narcissism seems impervious, he is wronged, maltreated, deprived. He even fights the prison staff. What cannot be projected and acted out turns into illness—the bad forces inside that torment him. In this way he had for years defied his authorities but also imposed an increasingly disabling burden of hypochondriacal anxiety on himself. This is a pattern which I was to observe in very glaring obviousness in the permutations of Rudolf Hess's paranoid behaviour.[2] In one phase we were all trying to poison him. In another phase he was tortured by dreadful cramps in his abdomen. When these did not cope with his inner conflicts and fears, he would hysterically "lose his memory", in other words dissociate himself from the intolerable outer reality, or more accurately, from the emotions this reality aroused in him. At one point the deep hate of the bad object broke through into a suicidal attempt.

KW represents a variant of Nazi terrorist at the opposite pole to the principled, fanatical "cadaver-obedience" zealots whom one can in a sense class with religious or ideological crusaders—within their group ethos highly virtuous and self-denying. In contrast, the self-seeking, amoral adventurer-swashbucklers were low-scoring on ideological fanaticism, though high on sadism, cult of manliness, tenderness taboo and paranoid features. One such, at KW's own level was *S1*, from *S2's* TKV KZ unit and tried with him. Though I was not permitted to interview this man, his history and behaviour were sufficiently documented to make some comment valid and perhaps of interest.

Born in 1917 at Magdeburg, *S1* seems to have hated, above all, members of Germany's liberal academic professions whom he delighted to hound to death on the drill square, shouting obscene insults at them. Though he tried to cut a very soldierly figure with clipped, military speech, what emerged at his trial was a completely narcissistic bearing and attitude based on seeking admiration for his smartness and ruthless efficiency. If he had an ideology it was that of an anti-democrat and anti-intellectual. His off-duty behaviour was described as that of a buffoon and joker, drinking and laughing and telling obscene jokes. Above all, the judge said, he had an egotistical pride in his uniform, in what the British army would describe as "bull", "a man without substance". When, sometime during his service, he was awarded the war service decoration (Kriegsverdienstkreuz) he is said to have "hollered with joy: 'I have deserved it! 300 passed through today. Now I must do even better!'" This man was sentenced for 46 proven killings, including a good friend of the late Dr Adenauer, though he had boasted of having shot 636 people personally and gassed some 1700 Russians. The court compared his personality and impenitence, with "crocodile's tears" at his "hard fate", unfavourably with the more principled bearing of S2 (Chapter Five).

Another variant of KW's pattern is exemplified by the record of one of Himmler's chief lieutenants, SS general *Odilo Globocnik*.[3,4] This Slovene-born Austrian combined a rabid anti-Semitism with a propensity for extensive black-market operations and currency dealing, and was as intolerant of taking orders or co-operating with his own higher authorities. Born in Trieste in 1904, he was a small builder. He became an underground Austrian Nazi in 1922. In 1933 he had to flee from Vienna because he was wanted for murdering a jeweller. He now joined the SS and rose rapidly to become the (as yet secret) Nazi Party leader for Carinthia. On the annexation of Austria Hitler promoted him to "Secretary of State" and made him Gauleiter of Vienna where he distinguished himself by riotous living, menacing anti-Semitic speeches and defiance of his administrative and party superiors, Buerckel and Seyss-Inquart. He is on record as having said: "I shall strive to make sure that in Austria only the Party has power and nobody else, neither a court of law nor any other institution"[5] In February 1939 the London *Daily Telegraph* carried an item from Vienna of official denial that Globocnik had been charged with corruption. None the less, later that year he was sacked for illegal currency speculation, and had to be replaced by Buerckel. Regarded even in the Party and SS as "the shadiest character" (dunkelster Ehrenmann), Globocnik was now signally favoured by Himmler who made him "his" Higher SS and Police chief (HSSPF) in Lublin, Poland. "This uneducated and impulsive man" is said to have evoked Himmler's gratitude for his loyalty and devotion in accepting at the Reichsführer's hands the onerous task of exterminating Polish Jewry. In this assignment, rationalized as a just reprisal in calling it "Operation Reinhardt" after Heydrich's assassination, Globocnik had four aims: (1) extermination; (2) exploitation of manpower; (3) seizure of all real estate owned by dead Jews, and (4) seizure of all hidden valuables, money and moveable property.

Globocnik was the creator of the first Polish extermination camps of Belzek, Sobibor and Treblinka, respectively with a maximum daily killing capacity of 15,000, 20,000 and 25,000. Pohl, as head of Himmler's "economic department", received as the harvest of Globocnik's work liquid assets worth RM 53,013,135, and real estate worth RM 100,047,983. Here we get a glimpse of the sort of SS chief whose directives the many BT's and KWs had to implement: the deep split between exploiting their victims economically and as manpower, and the ultimately always prevailing motive of destruction when both had been exhausted. We can also see, especially in BT and KW, how the inwardly denied qualities of greed, envy and "racial" inferiority of a common criminal like Globocnik presiding over the Gestapo units to which they belonged could impart a pitiless paranoid intensity to his minions' hate of Jews who could be saddled with just these projected characteristics.

It is known that Globocnik had lost heart in the latter part of his career of organized murder and robbery. When drunk he confessed to friends that he would have liked to have got out, "but he was too deep in and must win or perish with Hitler". Like Himmler, he took poison.

CHAPTER NINE

THE LAWYER TURNS HANGMAN

In my quest for something approaching a cross-section I needed not only "manual" killers at non-commissioned level but also some personnel at higher echelons of the "Final Solution" operation. I had given the Federal German authorities a fairly comprehensive list of men potentially available which included two or three highest-level SS generals, colonels, higher administrators, lawyers and SS doctors and scientists (such as those who devised the technological means of mass killing). The response was limited to a single volunteer in this class, to whom this chapter will be devoted.

PF had been a lieutenant-colonel in the SS (Obersturmbannführer) and had, at the material time, been the commanding officer of one of the *Einsatzkommandos* (EK No. 9), which were the units composing the *Einsatzgruppen*, the function of which was explained in Chapter Three. He was interviewed at length in a prison in West Berlin. He had been sentenced for life by the high court in that city in 1962 after being found guilty of the felonious murder of 11,000 persons in the areas of the Polish-Lithuanian cities of Grodno and Vilna and the White Russian (Soviet) town of Vitebsk. It may be of interest that the charge included the words " . . . jointly with Adolf Hitler, Heinrich Himmler and Reinhardt Heydrich", since this indictment related to PF's orders and not only to killing by his own hand. This number of murders had been achieved by the unit under his command in the four months July to October 1941 in the wake of the German invasion of the Soviet Union.

Curriculum Vitæ In this case the facts are culled from official documents and depositions to which I was given access. PF did not write a "biography" specially for me.

PF was born in 1905 in Darmstadt in Hesse of Protestant parents. His father was an official in the postal service. PF was educated in a modern high school (*Oberrealschule—in contrast to classical Gymnasium*) and left there before matriculation to become a bank trainee. He later passed his *Abitur* (university entrance) examination externally and studied economics and jurisprudence at the universities of Giessen,

Heidelberg and Marburg. The account stressed financial stringency during this undergraduate period. PF passed his State examination in Law in 1933, and proceeded to his (German) doctorate in Law six months later. He took up a junior appointment in the judicial branch of government service (the rank carrying the title *Gerichtsreferendar* in Hesse).*

In 1932 he joined the Nazi party and General SS. In 1935 Himmler's office summoned PF to report in Berlin. Here he was received by Werner Best, chief of the legal branch at the SS headquarters, and thereafter by Heydrich. An appointment followed to a desk job in foreign political intelligence operated by Heydrich's special service (SD). PF advanced quickly in rank to lieutenant colonel. In 1939 (when the RSHA was created) he was among those attending a top secret conference outside Berlin (Wannsee), in which Heydrich briefed designated senior TKV and Gestapo chiefs on the measures (mentioned at the beginning of Chapter Eight) to be taken in the wake of the invasion of Poland and later the Soviet Union. Among others, this conference was attended by PF's chief, SS General *Nebe*, commander of *Einsatzgruppe* "B" in General Brauchitsch's operational area, and by *Eichmann*. (*This document, part of the evidence, showed how close PF was to the policy-making group of the genocide project.*) Then in 1941, at short notice he was posted to take command of his EK unit. In October 1941 he was suddenly recalled to Berlin "on a disciplinary charge against him". He was relieved of all duties for some two years. In the autumn of 1943 he was exonerated and put in charge of another section of the RSHA under his old chief, Nebe. In 1945 (*like Himmler and many leading SS figures round him*) PF tried to disappear in Schleswig-Holstein under a false name. Some time later he resumed his proper name and obtained a job with a bank, in due course being promoted to manager of its Berlin branch. It was here that the war-crimes commission traced and arrested him. PF married in 1937 and there were two sons.

Resumé of Court Evidence and Summing Up The brief of PF's commando was given as

1. The creation of a "Gau" of "non-Germans" in a region round Cracow.
2. The corralling of Jews into city ghettoes in Poland.

* In contrast to Britain, German lawyers could advance up a career ladder in the judiciary without first becoming attorneys or advocates.

3. The freeing of the Reich of Jews by transfer to Poland.
4. The deportation from the Reich of some 30,000 Gypsies to this area.
5. Organization of deportations by goods trains.

The indictment detailed how PF's squads herded their previously arrested victims, mostly but not exclusively Jews, to remote areas, in woods, transporting them "under cover of darkness and in secrecy". Here men, women and children would be compelled to strip and then be lined up on the edge of prepared deep trenches and shot, falling straight into their mass graves. The next batch to be similarly executed would be waiting within earshot and even sight of these shootings. In their turn they would fall into the trenches on top of the bodies already there. There were no medical officers to verify death. It was left to local auxiliary SS levies from among "Volksdeutsche"*—and in PF's case Lithuanian anti-Semitic student-terrorists—to deliver the *coup de grâce* to victims found alive after the salvos.

It was established in court that when PF assumed command of his EK he made a speech to his paraded men, in which he announced "hard consequences for any who demurred at taking part in the destruction of Jews". He laid it down that in addition to Jews all identified communists must also be destroyed. He took his orders literally: "every man must fire", himself included, not only directing salvos but actually shooting "to set a good example". In his tactics of creating a climate of pogroms, PF used non-Jewish Poles, Lithuanians, etc. as instigators, after which his EK would intervene "to restore order". His bearing was described by some of his subordinates in evidence as "ruthless" (rücksichtslos), for example in dismissing objections to the herding and stripping of women and in his lack of consideration for the youth of some of his personnel taking part. It was clear to the court that PF presented himself as the zealous as well as ferocious executor of his Führer's policies. "It is true", said the prosecution, "that PF stopped the wild shooting of the Lithuanian auxiliary police, but he substituted for it the routine mechanical slaughter of the Chicago stockyards at the rate of 500 a day." It was further established in evidence that PF had severely punished any man in his EK who had shown some humane feelings to Jewish victims. He had had the clothing stripped from the executed presented to the auxiliaries and to persons who had denounced

* i.e. settlers of German descent and language.

Jews to his men. By the time the EK reached the Vitebsk area PF had delegated some of the shooting to a civilian militia recruited from among the local Jew haters and anti-Soviet members of the population, distinguished only by arm-bands, without even the semblance of "due legal process". This was shown to be due to a deterioration of morale among his own men who had to be issued with increasing rations of *vodka* to carry out their killing orders. Rather than shoot, they would bully the victims to jump into the pit alive, so that the local irregulars should do the final shooting for them. (*It was in this way that a number of intended victims, feigning death, managed to hide and later crawl to safety. These became important witnesses for many of the SS atrocities after the war.*)

In his defence PF used several arguments. The first was that he had received his orders and had "only passed on" his general brief to his subordinates "to kill all Jews". He minimized his personal participation and pleaded the need to obey orders from higher authorities whom he blamed for their inhuman policies. Secondly, he advanced the plea that he had asked for a transfer which had been refused, because his "nerves could not stand" what he was ordered to do, since he did not hate the Jews. Third, and most important, was his disclosure that a brother of his had been an inmate of Buchenwald KZ as an opponent of the Nazis, and that therefore PF did not dare show the least faltering from the Party line. In mitigation he further claimed that for the sake of showing his efficiency he made inflated returns of figures for the numbers of executions. "It was only perhaps a thousand" where the reports had said 11,000. Furthermore, he pleaded, "Vitebebsk had to be liquidated because of the threat of epidemics".

PF was, in fact, tried as the senior of a group of five from that 1941 Einsatzkommando, and some of his former associates seriously undermined his defence. The press reports of the court scenes stated that several of them, among them SS Major G., confessed fully, were openly weeping in the dock and would have none of the standard self-exculpations. Thus, Major G: "We killed because we were afraid we might lose our jobs, families and perhaps our lives. . . . " "If anyone *now* tells me he was no anti-Semite, he is in my eyes just a heel (ein Lump)!" An SS subaltern T. broke down in tears and exclaimed to the court "I have allowed myself to be abused (misbrauchen lassen) as a hangman's serf (Henkersknecht)!" A third man, like PF a protégé of the notorious Nebe (*an erstwhile respected police commissioner of pre-Hitler days*), said he could not understand how a man of Nebe's character could have lent himself to leading such an *Einsatzgruppe*. These SS officers also produced a remarkable piece of evidence for PF's irrational anti-Semitism. He had, it was stated, taken great objection to any captive Jews employed round the EK's billets using the same eating utensils as his own troops! (*A neat illustration of the operation of a taboo against the "unclean" as severe as any connected with the Jews' own kosher rules or the Brahmins' ancient laws about Untouchables.*)

The presiding judge in his summing-up used this piece of evidence to support his finding that PF's hate of Jews was established. He found him a man fully identified with his orders. There was, the judge said, no attempt by PF to evade, mollify or even question these orders which he had carried out with quite unnecessary ferocity, going far beyond even Heydrich's brief. PF's plea of having acted only under duress did not succeed and was not valid, because all he risked was an end to further promotion. As for PF's claim that he had asked for a transfer from his post, this was not motivated from any feeling of humanity towards the Jews, of which he had none, but solely because his nerves could not stand it. PF had created a model for the technique used by the *Einsatzgruppen* for which he now tried to shift all responsibility to his superiors. *One gathered that this trial had been regarded as a test case for the legal principle of "duress" pleadings (Befehlsnotstand.)*

PF was reported to have wept during the sentence, and in some ways to have demonstrated acceptance of his guilt. In his last plea he had expressed regret that he had not refused to execute his orders—"better to have committed suicide". As mentioned, he received a life sentence in 1962.

The Interview PF was interviewed by me, after I had read the documentation summarized above, at his Berlin prison in July 1969. The prison governor introduces us, and as he has shaken PF's hand I do the same. PF has under his arm a neat folder full of documents. As we sit down he is already producing papers for my perusal. This is a tall, gaunt, pale and faded man showing evidence of seven years' institutionalization. He has several scars over his lower lip and cheeks which I later discover are the proud acquisitions of his duelling student days. I am especially aware of his rather bulging pale blue eyes under heavy lids, of the kind I call "reptilian", rather unblinking and lifelessly cold.

I say "I do not smoke and cannot offer you a cigarette". Tears well up in his eyes: "I cannot afford to smoke now—my poor wife has to work, I cannot allow her to bring me cigarettes, she is so poor and so ill, she has diabetes." But instead of, as I assumed, continuing with the topic of his family, etc., PF eagerly fingers his papers and says with dramatic emphasis: "Herr Professor, there has been *no case like mine!*" and plunges avidly into telling me how it was his brother, home on a visit from the U.S.A., who got him into this mess by getting himself into KZ Buchenwald. I say I am interested to hear how PF got into his predicament—how he came to join the Party, the SS, the *Einsatzgruppen* and so to end with a life sentence.

PF now lets go his papers and tells me that he joined the Party before it came to power—in 1932 while still a law student. There were such bitter times then in Germany, the Germans were divided into Left and Right. When he started his first job as a *Referendar* in the Hesse Law Courts he dared not dress properly or even wear a tie in the street for fear of being attacked, jeered at and mobbed by gangs of the six million workless. The communists terrorized the merchants and shopkeepers. "So *we* (sic) joined the Party to bring about a better Germany." *PF makes a direct association next.* "In my home and family we only knew command and order (Befehl und Ordnung). I was born in military barracks. My father started as the sergeant major (Spiess) of the Guard of his Highness the Duke of Hesse. We had a good life then. Of course I wanted to become a soldier *(we shall see that PF uses references to his "being a soldier" a great deal)*. After all—the Guards! I was enthusiastic (begeistert) as a child." I interpose that, of course, absolute obedience was a cardinal point of the SS which no doubt appealed to him. PF replies: "The Kaiser demanded worse—he said 'When I order you to murder your father and mother you must obey!' The Kaiser's orders were like God's. . . ." He now switches to telling me that of course he was sensitive (empfindlich). "I always went to great lengths to avoid anything to do with death or corpses as a child. When I was very young my brother, 18 months older, took hold of me and held me out over the window-sill. Ever since I've had a dread of heights—a feeling it draws me down. I also feel terror if I climb a high tower or look down from an aircraft and so on. . . ."

PF now returns to his SS career. He relates how, soon after he had started on his legal appointment, in 1935, he received a summons by letter to present himself "in his uniform" at SS security office headquarters in Berlin. Here he was met by a Professor Hohn in the

Universities section of the SD who offered him a job to keep German student corporations (fraternities) under political surveillance. PF said this proposal outraged him: he was an old corps student himself and he had many friends, he regarded it as demeaning and unworthy. It was then that he went to see his old Hessian acquaintance Dr Werner Best (see *Curriculum* above), to tell him of the spying proposal. PF added: "It shows how naïve I was—I did not even know what went on in that building on the Wilhelmstrasse!" Best reminded him of his SS oath and duty. He also made it clear to PF that the SS did not approve of its members working for a local government not yet National Socialist.

It took the Nazis several years to "clean up" the always intricate patterns of local administration and get rid of local judges and other key personnel, and replace them with their monolithic totalitarian governmental structure. Hesse and Darmstadt were evidently late in being "assimilated".

PF's reluctance was rewarded by being, instead, assigned to the foreign service division of the SS Security Service (SD), which was then being built up in a villa in the Wannsee suburb of Berlin. This he accepted with pleasure.

I wondered what sort of confidential reports on this then young man's devotion and malleability must have preceded this selection.

PF continued how interesting and all-absorbing this work was, he felt he was "in on" high diplomacy and secrets of state. He mentioned how objective were the reports—"I can assure you there was no hate of Jews, but of course we learnt a lot of their international connections." Why, he said, not only did he have friends among Jews (*that hoary stereotype of the anti-Semite!*), but there were even Jews in the Party!

Well, how did it start? I interposed. "Ah", he said, "then came the order!★ But of course, our foreign monitoring service also brought proof of the concentrated hate the Jews abroad were fomenting against us—and understandably so, because of our measures." (*This clearly as a sop to me.*)

Feeling settled with good prospects, PF said, he could now get married in 1937. His wife and her parents were not in the Party—so there had to be all those enquiries about them and her pedigree. I said: "good SS doctrine". PF rather disdainfully replied that he had never really believed all that nonsense about Himmler's "Blood and Soil"

★ His words: "Dann kam ja Befehl" convey to me the sense that this necessarily changed everything. The "ja", like "doch" suggests something not to be argued against.

and Order of Chivalry. He quickly added that his two sons were born in 1938 and 1940, as if he did not want to recall the old SS follies.

He continued that in 1938 his older brother who had dangled him from the window as a child, and who had been in the U.S.A. for 12 years, came on a visit to Germany with his family. As he had not become a U.S. citizen, the Nazi government refused the brother a return visa, so that he was marooned at home, with all his affairs and belongings in Philadelphia. On the 9th November 1939 an abortive attempt was made to kill Hitler with a bomb in a Munich beer cellar. PF said: "One can understand it—but my brother was stupid enough to say out loud in public 'Pity that the bastard (Lump) didn't perish!' Of course this was promptly reported to the right quarters, and before anyone could spirit my brother away somewhere, the Gestapo arrested him on Himmler's personal orders, in the knowledge that he was Obersturmbannführer PF's brother." The brother was quickly tried in a "regular" court and sentenced to detention in Buchenwald KZ. Here he was soon "missing" (verschollen) and never heard of again. PF's reaction to my remarking how terrible this was, was highly significant. "Yes—it was terrible for me—it meant the end of all promotion (Beförderungssperre)! After all I had become a lieutenant-colonel in three years". Next, tears began to well up in his goggly eyes as he said "And my mother had a stroke when she heard the news." PF said he now had to take on looking after the brother's family. . . . And people began avoiding him ("Man rückte von mir ab"). "To think Himmler was behind this himself." Soon there began intrigues at the RSHA about his rather sensitive security job. "Now I was properly in the soup. I was of course under SD surveillance myself. And therefore I now began to ask to be transferred to a soldier's posting in the front line". PF used a vacation due to him to get some military training in a Waffen SS regiment.

Then suddenly came his summons to see Heydrich (*PF does not mention that he had before this attended the top-secret Wannsee conference referred to above*), who forthwith "granted" his wish to go to the front-line service and appointed him to take charge of the Einsatzkommando, as from the following day, with orders to proceed to Vilna, in Poland, where this unit was formed and based. Nebe, whom he called an old friend "also not a Nazi", was to be his group commander. When PF reported to Nebe, the latter said to PF: "I have looked after so many criminals, and now I have become one myself. Don't give your family any more trouble than it is in already"—a clear hint that Nebe could only indicate how far he was into the murder campaign and could do no more than warn him that at any sign of wavering on PF's part his family would be used as hostages. (*A well established Himmlerian technique which in German was put as "für Verräter haftet Sippe" (for traitors the family go surety*).) "And so how could I do other than take it on—with my mail and telephone under surveillance." But, he added, all that was without hindsight—now he knows he should have put a bullet through his head. But how could he have done that with a wife and two little boys?

PF now becomes very anxious, as he says: "You would not expect me to tell you of all the terrible things that went on in Vilna and Vitebsk and so on—all I can say is that I did my best to mitigate the cruelties and to fake the returns of killings to impress the authorities". I replied I knew what had gone on and could see he did not like remembering it—I was interested to hear what he had to say and to note what he could not say. So PF, with tears once more welling up, talks of how the SS practised coercion and moral pressure on its members, and especially on jurists who were compelled to work its own judicial system. The SS's basic law was that any SS man who failed to carry out an SS order was liable to be eliminated according to ancestral custom in disgrace and shame with loss of honour ("mit Schimpf und Schande ausgemerzt und mit Ehrenverlust"). This, according to PF, was promulgated in a secret order by Himmler on July 15th 1940. This was the order the Head of the SS and Police had brought into operation "before the body of generals (Generalschaft), every general and field-marshal—and none had raised any objection". So wasn't it natural that he was afraid?

But after a while, PF said, he suffered a "nervous collapse" while with his commando. "I was degraded into a hangman—I began to tremble and have weeping fits—I used to be so gay." He again started to apply for a transfer to more military duties. A friend of his in a Waffen SS unit, to whom he had confided his state of mind, had said "if we can get you to the front line it will take them a long time to catch up with you and try you". "Nobody believes me that I felt it." And then came "the crowning disgrace". Four months after PF had started on his murderous command he was once again summoned to the RSHA in Berlin—this time to be confronted with a charge that he had illegally kept back RM 60,000 for his own use, in the office safe. It was proposed to investigate this allegation, and in the meantime he was relieved of all duties. The memory of this insult brought more tears to PF's eyes. "I knew there was nothing in that safe when I had reported sick. Was it thinkable that I, a jurist and a soldier would do such a thing?" "Now I felt I had not only been degraded into a hangman (*PF was fond of quoting this sentence he had heard his fellow-prisoner T. utter at their trial*), but somebody in that office was determined to bring about my downfall." So, while the investigation dragged on, PF was on unemployed leave living at home for nearly two years. "Can you imagine how I felt as a soldier—the whole neighbourhood knew—night after night, seeing me sitting with my wife in the air raid shelter—what would all those women say: 'Why isn't he at the front—that's where he should be'?" And all the time fearing what those conspirators at the RSHA were cooking up—who had their knife into him ever since the affair of his brother. (*PF now becomes rather emotional and switches from 1941 to the present.*) He goes to his folder saying he is now preparing an appeal because he has nothing to reproach himself with—"before God and my conscience". Only in Berlin could he have been given a life sentence—that is what they are all saying in the Federal Republic. It was Judge Meyer—"who as we used to say in the SS was married into Jewry ('jüdisch versippt')—(adding at once) ah well, one can understand it—but what kind of justice is this when they hound a little man like me!"

He now makes a pathetic attempt at quasi-legal argument. "These judges who insisted that they could tell the court what only my Maker and I know—the subjective facts of criminal intent on which all justice must be based—took upon themselves to pronounce on these things!" PF now lists the disputed statements—let the Herr Professor judge what these fine gentlemen condemned him on.

True he had been a Nazi—but he was a decent man who had done his soldierly duty, because he was an eager, patriotic man. But the court had attributed to him (*a*) that he could not rest until the last Jew had been killed; (*b*) that he had exceeded Heydrich's orders by scouring every village and ferreting out the last Jew in it; (*c*) that even his asking for a transfer was not because he objected to this task but only because his nerves couldn't stand it! "Well—how does a man show he cannot stand it except by his nerves giving way?" I ask if this was really how he reacted. "Yes—a complete nervous breakdown . . . to be degraded into a hangman and murderer—nobody believes I felt it." Myself:

What were the symptoms? PF: Uncontrollable trembling (Schüttel-frost—a word I translate as *rigor*, as in fever), and weeping. I did not laugh any more.

It will be seen that PF had this experience so much on his mind he kept returning to it in almost identical form—as if to prove his judges wrong in denying him human feelings and a sense of guilt.

PF, once again with tears in his eyes, goes on to relate his intolerable assignment to the existence of the conditions of duress (Befehlsnotstand), and the unfairness of the prosecution and the Federal judiciary in not allowing this fact, when it is well known that a soldier dare not disobey orders. He attributes this vindictiveness to the influence of the Jews, just like the "impossible" prolongation of the period during which the West German state can bring former war criminals to trial. "Yes, that is the work of the Jews who cannot stop their need for retribution and punishment—(*and—once again quickly adds*) and who can blame them?" PF goes on with the review of his trial and its unfairness. He claims that his good defence witnesses were not even listened to. He instances how a Dutch woman with whom he had worked (*perhaps an SD employee of his pre-1941 work*) had visited him and offered to speak for him. She had brought other Dutch persons' greetings and thanks for having shielded them from Gestapo persecution. Back he comes to his "double" disgrace—first making him into an executioner and then framing him for a non-existent low-down crime of misappropriation of funds! That's how the SS used to get rid of its suspects and those who displeased the bosses—that's how decent men got into KZs—he "knew too much" so he had to be framed for some vulgar crime; then people could say "Ah, a swine after all". *It will be noted we are back from 1962 to 1941 again.*

PF refers by name to the man he thought had been behind this— this was the notorious *Schellenberg** who had for a long time wanted PF's job in the SD foreign department—Schellenberg's diary discovered after the war had proved it . . . a hateful swine of a man hand in glove with Heydrich. . . . It was only after Kaltenbrunner replaced Heydrich at the RSHA that PF was finally exonerated. . . . It was Schellenberg who was known to have stolen cash as well as blackmailed people. "I

---

* Schellenberg later replaced Heydrich as Himmler's special confidant after the former's death. He became head of the SD foreign intelligence department, and entrusted by Himmler with secret peace feeler missions behind Hitler's back when the war became hopeles for Germany.

could do nothing against them with that dossier about my brother in their files." PF rummages in his folder to continue his argument. The papers, it transpires now, are his own documentation for lodging an appeal. *This I perceive, is the reason why he had volunteered to be interviewed —in the hope of swaying someone to believe in and support his side of the story.*

He makes as if to lay various press cuttings, letters from his Dutch friends, etc., before me to read. I say that I cannot as an outsider and a non-German be of help by reading this, but would like to hear more of his own story. PF becomes visibly furious and agitated—he gathers up the papers with the words: "Oh, well, if you are not interested...." and half-rises from his chair. I say: "You have stated clearly what it was you couldn't accept in the judgement of the court—and in the task the SS thrust on you and I can understand how you feel—what about those in the service who could accept the extermination tasks—how do you think this was possible for them?" PF sits down again—soothed by my remarks, and says: "There were many of those others. The SS was full of desperate and bad characters." (*Note the distancing of himself from those bad others.*) He lists categories: (*a*) There were those who said: "The Führer commands, all is in order"—the unquestioning ones; (*b*) another type were those whose motto was simply "In the morning we shoot" (erschiessen wir—meaning the act of execution by firing) "in the evening we feast" (feiern wir); (*c*) the third group were those, like himself, who kept aloof from these types, and he was accused of being a bad comrade (unkameradschaftlich); (*d*) yet another sort were like the young law graduate SS officer who came to him at Vilna and said "I cannot do it" (ich kann das nicht) and PF had to say "Don't say that aloud!" and put him to work in the unit office. I ask PF to comment on the people who had such fun in high living and feasting. He replies that this was a defensive posture of bravado against a feeling of despair. After his somewhat scathing remarks about the bad fellows to be found in the SS and Gestapo PF now utters the familiar arguments that these poor SS men were really the scapegoats whom everybody could now blame and execrate.

I remark that PF has interestingly described three phases of a process in SS men: the starry eyed "cadaver obedience" to the Führer; the stage of doubt covered over by routinization of the killing, and drowning the misgivings by carousing and good fellowship; then his own inner withdrawal to the point of inability to accept such primitive denial. And there were those who could not even begin. I followed this up with the question whether there was not a time when PF himself was inspired and would have obeyed unquestioningly—in other words was he not also an enthusiastic Party man in his time? PF replied that he was never a romantic or a convinced ideologist. His motive for joining the movement was to help cure the hunger of those six million unemployed and hopeless men between the wars. *At this point in my interview note I wrote "the figure of 6 million haunts him"—implying he unconsciously bracketed it with that number of Jewish dead as the result of the "Final Solution". He used it also when he first mentioned conditions in Germany in 1932. This was my conjecture.*

I ask PF whether he attributed these hardships to the Weimar regime. He replies it was not so much Weimar as what the foreigners—the Versailles victors—had imposed on poor Germany. He becomes self-pitying at once, with moist eyes, as he goes on about his own hard times as a "working student" (Werkstudent) having to help pay his passage through his university period. *We see once again the high degree of self-centredness and the unconscious demand for ease and plenty. I refrain from verbal comment about U.S. and British students who do this regularly without such pathos.*

PF now says: "I see now that it was an error to deal with the Jews as we did." He had nothing to say in favour of pogroms and the "Crystal night". His father took him out to look at the damage to Jewish property the next day—and father was a Party member!—and together they saw all the burst feather beds and smashed furniture and shop windows. PF recalled how his father shook his head in disapproval. "And, Herr Professor, how the Jews have avenged themselves!" looking at me with the expression of anxiety and half-admiration in the undoubted belief that I was myself a Jew. I say that I am not in fact Jewish—when PF confirms he had assumed this.

I return to my endeavour to trace how far he was originally a Nazi fanatic and how a young man in his educational bracket was indoctrinated. I ask PF simply: "How did you progress so quickly in the Party and SS?" PF replies that his original affiliation was to the SA in a university troop. There he was a rank and file marcher and street fighter, taking part in the typical activities of packing meetings, sticking up posters, tearing down other parties' posters, processing through the town, etc. Then came a call to join a "leader course" of the SS (*to recall again, at this stage a part of the SA*) for which he volunteered. Here there was elementary military instruction—drill, small arms, smartening up. PF added that he deprecated the move from the voluntary principle to the structure of a closed "order" with a solemn personal oath (*which he none the less took*). He said the likes of him were always critical and somewhat ashamed of the old guard like Eicke or Sepp Dietrich.★ True these were brave men, but they were really the tough ("Rabauken"—see Chapter Three) element in the SS—these men and the "Streichers" were rather an embarrassment to him. He recalled what his father had felt on inspecting the results of the Crystal night pogrom. I remarked that those early militant days in the SA must have been enjoyable! This PF denied with some show of moral indignation. No, there was no pleasure in street-fights and punch-ups with the communist rabble, and he had little recollection of any boyish camaraderie or romantic hero-fantasies connected with that phase. "I was much too busy with my studies, I went to local troop meetings (Ortsgruppe) as little as possible."

It was obvious that, like KW and especially MO, this man represented the influx of "fine gentlemen" who thought themselves a cut above the roughnecks and had pretensions to leadership.

He now says: "In every nation there has to be a leading stratum—an élite—just as in England you have your Guards, the people who set an example of disciplined dedication, as it were." He felt this was a legitimate, justifiable reason for adhering to the SS, to set a more serious, refined tone. As for himself, he was soon so immersed and busy with the absorbing interest of the SD foreign intelligence work that he had no time for anything else in the service, "but I was always sensitive to that other element". There were, he enlarged, in the SS a lot of "no goods"— men who rose in it from nothing and who gave it a bad name. He gives the example of a "simple SS man" who, while in Berlin, had failed to recognize and salute Himmler dressed in hunter's kit. Himmler had not only personally abused this man but had had him punished. "Such small-minded vanity finished Himmler's image as a hero for me."

PF continues that such is the fate of human endeavours which begin with the highest motives. "Look at this present state (i.e. the Federal Republic—H. V. D.). The Jews are back again in places of power. What does the elder of the Berlin Jews care about me? These people just call me a murderer without thinking and condemn the SS wholesale. He doesn't know me or what I worked for. But this will also revenge itself

★ Sepp Dietrich was, as will be remembered, the commander of Hitler's SS bodyguard. He is said to have done most of the shooting of Roehm and his entourage in 1934.

—not only in Germany—look at the anti-Semitism in the U.S.S.R. and Poland!" But this was not to deny that there were bad people in the SS—*and not only in the SS* (with great emphasis)—who, as everybody knows, exceeded their orders and did wild things. He repeats his self-exculpatory arguments—I will not do so here.

PF here used the by now familiar manoeuvre of dissociating himself from "those bad men"—the others who did the bad things, unlike himself who had only worked from the highest motives.

I ask PF: "How long did you retain your faith in the goodness of your endeavour?" He thought it was in 1938,* over the merciless treatment of his brother and the moral stranglehold this produced on himself, that he became disillusioned. He adds hastily once more that he had no time to think—he lost himself (ging auf) in the technical developments and good comradeship of the SD job.

We may well regard this blinkered concentration on the prescribed task as perhaps the basic flaw in the Germans of that era—and others in many similar situations, when faithful routine becomes the defence against painful questioning of the values of what we are doing.

PF continues: "There are many people who deny they were ever Nazis, who still today, without thinking, or remembering what they had thought, will say 'Too few people were shot', whether they had been in the Party or not. You would be surprised to know where they all are now. (*He clearly wants to say these are murderously inclined people now in prominent safe positions in the new German states.*) It is we simple, straight little men who are now behind bars—these bigger, cleverer ones knew how to get away with it." PF cites the story of his successor in EK9 who stuck it out, was then put in a KZ by the SS for some (real or imputed) misdemeanour and "finished in the KZ with a lot of high ecclesiastics" where they dined off white table cloths waited on by SS orderlies! "And now he has a fine job as an administrator in a religious institution!"†
Next PF quotes the case of his opposite number, another lawyer, Dr B.‡ He served 2½ years in command of another EK and, with a task and record like PF's own, "only got a ten years' sentence" at Munich. "He denied nothing, but stood up in court simply affirming 'Those were my orders'." The same prosecuting state attorney had told PF that he had "nothing to fear—everything that could be done has been

---

* This was PF's statement—he was confused in some ways. He meant 1939.

† I have suppressed the name of this famous institution—H. V. D.

‡ A name on my list of potential interviewees who did not volunteer—H. V. D.

done". And yet that prosecutor had done nothing to help PF (the tears are once more in evidence). A further example of a "bad one" who had known how to wriggle out, was the (already mentioned) SS Major G., PF's former deputy in EK9. This man, a German originally from Moscow, had been recruited as a Russian-speaking interpreter. "He insisted on being my deputy, and then the dirty dog (Schweinhund) goes and betrays me as a crown witness. Here was another treacherous character from the SS."

PF is now back to the all-absorbing preoccupation with his "quite incomprehensible" life sentence—he just cannot get over it. Yes it was all those Jews sitting in court, shouting at him and barracking while he spoke. "One of my friendly witnesses had been threatened in an anonymous letter with shooting, and that Moscow man turned against me— that's what must have done it," So the SS had to take all the Jews' pent-up vengeance upon themselves.

I interpose that it was after all the SS to whom the tasks involved in the final Solution were assigned, so the world sees them necessarily as the quintessential embodiment of Nazi executioners. PF replies that it was the "Rabauken" who were the enthusiasts—the early SS men. "*We*, the ones who joined later, were the sensible ones who wanted to introduce reason, form a better ordered state (PF uses the old Prussian word 'Ordnungsstaat') once the time of the old roughneck fighters was over. Yes, Hitler had been my hero, but my regard for him diminished after the Gleiwitz incident which the Führer had thought up on his own."

The Gleiwitz incident was, according to sources, set in motion by Himmler on the eve of the invasion of Poland. It consisted of a carefully stage-managed night attack by SS personnel disguised as Polish soldiers against the radio station of the Upper Silesian German border town of that name. It was to serve as the pretext of Hitler's retaliation for "intolerable provocation". PF as a senior RSHA man would have been in the know.

But, continued PF, Hitler had not been bad. He had always thought of Hitler as a gentle, rosy-cheeked friendly chief whose mounting anger was a result of the hostile foreign press, as PF "had reason to know" through his job in the SD. "If Hitler had not had to make war the Third Reich would have lasted to this day." It was a fatal error to have treated the Jews as they were; they should have been included in the national effort. There were a lot of *good German* Jews. The trouble had been really those Eastern Jews who settled in Germany after the

First War. "Even the German Jews themselves rejected and disliked this alien element." Such, PF said, were the illogicalities and contradictions in the Nazi conduct of affairs. He becomes positively humorous when he now tells me: "You would never believe me—here I was for two years under a cloud of suspicion—and then in 1943 I was suddenly rehabilitated and put in charge of the SS office dealing with corruption in industry!" I say: "The 60,000 Reichmark was a good recommendation for a start", and we laugh a little for the first and only time. There is a perceptible lessening of tension and reserve, and PF turns without prompting to talk about his early life, as if he had been aware that I had been waiting for this.

He comes back first to the economic hardship he had suffered. His father had to take him out of the high school at 16, two years before the university matriculation, and got him his junior bank clerk's job, where he had to stick it for 7–8 years. Only when the financial crisis of 1929 caused him to be dismissed was he persuaded by friends to complete his university entrance examination and read law.

His earlier hard luck story about being a "working" student cannot be taken as accurate, since PF could not only attend the best universities but also join a high prestige "fighting" student corps with its considerable outlay on uniform, rapiers etc.

PF now talks with emotion and gratitude (and moist eyes) of all he owed his family (*I think really only his father!*). His venerable, dear father, now an official after retirement, was not only decorated with every possible medal in the First War but was loved in his regiment as the "company mother" (this was a customary expression among German soldiers when talking of their "Spiess" or company sergeant-major), and was popular and loved all over Hesse! PF had looked up to this kind, warm-hearted father and missed him terribly as a child when he was on active service. It was left to his mother to be the disciplinarian. Yes, she was too strict. PF recalls how he had a bad fall during his father's absence and lay on the ground yelling in great pain. The mother came out to him with her stick and gave him a beating for weeping. It was only after that had been done that she even looked at his leg and found that he had broken it. "Then she took me into the house." "Of course she was so *busy* that she did not have time." I ask how many of them there were to look after. It transpired there were three children: the elder brother, PF in the middle and a sister.

I next learn the other almost routine factor: how thrifty the parents were, and how good this was of them, for they sacrificed everything to give their children a good education and a better life (*higher social status is, I think, meant*). His dear father was so abstemious that he limited himself to one cigar a week after his Sunday dinner as his only indulgence. And now PF remembers how sorry he is for his wife (*the association with smoking*). Despite her age and diabetes the poor woman has to be a saleswoman. But at least he did the right thing by his sons who are in good posts. But after this brief excursion into altruism PF returns to his own hard fate, being in prison with common criminals who all think themselves quite a cut above the three poor SS men among them—the third being a gas waggon driver* who was given a 20-year sentence. Out of the blue PF continues: "Germans will only give their honest opinions if they know they are in no danger." Questioned, he infers that he cannot say what he feels in that atmosphere but also that none of the prisoners would dare show sympathy to the Nazis. His conversation now deteriorates into a grouse about conditions in the prison (*perhaps a compliment to my trustworthiness*). I reply that this is something I can do nothing about and make a move to rise and end our long talk, which had been interrupted by only a short luncheon break. PF now comes out with the remark how world events had shown Hitler to have been right after all. Why did the British not listen to him when he warned us about the war? Why was Rudolf Hess not listened to when he wanted to make peace with England? "What horrors would have been averted!" I mumble something about not being prepared to accept any undertakings by Hitler. PF now produces a document which consists of a Wehrmacht general's order of the day to his troops on the Russian front, in which any leniency to Jews is condemned, and which ends with the words "this unsoldierly bearing must cease forthwith!" PF looks rather triumphant as if to say "You see it wasn't just the SS!"

But he does now want to tell me of how well he had done as a good citizen after the war. Having gone to earth under a false name for a time, he decided to be above board. Under his true identity he got a job with a new enterprise in the timber trade, started by a friend of the late Dr Adenauer. Beginning as a joiner he rose to manage the timber processing part of this rapidly expanding concern. He was transferred

---

* I did not pursue the detail. Most likely he was the driver of an SS van used in mass killing by exhaust fumes before the invention of the cyanide chambers. MO (see Chapter Seven) was the second.

to the banking side and thus—rising again—he was transferred to manage the West Berlin branch with all the consequences he was now suffering. Finally PF asks me what I represent. I reply that I am a member of a project team which is interested in the phenomena in which he was involved, not in the individuals, and that his name would not be used in any publication that might result. PF seems reassured and points to a not very good copy of Rembrandt's "Man in a Helmet" hanging on the wall of the prison governor's office. This, he said, was his work. His sister pays for the paints and it greatly helps him to have developed this hobby. We part courteously.

Comment I had certainly expected a more subtle and impressive personality in this relatively high-ranking SS commander and doctor of laws—even though the German doctorate is at its best comparable to our LL.B. At no time did I feel that I was conversing with an educated or cultivated person. I allow for the fact that PF had left school at 16 and had what was probably a strictly "vocational" legal training; next for early diversion into the SS where he would have become immersed in a narrow bureaucratic circle of blinkered "apparatchiks" (to give them their Russian soubriquet); and lastly also for his seven years of prison. PF had never been other than a limited, lower middle class, status-and-promotion seeking philistine with a good-boy "underling" mentality. His cold, inhuman eyes that wept only for himself were an accurate pointer to his psychological make-up.

Though he denied ever having been a starry-eyed romantic who believed in all the more fanciful and millennial archaic ideological emanations of the Nazi movement, I would have classed PF as a real fanatic. To persevere in accepting zealously and unquestioningly any assignment the Party offered him, despite inner doubt and criticism, or even disdain, seems to me the hallmark of SS dedication. Whatever humiliation or evidence of corruption and intrigue he experienced or witnessed in the Order, such was his commitment that he was prepared to sell his conscience still to be in favour, to show his loyalty and iron manliness. We see in PF the logical extreme of Tertullian's *"credo quia absurdum"*. This was exactly what Himmler looked for in his "Order". He wanted them to be without personal will, ready despite any personal indignity or inner criticism to obey without flinching. It was just this quality which distinguished the SS in its hey-day from the old fighter's romantic revolt and sentimentality. PF had had many years in which to re-think, suppress, forget—and age. It would be difficult in his case to assess just how "devoted," cadaver-compliant an impression PF would have made on his bosses, nor how sincere was his "high-minded" urge to save his country. His own words showed how great was his ambition for élite status, for promotion, to be on the "inside" of the power group. Contrariwise, it is doubtful if PF originally paused to examine critically what he was joining. His was a "we" response, as he said, to the social pressures of that time on a young man typically pre-disposed to identify himself with the Nazi movement which promised to heal Germany's divisions, hunger and humiliated soldierly pride and to realize such mens' hate-laden aims to exterminate its real and imaginary opponents and enemies.

I need hardly take up space to reiterate those elements in PF's motives to become a Nazi which we may call "collective" themes, shared by many Germans of the period, some real, some the products of widely held culture myths like "the stab-in-the-back" legend of 1918 or the unique mission of the Germans as "kultur"-bringers.* At individual level there was no difficulty for me to score him very high on the authoritarian syndrome variables as shown by his eager—even craven—acceptance of subordination and "soldierly" obedience even to (at least retrospectively) bad leader figures; with a corresponding role-identification with their ferocity and inhumanity towards not only his victims but his subordinates. We could see his need to outdo others in his pose of manly hardness however palpably this was an over-compensation for a deep anxiety of being found inadequate, weak and vacillating. Projection was massive despite his present-day small concessions in the matter of "understanding" why the Jews were so vindictive—itself still a projection. This essentially paranoid attitude was not restricted to Jews, but spread to the working class, to the Versailles powers, to communists in Poland and Russia. Despite his attempts to preserve the image of the in-group's goodness, it was equally marked in relation to the power of the SD to destroy him, to seeing killers and criminals in many of his SS "comrades" as well as in the present German authorities who had it "in for him". He felt uniquely singled out just like *Captain A.* in Chapter Six. In other words, the more desperate his attempts to preserve some sense of his own goodness, the more widely had the attribution of badness and

* Léon Poliakov, our distinguished French colleague, is writing on the topic of the culture myth in this series.

persecution of him to the others to be spread. Thus PF shared with others in this sample an inability to carry the burden of an individual guilt conscience—he had, that is, barely reached the depressive phase. From this poorly developed sense of a "good strong" ego derived his ego-centricity and secondary narcissism, as a defence against hurts which he had repeatedly to swallow silently for fear of worse consequences. This process alone would contribute considerably to swelling the reservoir of hate of the bad object in him, entailing further ego-defence by projection and paranoid anxiety.

There is thus plenty of hate and sense of persecution as well as of mission and cleansing, ordering zeal to impel PF towards the Party and its *corps d'élite*, the SS. I have already mentioned the standard demographic variables as present. There was also the influence of wanting to make his bemedalled old-soldier father, himself a Party member, proud of his son, and go forth to redeem the shame of the 1918 defeat. This element aligned PF with the old order and discipline aspects rather than the pseudo-socialist innovatory aspects of the move-ment. He felt a special attraction for combating the noxious foreign enemies of the Germans, as a reprisal for all the wrongs done. This opportunity was offered by the foreign intelligence work at the SD central office and also in the idea of the *Einsatzcommando*. In 1935 PF still had enough ego strength to refuse at least the ignominious job of spying on his own peer-groups, the student corps, but not enough integrity, after "in his innocence" learning what went on in the RSHA, to wash his hands of it all and take his chance in some more reputable sphere. This is where his narcissism and status need as well as his identi-fication with the SS's purposes outweighed the more humane values He was sucked in by his need for self-importance, security and quasi-soldierly status.

I had mentally agreed with PF's complaint that the Berlin judge had been unfair in not allowing for the "nervous collapse" as being a sign of some "grace" in this SS colonel's soul. When he had gone deep into his unspeakably sadistic activity on the mixed motivation of his para-noid feelings and his identification with those of his superiors, some shred of depressive guilt and revulsion awoke in him. It appears he had confided his conflict to a Waffen SS friend as a rather halting step towards trying to get transferred, but essentially the only solution for PF, given his make-up, lay in the hysterico-depressive breakdown he suffered. The deeper conflict took over from his split, indecisive ego

and removed him from the field of action. The SS organization interpreted this neurotic withdrawal with more insight than the Berlin
judge—and acted with characteristic venom by framing him as a thief.
I felt pretty certain that PF's type of character would not have contained the capacity for such a common crime which belongs to the BT,
KW, Globocnik style of Nazi.

We should, at the risk of some repetitiveness, look at what can be
gleaned of this man's personality structure in the terms of his object-
relations, as the source of both the regressive readiness to identify with
the murderous purposes of the SS and of the ambivalence which he
seems to have developed towards this organization, resulting in being
disgraced within it. I hope to have clarified in Chapter One and in my
comment on GM in Chapter Seven the way in which the structure we
call the "bad internal object" can be viewed as being formed at an
early stage of life. I need here only attempt a diagnosis of the special
variant of this bad object that had been latent and was activated in this
man when the pressures against his inadequate ego-defences became
too strong. Fatally for PF he was also impelled and pulled into the
Party and SS by his good, even idealized object—his father, the only
figure in his past unambivalently loved, with the possible exception of
Werner Best (SS legal branch—later "disgraced" for humane scruples)
and Nebe whom he regarded as well-wishers. Thus PF's internalized
model for identification was the standard one of the brave, disciplined
obedient old soldier—time-server of the Kaiser's golden era. This old
man had himself, predictably, become a Nazi party member, though
he appears to have induced in PF some criticism about the lawless
violence. He may even be the source of that dawning awareness in PF
who dissociated himself at once from the Rabauken (even though his
11,000 dead would have out-classed their records). It is of no consolation to the victims that their senior executioners were purists acting
from a sense of ordering, cleansing mission, and of "soldierly" duty—
as bogus in PF as in many others—not least in Himmler himself. Like
MO, so PF managed even to represent *his* stockyard routine as a great
improvement on the "wild" shooting by the bands of Lithuanian
auxiliaries, simply because it represented to him his German thorough-
ness and orderly way of doing a job.

But if PF had become a Nazi and—so far—an armchair SS officer
simply from an uncomplicated love of the values of his fathers, he
could have remained in the SD office and secretly mourned his brother—

the victim of a hard but loved regime. But this would be to reckon without the influence of the bad internal object which, not without good reason, had been called the "inner saboteur" by W. R. D. Fairbairn. I would assert on the evidence I have presented that PF was driven to offer proof of utmost loyalty and devotion by his mounting inner doubts and consequent rising paranoid anxiety activated by his brother's fate at the hands of the ruthless and place-hunting inquisitors of whom he was one himself. More brothers than his biological one turned traitors on him—sought his downfall. We here recall PF's deathly fear of falling as a small child at the hands of his brother, leaving a permanent, admitted scar in the shape of a phobia of heights. I further recall yet another fall—when he broke his leg and his mother set upon him with a stick to beat the cry-baby out of him before she even was human enough to see what he was crying about. In contemporary psychoanalysis such traumatic recollections in a patient's self-presentation are deemed important not primarily as isolated events but as disclosing a "view into the interior". In PF's case we are afforded a glimpse of how far back dates his sense of being surrounded by hard, unloving, even murderous figures, with his good daddy not there to save him. Here there is a reversal of the stereotype derived from many studies of the German family. It is the *mother* who must be in this case the hated and dreaded figure without mercy—whatever the personal and cultural reasons for this soldier's wife's attempt to act as a stern father substitute. I think that in so far as PF was relating a fact of his own experience, we are justified in recoiling as much from this piece of cruelty by the mother against her own child as from a typical SS man's atrocity. It is then less hard to visualize what damage had been done to PF's tender-dependent relational capacities. I have, in Chapter One especially, outlined the psychological consequences for a child of having to assimilate such a parental response to its need for love and succour. I there developed the theory that this early, recurrent need to deny hate for and in the needed "good" parent gives origin to that introjected and walled-off "complex" or enclave of represssed but still active feelings invested in the bad object at the heart of this stored memory. The younger the age at which this happened the less modified the primitive total murderous hate felt both *against* the bad object inside and as emanating *from* that inner enemy. I cannot stress too often the light that this clinically derived hypothesis has shed on the sources of paranoid feelings and the compensating defensive compulsion towards keeping it out of sight by conformist obedience and defensive idealization of the bad object. This submission and devotion are man-oeuvres to preserve the "goodness" of, or at least secure some pro-tection from, this terrifying agency which is felt to be both inside and outside. Here then, is the other half of PF's unconscious personal openness to respond to the SS's treatment of his brother in the way he did. There is no evidence that he did anything to help his brother, or that he took any steps to withdraw from the plan to form the *Einsatz-gruppen*. On the contrary, he had to show how much he hated sons who did not revere their parent figures, however cruel and inhuman. He could not, as he was free to do, reject the job for which Heydrich, possibly maliciously, had selected him, because he felt an inner com-plicity and echo of the need to avenge himself in cruel form—on Germany's collective scapegoat enemies. As in his humbler confrères, the lure of being a "master over life and death" instead of a despicable victim, activated the latent identification with the internalized per-petrator of atrocities. This seems to me to be the basis of all such "frightfulness" under conditions when the ego–defences are weakened and positive incentives to displaced acting-out of the pressures of paranoid hate are offered.

PF, however, seems to have been unable to sustain his terrorist role. Possibly the maltreatment of women came too close to his own defence against matricidal fantasies. It could have been the effect of parallel good-object identification with his father who disapproved of violence against civilian victims. The earliest sign of this was PF's humane act of shielding his new subaltern by putting him into the office. He evidently also let his men weaken, handing the shooting over to the local auxiliaries. In the end the pressures from conflicting streams of motivation produced the mental short-circuit of the hysterical break-down—the sort of traumatic neurosis that removes soldiers, terrified of further carnage, from the battlefield. After this manifestation of PF's exhaustion of his hate, the aspect of the terrified victim of the persecutor internalized in himself as a "bad conscience" reasserted itself in its infantile form of uncontrollable shaking and weeping. From now on he was really a broken man; all his grand SS panache in the dust. The SS had suddenly become full of bad characters. He could save the remnants of his ego by finding almost everybody a killer or a thief except himself. He was now the poor self-pitying "little man", the decent one who stood aloof from the Rabauken and the cheerful assassins, and whom they had extruded. This was where his paranoid hate now went—to the false accusers, and to the women in the air-raid shelters "who would talk". One was not allowed to be sensitive or afraid of death and violence, it led to pitiless retaliation and female scorn. The trial revived this deep hurt of the child not allowed any tenderness, having his smallness and humanity beaten out of him by a harsh unfeeling world, taking away his dignity and wish to be good.

This seems to be the commonest theme linking at least six out of these eight men and their availability for killer roles in the Third Reich. I return to it in the next chapter.

I should like to compete this chapter by briefly citing the record of a man whom I should have seen, had he not been meanwhile discharged from prison at the end of a shortish sentence and remission. The interest lies in the similarities and contrasts with both PF and GM.

DL was a lower-middle class man born in Danzig in 1908. Employed by a Jewish firm as a salesman in that hotbed city of German irredentism and nationalist fervour, he joined the general SS in 1934. In 1936 this involved secret enrolment in the Nazi "auxiliary police" which after the liberation of the city in 1939 became TKV, with concentration camp duties in KZ Stutthof, after some skirmishes with Polish rearguards. The inmates were Poles, Jehovah's Witnesses and various "asocial" Germans; later East European Jews. The evidence showed that he had, at this stage, repeatedly asked for transfer to fighting units which was always refused with various degrees of threats and appeals to his SS oath. His aversion became known, and he was, like GM, trained as a sick-bay attendant, first for the SS, then in the prisoners' hospital, with instruction in the techniques of lethal injections and "disinfection" by Cyclone-B gas. At his trial he had not only turned crown witness but gave a convincing picture of a consistent flinching from the "sick-bay" methods of studied neglect, brutality and murder of unsuspecting inmates by injections, shooting through a slit during "medical examination" and so on. Unable, from dread of retaliation by his authorities, to mutiny openly, his "nerve broke" during such a shooting session in the medical room. He was himself transferred to a quiet backroom job—no worse consequences followed. At the trial he gave an interesting commentary on how his lack of moral courage to defect early had sucked him into these abominated activities, because he was not only afraid of his superiors but even more of his comrades for being a "sissy". He said: "I had tried to be a hard and loyal SS man", and he had put on a special act of ferocity when there were others around.

His sentence was for complicity. He seems to have impressed the court by his lack of defensive self-justification and genuine remorse. The prison record spoke of him as "having learnt his lesson".

My point in quoting DL is the demonstration that men did survive who knew how to show they could not face being "hangmen". Even neurotic reactions were effective. The chief difference, therefore, between those that persevered in the atrocities and those who managed to avoid doing so seems to be inside the man's own mind—the degree of hate and paranoid-projection between self as pitiless authority and self as victim *of* a pitiless authority outside.

CHAPTER TEN

HOW COULD IT HAPPEN?

The foregoing pages have presented the concepts and hypothetical assumptions with which eight men convicted of brutal mass murder of defenceless persons were interviewed, and also recorded the impressions those interviews had made on me as a seasoned psychiatrist. I must now try to advance towards some conclusions from what I have learnt about the way human beings can be brought to commit organized brutality and mass murder. The selection of the German case, for reasons stated earlier, had the merit for our project that the perpetrators were persons belonging to an "advanced" society in the heart of the European family of peoples, sharing a common cultural and historical heritage. The findings and inferences were consequently more likely to be applicable to other members of that great family and its descendants overseas. This application could not with any confidence be extended to massacres and genocide in epochs and places far removed from us in space and time. Storr[1] and Cormier[2] hold that in some older cultures with different value systems mass murder of the defeated or subjected by their conquerors was part of normal "political" practice; it is only in our era that this deplorable characteristic of *homo sapiens* has begun to be defined as an international crime.*

Two commonly encountered thought-stereotypes about the Nazis will, surely, already have been weakened or eliminated by my interview reports. The first is that these SS killers were "insane" or uncontrollable people, in any generally understood clinical sense. This makes the assessment of their "temporary" systematic, murderous activity all the more baffling and psychologically important. The second widely believed idea—that Hitler's terror and extermination activities were exclusively and narrowly focused on Jews and thus a murderous exaggeration of anti-Semitism alone—is also found to be untenable.

---

* Even if we granted that Nazi Germany had relapsed into killing conquered strangers, e.g. Poles, in this "normal" sense, we are still left gasping when we reflect that the mass murders began on their own flesh and blood during the "euthanasia" phase, just as Stalin "liquidated" millions of Russian peasants as obstacles to his plan.

HOW COULD IT HAPPEN?

It was already stated in Chapter Three that the "Final Solution of the Jewish Problem" emerges as only an instalment of Hitler's and the Nazi party's destructive millennial dream of a world entirely dominated by the Nordic, Teutonic supermen and forever freed from all rival races and "noxious" influences (including political or religious dissenters from Nazism) even within their own nation that could challenge or imperil this dominion. If there is clinically recognizable "insanity", it is to be sought in the unchecked proliferation of this megalomanic fantasy system translated by the Party's ruling élite into a policy of state. The history and background of some currents of thought that finally coalesced into the ideology of *Mein Kampf* and because the political programme of Hitler's Reich, briefly sketched in Chapters Two and Three, are not the main focus here, though they are an essential part of the whole macabre theme. Poliakov and Scheffler treat them more adequately in companion volumes, and much else has been written about it.

My task has been to throw some light on how that ideology and its disastrously destructive implementation came to grip individuals such as my interviewed men and make them its available and willing tools. This will involve on the one hand some discussion of the special claims a state or a political authority has on its subjects' loyalties and obedience. On the other hand it will necessitate an examination of the latent capacities of "ordinary" men to harbour and, under given conditions to activate, *murderousness*, and—when the given conditions have ceased to operate—to return to inconspicuous, "ordinarily" law-abiding reasonable existence. In a casual encounter such men as the eight interviewed could pass muster as "normal chaps". The fact remains that they were part of the tiny fraction of the German and Austrian populations that stayed in, and carried out what was done by, Himmler's death units.* For the many who mouthed and enthusiastically cheered the ideology and its ruthless practice, there were the few who *actually* did the "manual work". Whether, if in 1941-45 every TKV and Gestapo and Einsatz-group man had disappeared, Himmler would have readily recruited as many others to take over, must remain an unresolved problem, which I personally would tend to answer affirmatively. There was no difficulty in getting medical and nursing personnel to kill 100,000 German mental patients! It is also true that for every TKV

* In 1937 TKV strength was only 5000 men, other SS activist cadres 12,000. (Buchheim, op. cit.)

or Gestapo killer who shot, throttled, injected or gassed defenceless human beings with his own hands, there were instigators and accomplices in ever-widening circles, from the bureaucratic armchair administrators to the shunters and drivers of trains and trucks and all the technicians, doctors, petty officials and clerks who were essential to the enterprise. Though to varying degrees in the know, these helpers did nothing to oppose it. The same is true of the majority of senior commanding generals and civil governors under whose jurisdiction mass extermination and atrocious slave labour regimes were tolerated and even aided and encouraged. All this is history, fully documented at Nuremberg by the War Crimes Tribunal. But I repeat they did not do the *actual* manual work.

1. Aggressiveness and Murderousness

The consideration of my findings and their interpretation imposes on me a need to review the connexions and the difference which exists in human beings between aggressiveness as a general predisposition, and the much rarer special case in which aggressiveness manifests itself in the act of *murder*—or culpable homicide. I had already made fairly obvious subdivisions of "aggressiveness" when examining my wartime group of 138 German prisoners. In Table I, partly reproduced in Chapter Four, I classified "Sadism" responses into "Anti-Social" and "Social". The former consisted of three variants: (*a*) overt, gross cruelty with some evidence of its being enjoyed by the subject; (*b*) harsh, domineering behaviour and (*c*) indifference and imperviousness to the show of sadism by others or to the suffering of the victims.* The *social* variants implied a greater degree of conscious or unconscious control over aggressive behaviour, yielding (*d*) "normal" (not really "sadistic") capacity for self-assertion and anger coupled with human warmth and lacking viciousness; (*e*) an over-compensatory suppression of aggressiveness, resulting in a gentle, submissive, apologetic attitude, and (*f*) a strong reaction formation against cruelty shown by such things as blood phobias, pacifism, moral aversion from all forms of aggression, etc. This classification reflects, of course, the general psychodynamic views on how, in personality development, the ego deals with the feelings of rage and hate. Variants (*a*), (*b*) and (*c*)

---

* This is the mental state closest to Gilbert's "schizoid" personality, in his "SS Robots" paper (see also footnote on p. 114, Chapter Five.)

represent "raw" aggressiveness against which no strong defences are deployed in the mind. In the case of (a) and (c) there is a link with the abnormality of the Western European personality disorder which we call aggressive psychopathy—close to the failure to grow an adequate, "depressive" super-ego based on the recognition of others as needing love and sparing them pain. Variant (b) was conceived as an index of an identification with a harsh, loveless and persecutory authority figure, whom the subject was emulating, at least when acting in his role as soldier, official or superior. I conceived that these personality traits demonstrated a kind of "naked" outwardly directed aggression with too little counter-action by more tender, civilizing components in human feeling. Such a "softening", humanizing layer was either not developed, or else had worn thin (brutalization), or had been sternly suppressed. We shall find this theme a central one in later discussion.

To complete the interpretation of my use of the "sadism" variables in Table I, (d) was the most "normal" because thought of as the ability to use aggression undestructively and therefore as under control of a more mature ego or self in which the loving and reparation-making impulses of the personality were integrated with and balancing the aggressive ones. We may say that here the subject had passed through and beyond the depressive phase. Variants (e) and (f) showed, on the other hand, that while the over-submissive, anti-aggressive person was valiantly struggling against his own, and thus, by projection, also against other peoples' aggressiveness, he *was* still struggling! His was a less secure or more neurotic control; he had turned aggression round either against himself in submissive, propitiatory self-abasement, or in total rejection, guilt-laden and fierce! This was the effect of still being "stuck" in the depressive phase of personality development in which harsh and punishing authority is internalized but turned against the self and its projections. While from the viewpoint of immediate effect such a disposal of aggressiveness may be described as "on the side of the angels", it is not hard to sense the insecurely controlled hate that hides behind the excessive gentleness, contrition and "pacifist fervour" of such persons. I must repeat that this analysis is a wholly general one, by no means confined to Germans.

Until I had steeped myself in the life histories and observed psychological data of my eight SS men, I had, perhaps naïvely, assumed that their profiles would uncomplicatedly conform to my three "antisocial" variables, singly or in combination. This, however, turned out to be true only of their behaviour at the height of their SS careers and service with the "death squads". Let us take *S2*, and the story of his, as of other TKV cadres', gradual conditioning, brutalizing and indoctrination by model—and norm-setting senior trainers. We might have scored his aggression in his Iron George phase of adolescent street-fighting as "normal" or (*d*) class aggressiveness. Here was a rough lad who enjoyed punch-up encounters with their give and take as fair game and fun against other youths belonging to the Left-Wing militant group. These were the "skin-heads" or "rockers" of their period but geared into an exciting "patriotic" movement which progressively sucked such unemployed lads into its brutalizing group ethos.

To the significance of the systematic brutalizing effect of the Nazi culture pattern I will return later. For the moment I want to focus on the *internal psychodynamics*, on the possible *predisposition* to feel drawn to the "lure" of murderous acting-out by inner pressures, and on the "flash-point" or crisis in which "normal" lusty or even socially counter-acted aggressiveness passes into cruelty and ruthless killing. Somewhere along this path of escalation S2 "lost the last of the Ten Commandments", the remaining personality restraints against the emergence of the most primitive—and as I hope to show—infantile murder lust. Similarly, his seven companions in my series at some point crossed the line between their previous "law-abiding" lives and their subsequent killer careers. And—their SS roles ended or interrupted—these same "fiends incarnate" in various ways disappeared quietly into civilian life, in some instances resumed orderly and normal careers, and are in prison "the easiest convicts to handle"! This remarkable phenomenon must somehow be elucidated by reference to what knowledge we possess about the psychology of murderers in general, leaving aside for the time being the element of ideological rationalization which has never been lacking in the bloody history of massacres. The records of depth studies of convicted murderers are as yet scanty.

Dr A. Hyatt Williams, who has published psychoanalytic studies on a group of convicted killers treated in a British prison, seems to me to have advanced furthest into this difficult terrain. I shall mainly use his concepts and insights, as well as some recent statistical material presented by clinical psychologists working in Broadmoor Hospital, England, with mentally ill murderers, in trying to understand the connections betwen personality development (and distortion) and that often hidden reservoir of deadly aggression which can lie dormant, burst into destructive action, and again subside leaving a variety of sequels such as deep guilt feelings, or denial and forgetting, as if the killing had never happened.

Hyatt Williams[3,4] had at the time of his latest publication to date studied seven murderers—also serving long sentences. His observations on the inner life of his patients are much more complete than mine because Williams was in a continuing therapeutic relationship with them and a regular part of the prison scene. I find his provisional conclusions on the structure and dynamics of murderousness of great support as I come to review my own observations on the SS men reported in the preceding five chapters. Commenting on the remark of a wise old C.I.D. officer, that often murderers had "led hitherto blameless lives" (in the legal sense), Williams agrees with this fact, but shows it to be belied by the reality inside the killer's mind.

> Murderers vary tremendously—from ones in whom the violence is bubbling over the brim, to those who are quiet, worried, white-faced men whose intense calmness covers up the most deadly of fantasies . . . in general the convicted murderer is pleasant enough to talk to and peace-loving in everyday life. . . . What appears clearly only after a close rapport has been established . . . is that somewhere within the psyche of the murderer there exists an enclave, a split-off encapsulated area, of deadly ruthlessness. . . (1969).

Hyatt Williams finds, as do other researchers, that the "obviously violent" are the very immature, the psychopaths, who have not grown any controls or defences against their "bubbling-over" aggression. Storr[5] characterizes such psychopathic violence as casual, dictated by impulse and momentary mood, indifferent as to its results. Violence is, as it were, part of such personalities. None of my eight men strictly fell into this category, since their violence, even if we include their street-fighting (e.g. S2, Captain A) was never impulsive, but only occurred within their "party" or "service" role, however congenial it might have become. My men fall rather into other categories of murderer, as also differentiated by Hyatt Williams—by no means lacking in personality defences in general, but "containing within them important split-off parts of themselves which broke loose and were violently projected, resulting in murder . . . desperate furies can remain cordoned off . . . for years, but can erupt at a time of stress or illness. . ." (1960).

At this point it is valuable to gain some statistical perspective. R.

Blackburn[6], senior psychologist at Broadmoor Hospital, has classified 56 homicidal patients tested on admission by the well-known Minnesota Multi-phasic Personality Inventory (with some added variables) for discriminating personality types. This study was to some extent stimulated by the finding by many investigators that "few murderers were hardened criminals", and the surprising occurrence of many *"mild-mannered individuals"* among murderers. The validity of *four* main sub-groups or types which emerged from Blackburn's scrutiny was found to stand up well to statistical analysis of a stringent kind. I abstract the essentials of these psychological categories:—

> *Type 1* or *overcontrolled repressive* (30 per cent of the group) yields an essentially normal profile, but is marked by a higher level of defensiveness, impulse control and denial. Their only symptoms are mildly depressive. They are described as "overly conforming, strongly controlled and lacking in hostile or aggressive tendencies", suggesting that their usual way of dealing with emotional arousal is by denial or repression.
>
> *Type 2* or *paranoid aggressive* (23 per cent), are the most disturbed, with very high levels of anxiety, hostility, prone to act out, clinically resembling or identical with paranoid schizophrenics. They lack inhibitions against expression of anti-social attitudes and behaviour, but their social anxiety and introvertedness distinguishes them from the primarily undercontrolled impulsive type.
>
> *Type 3* or *depressed-inhibited* (14 per cent), score high on most symptom variables, but especially on depression and social avoidance. They also exercise strong impulse control, with high "General Hostility" predominantly directed against the self.
>
> *Type 4*—the *psychopathic* (13 per cent) characterized by moderate degrees of anxiety, paranoid suspicion, and an absence of neurotic or psychotic stress. Poorly socialized, they lack social anxiety, but abound in hostility directed outwards and in impulsiveness.

These last are the same as our under-controlled, immature psychopaths. In the remaining 20 per cent there were overlapping or highly individual profiles not further dealt with in the paper.

As Blackburn himself points out, the finding that nearly half the group (44 per cent) falls into over-controlled categories suggests (as Megargee quoted by Blackburn had done) that these normally inhibited, mild-mannered individuals are likely to commit *extreme* aggression when they *do* aggress, either because the level of instigation is high enough to overcome their strong resistances, or because they lack internal cues for "when to stop" once the normally withheld aggression is set in motion. These types were defined in murderers who were "abnormal" in that psychiatric evidence had effected their confinement in a psychiatric security institution rather than in a "normal" prison. Blackburn has little doubt—though as a statistical psychologist he is cautious—that his findings may hold good also for murderers in general, of whom they represent 25 per cent for the year. As Black reports, also from Broadmoor, in a paper read to the Royal Medico-Psychological Association,[7] the *over-controlled* groups as well as some under-controlled among the inmates accounted for most of the homicides; whereas the "aggressive psychopaths"—the impulsive, *under-controlled*, predominated in the lesser offences against persons: wounding, assault, etc. The murderers by contrast, in this random series of convicted (and surviving) aggressors in Broadmoor, turned out to be the less impulsive, more controlled, introverted personalities with less scoreable hostility, higher social conformity, fewer previous convictions. Their victims tended to be family members or well known to them. It may be noteworthy that among this predominantly British home-born series the main abnormality necessitating Broadmoor admission was found to be depressive illness. Black attributes this to bafflement, guilt and genuine depression that *"behaviour foreign to their experience"* (my italics—H. V. D.) had resulted in genuine personal tragedy. A quarter of all murderers in Britain follow their act by suicide.

These studies support the view I have to come to, contrary to my expectations, that the eight SS killers were not simply primitive, impulsive psychopaths. Had I known this I should not have asked for a guard when about to interview the most fearsome one among them, Captain A. The prison governor knew "he would harm nobody"! I learnt how much more complex the problem of explaining these SS killers and many like them must be, whether as formal "categorization" or in the more aetiological terms of psychopathology. Black (op. cit.) warns us not to seek the causes of murder only in definable psychiatric illness. I have now focused my task on the questions:

(1) What could be learnt from my men about Hyatt Williams's "split-off parts of themselves which broke loose"? Are some of these deep "enclaves of deadly ruthlessness" common to the personality structures of my sample and to British "civilian" murderers?

(2) Are the glimpses I had of the infantile, paranoid pre-existing motivations derived from internalized hate-love objects confirmed by analytic work in depth? And if so, are they all the same or are there variants?

(3) What were the favouring conditions which raised the level of instigation to the point where the inhibiting forces could no longer hold the "encapsulated" murderousness in check? Were these men quantitatively more murderous than others, for whatever reasons; or were the releasing, instigatory conditions stronger and more compelling? The answer to this question seems to me to be the real goal of this present enquiry. That is, we must try to understand the reciprocal influences of societal pressure (political decision taken at some high administrative level) and the intrapsychic predispositions in men at subordinate levels— at least in the German context, but probably also in other like contexts.

2. The Murderous Enclave in the Personality

Hyatt Williams does not report on Gestapo men or KZ personnel. His subjects and patients are people who were convicted of rape-murders of women or "revenge-retaliation" killing of scapegoats for bad objects significant in the murderer's inner fantasy life. Like myself, Williams finds the most widely applicable explanatory theory for the genesis of this reservoir of latent hate in the post-Freudian psychoanalytic formulations of Melanie Klein (which Fairbairn has elaborated into greater coherence). These concepts were summarized according to my understanding of them in Chapter One. May I just recall that there I traced the early phases of an infant's developing psycho-biological relations to its objects and its own evoked emotions about them. There is a massive technical literature on this subject which deals also with the perennial problem of where aggressiveness comes from, how far it is inborn or is a derivative of the budding sexual impulses and so forth. Anthony Storr (op. cit.) has endeavoured to deal with this most fundamental aspect of the psycho-biology and ethology of aggression and killing in a companion essay.

I do not attempt to answer the ultimate problem of Man's hate—as it were of original sin—here. Like Hyatt Williams's studies, I stay on the next level of abstraction—nearer to clinical realities—of taking the phenomena of murderousness as observed facts and searching for the socio-psychological vectors for their control and release. Already in 1939[8] I had formed and expressed the view based on analytic work with severe sado-masochistic perversions and with other crippling disorders (in which the transformation of murderous rage into obsessive-compulsive behaviour and dread of aggression were the central theme) that the source of these phenomena was to be found in the total need for security and dependence on a giving and loving mother, and in the feeling of helplessness experienced when that need was not met. The defences of internalizing and so "owning" the elusive, loving-frustrating object, at the earliest, least rational and most vulnerable levels of an infant's development I found to be the same as those systematically described and worked out by Klein and Fairbairn. It is perhaps the long bodily helplessness and inability to give expression in appropriate movement to its feelings (as compared with the more rapidly maturing physique of other animals), that determines the human infant's rich early fantasy-formation. These fantasies are of the greatest importance for all later development. They fulfil the paradoxical wishes of the helpless infant for plenty and of a plenitude of power to have anything one wants, and also of power to dominate and destroy the objects that thwart and withhold gratifications.

Thus Hyatt Williams reports as one of his cases that of a 26-year-old man (1960), whose repeated acts of rape and finally of a rape-murder resulted from a split in his mother relation. There was a depriving mother and a gratifying mother "inside" this patient. He had since puberty felt compelled to track down females and *subject them to his will*. The reality in his early life had been the appearance of a series of younger siblings and his sense of rivalry, jealousy and envy. The "bad mother relation" had been split off and "buried", in order to preserve his good mother relation. The goals of his fantasies were not only to restore the blissful breast relation of before the rivals had appeared, and to control this absolutely, but also to destroy the mother figure if she could not yield all the gratifications he sought in which sex was fused with the greed for sucking. As the case progressed Williams found a still more remarkable fantasy: the need to murder the resisting, unyielding (hence "bad") mother-figure came not primarily from wanting to silence the accuser (hoping to escape detection) but mainly from the *guilt-determined* wish to prevent this persecuting, haunting bad figure from getting inside the murderer's mind again to continue the eternal inner persecution. The woman this man in fact killed after rape was an older woman to whom he gave a lift in his truck, and who reminded him of an envied brother whom a *foster-mother* during wartime evacuation had preferred to himself. It became clear that the man had internalized a whole complicated hate-envy relationship—always short of the depressive capacity to feel and accept the pain of frustration and reparative guilt. There was in his daily life an *apparent* giving in, in fact a marked passivity and inability to express any open jealousy or envy—he was in most ways a compliant and "good" mother's boy. The climax which started Hyatt Williams's patient on his raping "prowls" was a homosexual episode in adolescence. The brutal man to whom the youth acted as passive partner had made him choose a female name—and the youth chose his mother's. But during one particularly callous act, the young man suddenly mentally switched from a passive to an active role, showing, as Williams says "that he had incorporated all the cruelty and callousness of the man". There had happened a turn-over from being the "hunted" to being the "hunter". A further detail is of great interest: the prisoner reported a dream in which he was looking at the face of a woman in a mist. "A nice face— I like her and do not want to murder her." The mist cleared—it was a mirror *and the face was his own* (my italics—H. V. D.). Soon after this, he could experience during his therapeutic hour a coalescence of his raping and his homosexual passive impulses—as it were the hunter and the hunted at the same time. There was also much evidence that this killer at other times had tender and generous impulses towards women who gave themselves lovingly. What he could not stand was resistance to his complete mastery, based on the now revealed rage at being the deprived child of the "bad", nurturally unloving frustrating part of his mother as internalized, whose hate and disapproval haunted him as a power that exacted his compliance and dependence. During the prolonged doctor-patient relationship, Hyatt Williams could also discover the fantasies which had actively preoccupied this killer's mind long before their dynamism short-circuited into murder. These were, significantly, of seeing a baby at a woman's breast, of snatching the baby away and demanding from her that he, the patient, should be suckled and have coitus—else he would destroy the baby.

Recalling several of my SS group, these observations and findings seem to enhance our insight into the deeper motives that impelled them into the murder area of their organization. I am thinking first of

KW, "prowling" alone through the Warsaw ghetto, with whip and gun, full of his clearly expressed attitudes of being both irresistible to and greatly deprived by women, shooting them at his whim, at times with their babies; even paying out a colleague by killing his Jewish mistress. The conversation with his cell-mate in the remand prison disclosed the close and ominous connections in KW's mind between sexual fantasy and killing. I also recall the regularity with which most of my subjects described the privations of their childhood, conveying the clinical impression of a "good brave boy" who did not complain but was also deeper down full of self pity and resentment at his hard fate. We have already noted the link made, *inter alios* by Wangh[9], between this feeling in German youths and their often real under-nutrition and insecurities as infants during and after the First War. MO (with his vaunted pride in large families) and GM both wanted to exterminate "useless mouths to feed".

But this unconscious link between a depriving object and hate against it, legitimately to be related to general depth studies of murderers, does not exhaust the findings. A second case, investigated in detail by Hyatt Williams (1960), had close affinities with at least one of the SS killers—BT. This case was of a young man with a brutal but moralizing father whose severe beatings often left the boy bruised. The mother was unable to shield the son from this violence so that he felt betrayed by her. None the less this murderer was always gentle with women. As a child he had refused to kill field-mice at his father's orders and wept when the father sneeringly forced him to do it. This had recurred over putting down unwanted puppies and their pet mother dog. But when he came on the father beating his sister (to whom the patient felt close) he threatened the father with a gun. This seems to have been the switch from "hunted" to "hunter". The weak maternal object could no longer keep his hate of the bad father in check. To enhance his deficient sense of potency and overcome his despised passivity, the young man in adulthood took to collecting pornographic pictures. When one day in a "blue" bookshop the owner reminded him of his father, he made as if to steal some pictures. When the shopkeeper resisted he shot him dead. The interesting thing is that already this man had been carrying a gun, though not yet aware that he wanted to kill a father-surrogate who clearly in fantasy had stood as a brutal aggressor, an Oedipal castrator. So on impulse he killed this sorry substitute for withholding the equally sorry pseudo-sexuality. This case reminded me of BT's similar childhood memories of the "dangerous" father killing defenceless animals, the burial of the introjected cruel father-figure under a moral, gentle and smug exterior of a religious mother's boy with its demanding obsequious conformity and passivity.

BT also illustrated another aspect of murder—the greed and envy which aims to take all the good from the victim, as he did with Jews' valuables. (Others in the SS "economic office" must have had similar tendencies, if we recall the great organization for extracting gold dental fillings and robbing the victims of every possession, which filled great warehouses in the extermination camps with jewellery, watches, clothes, shoes and even toys). Like Hyatt Williams's second murderer, BT's prayerful, passive relation to his mother was switched to his dormant brutal father identification under the influence of his role as leader of a Jew-hunt. His sadism score, so to speak, changed at this point from (f) to (a) and (b). Even more primitive and also easier to see was GM's acting-out of his deprivation and hate fantasies with a direct projection of the weak, starving, incontinent child into his victims. He even consciously admitted that he was doing this to those he knew to be his social superiors. The most abject of all the qualities —envy—gains its satisfaction by destroying and tearing down the good things in others which one cannot have.

Hyatt Williams (1969) states the psychoanalytically discovered proposition that the infant's primary instruments of inflicting fantasied harm on its mother are "urine, faeces and flatus; sucking or scooping out good things; putting in bad, scalding, smelly things". It need scarcely strain any reader's credulity when I relate the often highly ingenious methods in general use by the TKV (and evidently imported by the founder-trainers from the Feme-rituals), as evidenced by my interviewees, to the symbolic elaboration and reinforcement of these humble nursery murder weapons, Freud's "anal sadism". We have seen the various uses to which hose pipes were put in camp S by S2 and his amanuensis BS: drenching, oral assault by the nozzle in the mouth (related to forced feeding and giving diarrhoea) bursting people open, etc. We have also cited the predilection of the same men for throwing their victims into cesspits or shutting them into toilets, not to mention GM's special and indescribably cruel faecal humiliations of his "patients" —or the replacement of beneficial injections by poison by him and his medical confrère MO. Guns, truncheons and whips made from an ox's penis are more obvious symbols for phallic power, merging into more universal modes of inflicting death, pain and humiliation. So much for motivations.

3. DEFENCES AGAINST MURDEROUS IMPULSES

Something should also be said about the comparison of my sample with the cited material from British observations on the mechanisms of defence against murder, which is the same as the problem of a restraining conscience and the fluctuations of its effectiveness. My case material has, I think, shown that seven out of the eight men had various kinds of inner restraints and inhibitions which will be discussed in the light of general psychological insights into these complex matters. The only possible exception was *KW* whose actions and general overall personality picture made him closest to the category of a delinquent psychopath. He seemed impelled by whims and appetites and was using hysterical symptoms to evade unpleasant reality and discipline. The only evidence of a rudimentary sense of guilt (as an apprehension of retaliation by "fate") was his hypochondrical anxiety at bad things happening inside his body. He was the only one who gave constant trouble to the prison staff. KW could perhaps be squeezed into Black-burn's *Type 4*, of which he had all the listed traits. It is also typical of the psychopathic delinquent that the infantility of his feeling and reality sense make him, so to speak, "genuinely" unable to feel that he has done anything wrong, because while at the time of his criminal act he knows what he is doing and what will happen if the tiresome authorities catch him, there is no "adult" foresight or warning system to stop him. He even *boasted* to his cell-mate about his killing, heedless of his danger in trusting the unknown man.

Before completing a review of the "moral state" of the other seven men as far as my data permit, further consideration of the available insights on this topic will enhance the value of my findings. First, we can exclude Blackburn's *Type 2* which contains the really insane murderers. I shall presently try to deal with the marginal case of Captain A. in relation to this statement, since his was the mental condition nearest to a clinical paranoid state. At the relatively superficial level of study used for Blackburn's assessment, it would seem that the internal dynamics of my sample (KW apart) conformed predominantly to *Types 1 and 3*. That is to say they passed as superficially peaceable characters who gave no trouble, were courteous and "mild-mannered" in ordinary contact; but some of them showed some evidence of passing or lasting depression, including some expressions of remorse and of suicidal preoccupations at some stage after capture. In terms of the Klein-Fairbairn object-relations theory of ego development, the SS sample showed an uneasy oscillation between mainly paranoid phase (i.e. "fear") consciences and the depressive phase (or "guilt") consciences.

Though unrelated to Blackburn's researches, Hyatt Williams's depth studies of other killers in gaol valuably fill in the content or dynamics of the numerically larger Broadmoor samples. Writing of the pain of guilt-depressive tension inside human beings, Williams (1969) says:

> In every one of us to some extent (and in some of us to a decisive degree) . . . the depressive anxieties cannot be tolerated, so that there occurs a relapse into a state where persecutory anxiety again predominates.

This seems to be a marked feature of the criminal, in whom all psychic pain is felt as persecutory—even if it arises from the pangs of guilt. "Conscience pain", continues Hyatt Williams, "which most people feel as a guide, acts as a goad to criminals." The savage, cruel "conscience-figures" or bad internal objects have to be defied, by regression into the paranoid phase of dealing with them.

> There may be action the aim of which is to evacuate the whole threatening situation, sometimes into a victim—wife, mother, father, brother, sister, child. More usually the action is against a scapegoat victim standing for . . . the near relative. This is more dangerous, as with the scapegoat there is not the tenderness or regard which could help to offset the hatred and destructiveness.

The strange unconscious relationship in this situation makes the potential criminal, himself perpetually menaced by what is essentially a part of his inner make-up, threatened in his very existence as a weak, helpless victim. It is this intolerable tension that is projected "outside" into the scapegoat-victim who is thus also perceived as the attacker. Dehumanization or rather demonization—turning the victim into a devil who must be killed—is naturally easier if no ambivalence towards a near relative complicates the paranoid projective identification "out there" with the other who now carries all that is bad. This, in passing, is of course the essential mental content of anti-Semitism or anti-coloured prejudice, etc.—seeing in these minorities the peculiar blend of devilish mysterious power with despicable weakness. This need to project inner badness is also the most logical explanation so far devised for the statistically and clinically established fact of the closeness of murder to suicide, as fantasy or fact. A minimal shift in the balance between depressive and paranoid feeling at a given time may result in one or the other. Both murder and suicide thus can be essentially attempts to avoid or eliminate intolerable mental tension: the former by projection, the latter by killing the internal persecutor, or in another sense succumbing to him.

Dr Walter Bromberg, a noted American researcher in criminal (forensic) psychiatry, had already in 1951 drawn our attention to the phenomena of projective identification in murderers.[10] Reporting at depth on a young alcoholic wife-murderer, Bromberg described the latter's frankly expressed horrific dread of being himself castrated, dismembered or of his body being destroyed, based on fantasies of the terrible things his father would do to him. Under alcoholic intoxication Bromberg's patient would express these delirious *fantasies* in words and actions closely reminiscent of my SS torturers' *practices*: penises would be cut off, urine dashed over himself in his cell. The crucial experience of this murderer's "switch" from being an *over-compliant*, conscientious and duty-ridden victim himself to killing his long-suffering wife, came after a highly symbolic experience of "passivity" —an operation for piles. He began to fear that he was now turning into a woman, and had to counteract this growing sense of helplessness in surgeons' hands (based on the above terrifying fantasies) with more drinking. The nucleus of this passivity-dread was, however, a pro-jective-introjective inner relation to a depriving mother-figure who was threatening to become manifest in himself and whom he had to deal with by becoming his "father". This internal "female object" had to be killed "out there" in revenge. The childhood was an insecure one, and the patient had had a long-standing need to prove his potency, his manhood and his efficiency in the face of his inner dread of being starved and helplessly unmanned by the powerful object—functioning as a destructive, masochistic core of this severely split man's make-up, with both the bad aspects of his parents warring inside him. It is highly relevant to our study that, in order to counteract the inner sense of sado-masochistic turmoil and of persecution, Bromberg's patient not only developed the pattern of over-conscientious, anxious compliance, but actually *joined the police* (my italics) as if to "bribe" his merciless inner tormentor and convince himself that he was on the side of the forces of order. Here he managed to serve with an apparently unblemished work record. But at deeper level there was, increasingly compelling, the murderous revenge motive for his internal "bad" mother's fancied neglect and wounding of his infantile omnipotence need. In this case of Bromberg's the displacement was the banal, everyday one from mother-figure to wife—the marriage therapist's daily experience with hen-pecked or impotent or adulterous husbands, in whom death wishes against the spouse are common.

What is significant is the general pattern, rooted in infancy with its extreme emotional polarities between helplessness and total omnipotent power needs of the paranoid phase, that uses primary body symbolism (breasts, buttocks, genitals, excrement, etc.) as the basis for its imagery. It is this early link which gives so much of the world's savage murderousness its "sexual" colouring, and even misled Freud himself for a long time in postulating only one source of sado-masochism—the sexual or reproductive instinct in its childhood precursor manifestations. It was probably the influence of the horrors of the First World War that made Freud at last affirm the existence of the aggressive impulse in man. This he named the death instinct, a term that was, rightly, much questioned by psychologists—many of them his followers—and biologists alike. The material of our study, as well as the condensed quotations from findings by recent forensic psychology and psychiatry, has brought us closer to a clinically based reformulation in the light of post-Freudian work. Whatever one may feel or think about the abstract concept of a "death instinct"—whether linked to genes or other anomalies in body cells—in Hyatt Williams's phrase there clearly exists in many people a buried, split-off "enclave of deadly ruthlessness". This remains for most of us a safely encapsulated area round which relatively healthy parts of the personality based on the likewise existing "good object-relations" can develop. In the majority the murderous potential is counteracted by the life-affirming aims, but we can see that the safety of the boundary wall will vary over time with the state of health, the strength of the instigatory motivations and the degree of frustration of the positive forces in even the same personality.

We are now able to give fuller significance to my "sadism" variables in Table I. We can appreciate the psychic effort that many people have to expend to keep the extreme aggressiveness of the death enclave safely insulated by the selection of "depressive", reparative mechanisms at their disposal—from severe obsessional counter-rituals to good works, extra-kindliness and ethical severity. The "blue-print", however, is there because of the vicissitudes of human development, most emphasized in those in whom the conditions of child-rearing discouraged the successful negotiation of the maturational watershed from paranoid to depressive and thus to recognition of the Other as a whole other person to preserve and protect.

That the death constellation was strongly activated in the Nazi movement, and its pseudo-mystical ideology and symbolism, emerges clearly from the voluminous death-and-glory literature of the period which reflected itself in the macabre trappings of the SS and in the masochistic fervour of the storm troopers and SS men themselves. I have already quoted in Chapter Four one or two choice excerpts from the Old Fighters' documents with their idealization of complete surrender and loyalty "unto death" to the Führer's will. I have also referred to the writings of Erich von Salomon. The terms in which such "cadaver" devotion is expressed leaves little doubt of a quasi-homosexual passivity that saw death as a fulfilment or highest apotheosis of their dependency—and love—needs. Thus, the young man who still had his ears boxed by his father at 19 years of age writes of his "fanatical devotion (Verehrung) to Hitler as a will to complete self-surrender (Wille zur vollen Hingabe)". Another (No. 10) writes, after Hitler had squeezed his hand and looked into his eyes, of "an oath of fealty unto all eternity". An SA father writes of his son who had succumbed to influenza after being wounded in a street battle: "Until his last breath was Adolf Hitler his All." "We have finished with life—we bear the Death's Head and have only one aim." I have already stressed how these same professions of faith and loving sacrifice are coupled with the most blood-curdling accounts—in fact or fancy—of ruthless sadism towards the "enemy"—be he democrat, Marxist, Catholic or Jew or even just timid bourgeois—in whom all evil and murderous intent against the writer's group are felt to be incarnate. The deification of the great Leader which we already saw in the German naval diarist of 1917-18 and which occurs again in the "cult" of Hitler, is no less a characteristic of paranoid feeling that the dehumanization of the correspondingly polarized scapegoat counter-object. W. Bromberg (1951) quotes Freud's famous pupil Schilder's "paradox" that "murder is suicide and suicide is murder". The attitudes to death at this level could be seen both as the achievement of perfect surrender to, or union with, the incestuously tabooed love object, the final gratification of dissolving oneself in the other, or the dissolution of the other in this dreaded-desired dismemberment and disappearance of the object that had such omnipotent power which one wants to make one's own.

My interviewees have, I think, supplied evidence of a certain regularity of occurrence of this paranoid splitting process as an inner-psychic mode of trying to by-pass the intolerable conflict between, on the one hand, the dread of the destructive object formed in infancy with the unassimilable, helpless hate and rage thereby engendered against the object, and on the other hand, the need for love and protection as essential to survival. Therefore the hated object could not be the target of even fantasy attack. Even though I could not, in the conditions of my interviews, adminster any formal tests, such as the Minnesota one, nor take the months to explore their fantasy worlds in depth, I could make some clinically obvious deductions largely recorded in the commentaries following each interview report. Here I should like mainly to highlight the characteristics they had in common, pointing to their inner predisposition as carriers of the "death constellation" which we now see as rooted in the schizoid-paranoid level of development.

(1) *Captain A.*—the clinically most paranoid person among them, had by the time of our interview irreversibly solidified his inner pantheon of persecutors and retreated into the pathetic role of a powerless little fellow "they" were all trying to destroy by their ruthless machinations. I described his hold on reality as precarious. He no longer even manged to keep the "international Jewish conspiracy" aspect apart from "German justice" or indeed the SS leadership in his imagery of their pitiless hounding of him and his SS peer group of poor obedient scapegoats and guiltless victims. His preoccupation was still with repudiating the pain of responsibility for his own aggression, that is for the near-conscious promptings of his long repudiated Christian moral norms. He spent his time dreaming of ways to prove his innocence. He gave evidence of his own death-wish as a possible relief for his utter paranoid loneliness, when he could have joined the only "good" comrades he knew. His world image was entirely in terms of powerful manipulators against whom he was powerless and whom he must obey sullenly like a yoked ox, contrasted with a dead, unattainable world of loving, indulgent fathers. *He* was not aggressive—*they* were the ones who made one do things. The manipulators as internal to himself could not be accepted. Yet Captain A. was far from a complete paranoiac psychosis. He knew how to dodge

arrest, how to behave compliantly in accordance with his predicament —e.g. in prison. Perhaps this is the classic structure of the potential violent criminal who would not be admitted to Broadmoor, though close to Blackburn's *Type 2* ("paranoid-aggressive"): self-centred, hardened against guilt, hating both pitiless authority and helpless weaklings, the twin poles of the authoritarian personality and—as we now see—also of the object-relation contained in the "death constellation". This structure seems to be common in the lower officer echelons of most political police forces of authoritarian regimes—the bull-necked ferocious interrogators and torturers from South Africa to the Soviet Union, who have, like Bromberg's case, joined their persecuting authorities and thus "bribed" their inner bad objects to leave off hounding *them*. There was no evidence that Captain A. had elaborated any personal fancy methods of torture.

(2) The case of *BS.*—the "equable killer"—posed a different problem. There was, first, the hint of an organic contribution to this man's readiness to regress to a level of fiendish cruelty and unconcerned murder in his history of an attack of encephalitis ("head 'flu") in 1936. This virus disease is known to be followed by a wide variety of residual symptoms: a degree of loss of mental capacity, deterioration of memory, shallowing of emotional responsiveness and (more often in children) a change in personality in the direction of vicious cruelty, with outbreaks of ungovernable rage. BS's disturbed sleep and his own claim as well as the SS medical report could all add up to the otherwise hard to understand continuation of his violent behaviour.* Authors like Hyatt Williams and many others stress the role of illness or intoxication† in lowering the threshold of resistance (ego-defence) to the irruption of the "death constellation"—though they usually have in mind an acute crisis and sudden murderous violence. The fact remains, however, that BS could leave off and become a hard-working civilian craftsman, once the social sanction demanded this for his own survival. It is more probable that, whatever the contribution of organic nervous system factors, BS was making unconscious and partly "malingering"

---

* W. Backhaus, in his book *Sind die Deutschen verrückt?* (Bergisch Gladbach, G. Lubbe, 1968), offers evidence from German sources that Hitler may have been the victim of this disease at 12, from which the later behaviour disturbances could have originated.

† "Intoxication" is here used in a wider medical sense of general systemic poisoning, not only by alcohol; e.g. by uraemia, diabetes, or bacterial toxins.

use of them for his own ego-defences now. Like Captain A. he clearly liked the SS and its relation to the exercise of authoritarian power, and now felt an equally "done down" little underdog. To these victims of unemployment, ideology had almost nothing to do with their attraction to the Party and the SS. These meant to them a fulfilment of the need to "belong" and "to be somebody". It should also be remembered that BS, unlike Captain A., had volunteered for front-line service and thereafter experienced some return to a more rueful frame of mind. It is likely that his posting to the fighting Waffen SS was a man-power effect, rather than due to BS's insistence. It is none the less interesting that the experience of real discipline brought about a switch to a humble, punished, demoted attitude. Only before the court he recalled his TKV role and put up a defiant, "I deny everything" act. Somewhere, in recollection during my talk with him he had returned to admit elements of a more "depressive" evaluation of his role and actions, realizing what deprivation and cruelty had meant to his victims. The notion of splits and different levels enables us to reconcile the facts of the co-existence in BS of this attitude with an equally clearly persisting paranoid sense of persecution by the Federal judicial system, by the "Jewish witnesses" and of being a hounded, powerless little man whom his own lawyers, wife and relations had abandoned.

This fluctuation between a precariously maintained foot-hold in the depressive, responsible position and the readiness to slip back into the obviously more "comfortable" congenial paranoid mode of dealing with the stark horror of their factual record is the main common factor of these SS killers. However much, in their various ways, they evaded or denied their direct experience of Oedipal fear, hate and deprivation, by idealizing their parents' actions and attitudes, the note of resentful self-pity and frustrated envy and greed was always clearly sounded.[3]

(3) S2's split was the most watertight. His denial of any sense of resentment or badness against his early figures held. Whatever he had identified with was totally good, and what his good objects decreed as bad remained totally bad: Poles; Weimar judges; all KZ inmates. But he could also shift his identificatory models at the drop of a hat once one set failed and another took over. From evangelical fervour to SS ideology; from SS to MVD camp commandants; back to the good little pastor's boy. He was thus, in a strange way, the most whole-hearted killer and the most appealing small child, with scarcely

any central ego with any values or permanence other than the need "to do what was demanded of him". Thus he stood "foursquare" in court —with bowed head it is true—because the social setting now asked this of him, as part of the honest, brave little boy act. He was the least guilt laden, least depressed and also least paranoid, because—so I think —he had most completely split-off his early object-relations. He showed early on that he had rejected insincere parental pretensions of protecting and fostering the goodness of their child. This sort of hate was now displaced to the left-over Weimar guardians of legality, as prescribed by Nazi propaganda, which was such a clear expression of collective resentment against the "bad" parents who had betrayed their sons. And S2's really had.

(4) The two "educated" men, PF and MO, had perhaps most trouble in warding off clinical depression since conviction. I have fairly fully described the evidence of how they had, as I saw it, dealt with this problem. Both constantly came back to the wrong done to *them*, and to their self-righteous condemnation of all the swinish, cruel, corrupt or self-indulgent people who had surrounded them. Both of them had clearly had high principles of the Protestant ethic instilled into them. Both were narcissistic prigs with a near-total inability to tolerate their deflation and terrible fall. Neither MO nor PF (nearer to a potential of depressive guilt) had followed his severe conscience, but had succumbed to the lure of power and status close to the centre of SS power. The continuing pretensions of these two men to represent decent, "clean" innovatory high-mindedness in the midst of murderous badness, exemplified that "bribing" of the super-ego into almost total moral blindness with which many historians have charged German intellectuals. As I said in my individual comments on their cases, the phenomena of basic identification with a pitiless, ordering all-powerful authority were exactly as in the lower orders of the SS, covered over—especially in MO's case—with a lot of philosophic and biological rationalizations of man's inhumanity. There was in these two men the same desperate struggle to avoid the pain of real depression and the clinging to every kind of projection and subterfuge. Their humane consciences—of which they were aware—had been not a guide but a goad, to be denied in the name of their eager choice of the blandishments of status, power and "soldierly" manliness. But then— had their humane consciences won they would never have joined in the first place.

Certain common factors stand out above all in *all* the eight, as traits associated with German culture in general. The first is the already much mentioned emphasis on "Discipline and Order", both as objects and as dispensers of these Prussian virtues—cadaver obedience idealized and also, more literally, enforced. We know how close, in clinical paranoia, lie delusions of persecution and delusions of grandeur. In the solipsistic world of the paranoid phase these twin aspects of deadly ruthlessness co-exist and switch round. The fantasy demands recognition of the self as all-powerful, but can therefore only see the outside world as all-powerful, capable of as much harm and destruction as oneself. Neither subject nor object is seen as human, but only as embodiments or stereotyped images of power or weakness, of enemy or friend. Hence the reassurance of merging with an impersonal *role*. Hence the terrible effect, once a person with this constellation—even if it does not irreversibly become the sole content of consciousness as in the full-blown disease—"feels his feet" in an executive role and switches from abject terror and "cadaver obedience" to "all-powerful master over life and death"—a phrase much used by the Federal judges in their summing up of my interviewees' cases.

Military tradition—not least its German variety—has always held that "a man cannot command unless he has first learnt to obey". In these SS men (as, I suppose, in most Totalitarians with a claim to be the absolute rulers of docile and unresisting subjects) this sado-masochistic prescription is seen to have been carried to its logical extreme. Craven and haunted by dread of merciless retaliation, they became almost totally destructive themselves. To account for this gross perversion of a passing general psychobiological phase of infancy, I recollect that, in contrast to my war-time findings in German captured soldiers, there was in my present group an unexpected and spontaneous stress on the power and severity of *Mother figures*. This was clearest in PF, GM and KW; only a little less stressed in the "must be a good boy" recollections of BS and BT, while S2 spent his later childhood with an aunt; his mother had been ready to leave him behind. Captain A.'s recollection was repressed; only MO seemed to have the more "classical" Prussian attitudes. All except MO stressed the hardship and privation arising from the absence, death, post-war ineffectiveness, etc., of their fathers. MO had idealized his. I recall also Wangh's remarks already cited in Chapter Two (p. 46) and in my commentary on GM in Chapter Seven (p. 175) on the subject of the mother as a more terrifying father-substitute. The earliest and most destructive "bad objects" that are internalized are maternal, female ones. Hyatt Williams's and Bromberg's examples, quoted above, support the hypothesis that real murderousness may be rooted at this very early primitive level. The primary absence or under-representation of a complementary protective father-figure then leads, in a male child, to an undue tie-up with an internalized mother-figure; thus to a weak ego-development— even weaker than if a brutal father had been the first or main bad object to which to submit. This, especially in a patriarchal-authoritarian culture pattern, such as in pre-1939 Germany, would be likely to be followed by a split resulting in the "enclave of deadly ruthlessness" containing also the correlated sense of being helpless, dependent and passively-feminine in a loveless world. From this the over-compensatory, typical authoritarian traits of denial of weakness, tenderness taboo, denial of the importance of women, cult of manliness and wish for a powerful father-leader would be an expected sequel—not the only possible sequel, but one we saw as characteristic of the typical German solution. That our findings would then include also the fixation at the paranoid level, with all that this connotes, is thus not so difficult to accept. It is certainly in line with Nietzschean defiance of the unmanning, Christian weakness of being a mother's boy, and so feeling a powerful and ruthless "blonde beast". Perhaps my group of killers differed chiefly in this from their fellow authoritarians: they had particularly destructive mother-images.

This train of thought has brought us from intrapsychic predisposition to the social and group pressures that could act as the precipitating factors powerful enough to release murderousness.

4. Obedience, Group Ethos and Brutalization

The first thing that needs to be said, when we leave the individual predisposition to murder and turn to the conditions of its release or instigation, is to stress the great difference in this regard between the killers investigated by the forensic psychologists cited and my SS men. With the dubious exception of Captain A and KW none of these SS men would have been likely to become "common murderers" in normal conditions. Their instigatory triggering was not a sudden, solitary experience, but a process extending over time, shared with team mates in a facilitating group setting. It was, as we saw in S2 and the relevant quotation from Hoess's autobiography (Chapter Five) a *conditioning* process which in this context we can term *brutalization*. It was a process which had started in several of my subjects in the rough cameraderie of increasingly violent street and meeting-hall fighting and in group indoctrination after joining the SA and SS. At this level it was without question voluntary and expressed the murder constellation in precursor form—as in the SA song about mass murder of the clergy, or in the stereotyping of the "enemy" even in small towns where, e.g., the socialists were people they would have been to school with or knew by name. I found this form of slow release also formulated by Hyatt Williams (1969):

> What happens acutely in the catathymic crisis* often takes place more slowly in the chronic process of brutalization. An end result of this process is that killing and malicious wounding, together with indifference towards the life and well-being of the victim, become part of the ordinary *modus operandi* of the criminal. It is this kind of brutalization which one sees in gang warfare, extortion, armed robbery. . . .
>
> Manic defences characterize the brutalization. They are not confined to criminal brutalization. They were described by Melanie Klein and consist of splitting, denial, idealization of omnipotent control, and projective identification. They are most integrated when they appear at this juncture. Forces working for good within the psyche and those working for evil are in conflict. Brutalization consists of a progressive expansion of the forces of evil at the expense of love, kindness . . ., etc. The brutalized individual is governed by hatred and distrust with a tinge of death rather than life, with destructiveness rather than creativity. Power is sought so that the pain of need and dependency can be avoided.

This passage, though not so intended, could have been written on perusing the "Old Fighters'" biographies or after interview with PF, when he described the manic defence of the *Einsatzkommandos'* men by splitting their murder by day from their "jolly" revels and cameraderie by night.† Implicit is the facilitation of this brutalizing repression by *group affiliation*.

---

* A term used by Wertham to describe the breakthrough of violence in his *The Show of Violence*, 1929.

† Samples of this capacity for splitting are recorded by *Hermann Langbein* in ". . . Wir haben es getan" (Vienna: Europa, 1964), being excerpts from private diaries and letters of Gestapo men in Poland, as well as of an SS medical officer at Auschwitz, who was a professor in a medical school.

Frau von Baeyer-Katte[11] has skillfully depicted the process of re-gression towards the acceptance of Nazi group norms or ethos in various social contexts after the Party came to power. At mass level there were the constant uniformed triumphal marches, day-long singing of the Party's "Horst-Wessel" song, in short the build-up of a "We" feeling, from which no patriotic "decent" person could stand aside. One had to cheer, too. It now became easier to succumb to the subtly introduced blackmail of Party pressure through the appearance in offices, industrial plants, etc., of uniformed or at least openly Nazi "believers". In the climate of Germany of those days such people easily became paranoidally regarded and feared as planted secret in-formers. Thus conformity—always a strong social motive—by collu-ding with those early elements of terror, in the shape of "authentic" representatives of the new and required group ethos, replaced individual rational criticism and moral judgements. People had to vie with one another in public to mouth the right sentiments. It became a spiral in which each suspected the other of being "authentic" and thus chal-lenging loyalty. At *first* a person with an averagely humane conscience would condemn himself for this lack of moral courage and self-betrayal. This became too intolerable—so the second stage was a denial: surely there had to be *some* truth in what Nazi beliefs he had to assent to in his group. "He was not a hypocrite", he did want to accept what was good. By the time such a person saw, for example, a respected Jew or anti-Nazi "disappear" from his office he had already to say to himself: "Surely I am not supporting criminals—these methods cannot be crimes—they arise from tragic necessities of fate—I am wit-nessing a great happening in history", etc. Here, writes Dr v. Baeyer-Katte, we already witness the break-through of the "destructive drive" (Hyatt Williams's "death constellation") into the framework of private attitudes. This becomes overt in the *fourth* phase of spiralling down the scale of de-individualization when the painful memory of the injury done to a hitherto respected human being is replaced by dehumanized stereotyped anti-Semitic and prejudiced opinions and utterances.

Frau von Baeyer-Katte, quoting a number of personally observed histories of this kind, concluded that even in 1933 the unconscious of many such conforming, "well-intentioned" nationalist patriots already divined what the new regime betokened, and their inner "enclave" fashioned in the cultural mould responded with dread and the capitu-lation of all resistance. But if this was happening in the "higher" middle class circle which was Frau von Baeyer-Katte's main field of observation, how much more easily would this escalation occur in men already enrolled by insecurity, ego-weakness and social resentment as fighters for the very movement that was the expression of their inchoate feelings, and promised release from their unease in the unstructured freedom of a despised democratic regime in which they had had to be the reluctant keepers of their own consciences? We have seen that, even so, in several of my eight men there were at first moments of anxiety and drawing-back from atrocities: GM from violence to women; BT from KZ duties on German inmates; even Iron George was aware of the watershed he crossed when his simple "ten-commandments" morality was required to be renounced at the compelling behest of his successive Nazi father-figures, more potent than the legitimate arbiters of right and wrong.

In Chapter Four I reported the high incidence of the motive of *affiliation* to a like-minded group as scoring higher even than simple longing for a leader, and second only to the prescribed Nazi paranoid scapegoating in the Old Fighters' self-attributed reasons for joining the SA (and SS). I have also drawn attention to the use of "We" by several of my interviewees, as a "cover" and an attempt to bypass individual responsibility and pass it to the group: "*we* all joined", "*we* shot", *we* helped shove them", etc.

Freud's classical study of regression inherent in group behaviour and dynamics[12] is still the best theoretical model for explaining the phenomena of certain affiliative groups animated by aggressive intent resulting from social despair. Freud, following Le Bon, lists among the characteristic traits of behaviour of persons in such groups: (*a*) the dwindling of conscious individual personality; (*b*) the focusing of thoughts and feelings into a common direction; (*c*) the dominance of the emotions and the unconscious over reason and judgement; (*d*) the tendency to immediate carrying into action of the intentions as they emerge (p. 91). Perhaps the most important of Freud's additions to the already existing hypotheses on groups (such as Le Bon's or Wilfred Trotter's) is contained in a footnote! In it he says that under "primordial conditions" (of which more anon) the "will of the individual was too weak. . . . An idea did not dare turn itself into a volition unless it felt itself reinforced by a perception of its general diffusion". It is generally accepted that people in groups or crowds (e.g. a demonstration or a pogrom) gain a sense of irresponsible power. Nor has it escaped observers of group behaviour that the individual, at the same time as being carried by its élan, may be aware of its compulsion on him and of the peril to himself were he to stand out or oppose its imperious direction. This is, of course, the source of "In-Group" and "Out-Group" feelings.

Freud's innovation in the study of groups is also typical of his influence on social science. He penetrated behind the unexceptionable phenomenological descriptions of Le Bon, Trotter or McDougall to point to the evidence that libidinal object relations are at work. He thought that a group primarily coheres because it meets the need of its members for the equal, shared love of a leader—or of a common ideal or goal symbolized in a human figure. He derives this from a theoretical biological model of the "primal horde ruled over by a despotic male". As a valid proposition in ethology or anthropology Freud's prototype for the origins of human grouping is open to objections. Norman Cohn[13] has shown that militant groups under charismatic leaders arise in response to feelings of being oppressed or deprived, usually with a paranoid creed, in given social situations. The despotic leader certainly has much in common with Nietzsche's dream of his Superman: powerful, ruthless and independent; somebody to overawe and compel the common obedience of the weaker dependents for their own protection. In our present connextion the concept has the greatest relevance when we link it to the widely shared common factors among the insecure young Germans who flocked to Hitler's banners and were *affiliated** by much totemistic ritual into the brotherhood, for example, of the SS. The intrapsychic processes of the phenomena, as I have stressed through these pages, can be subsumed as the need to identify with or rediscover a "good father" who loves all his children alike and thereby become brothers in and through him. Freud, with characteristic pithiness, says that the illusion that the members of a group are "equally and justly loved by their leader" is "simply an idealistic remodelling of the state of affairs in the primal horde, where all of the sons knew that they were equally *persecuted* by the primal father, and *feared* him equally" (pp. 124-5). The fascination and devotion evoked in the affiliate towards the leader is thus closely related to the individual's ambivalent and thwarted primary love needs in the phased development of his parent-ties. The ties of identification can simultaneously make the affiliate feel powerful through the shared

* The word comes from Latin "filius" and means "to be received as a son".

omnipotence of the "father-leader" and of the common, one-pointed herd-like direction; and at the same time also feel a powerless, dependent tool or cog, in awe of the group's power to threaten and persecute him if he falters.

> The leader of the group is still the dreaded primal father; the group still wishes to be govened by unresticted force; it has an extreme passion for authority; in Le Bon's phrase, it has a thirst for obedience. The primal father is the group ideal, which governs the ego in place of the ego ideal (p. 100).

I have quoted some verbal evidence of that gushing feeling of "maiden-like" surrender and hypnotized doting which some of my interviewees and many SA and future SS men manifested for Hitler, or for figures like "Papa" Eicke at local levels, as well as for the *Idea* of the Millennial Reich. We have also seen how on the melting away of the whole Nazi group structure and the suicides of the leaders, after the Allied victory, individual norms could reappear and the previously concealed, denied or split-off hate for these deified figures could become manifest. Fairbairn[14], in an essay on military demoralization that sets in when the leadership ceases to provide the image of the idealized object for identification and support, writes:

> The problem of separation-anxiety in the soldier (i.e. from his customary security-giving good objects—H. V. D.) is anticipated under a totalitarian regime by a previous exploitation of infantile dependence, since it is part of the totalitarian technique to make the individual dependent upon the regime at the expense of dependence upon familial objects . . . (which) really constitutes the "degeneracy of the democracies" in totalitarian eyes . . . only under conditions of success can the regime remain a good object to the individual. Under conditions of failure the regime becomes a bad object . . . (p. 80).

This process must be seen also the other way round. The emptier, the more bleak and threatening the familial world, the greater the lure of finding the good object for sheltering under in the group and its father surrogates. My men had all but renounced their depriving familial world for the promise of totalitarian mothering and fathering, bringing their latent murder constellation as a sort of masochistic offering of obedience to leader figures who actually advocated and did what their fantasies had only guiltily dreamt about. This guilt could now be progressively displaced and fastened upon the group leader(s) who thus temporarily resolved the inner split between "good" and "bad" in becoming loved while also incorporating the subject's own murderousness—a pseudo-integration of a weak ego by surrender to the group. This was perhaps the final releasing function of Hitler at the top level. Such also was the importance of Eicke and similar' 'loved" assassins at face-to-face level in the SS training scheme. We recall PF's idealization of Nebe (his SS commanding general), when he "touchingly" opened the way by declaring that since he had now become a criminal why should not PF do likewise, "to save his family further trouble". This really meant he need not trouble any further about his family either! And what a revealing glimpse we have of Nebe's own cynical, brutalized acceptance of his own pitiful regression seen with such horrifying detachment.

There is ample evidence how greatly Germans were culturally conditioned to idealize paternal sternness and disciplining as a beneficent process, especially in its military setting. I recall BS's admiring reference to the "tortures" he had to go through when being trained to be the complete SS man. Schaffner[15] found this same high esteem of "hardening" by military drill (Schleifen—whetting) in 60 per cent of a 2000 sample population surveyed within months of defeat in the U.S. Zone. The same sentiment was a recurring stereotype in my wartime interviews.

In the SS (TKV) training the military drill gave the troopers the bogus manic reassurance that they were "soldiers" as some of their instructors had indeed been in 1914-18. The essential training, however, was clearly a group conditioning in restructuring ego-defence away from the familial and *social* end towards the *anti-social* end of my "sadism" ratings. It was, in fact, planned brutalization or breaking down of the psychic boundaries guarding against the break-through of the murderous death constellation, but under the exploitation of the "military" ideal grossly perverted and debased. Eicke himself introduced both ends of it: the jolly, permissive group daddy dispensing beer as rewards to the brave lads who had not fainted; and the inexorable bad object to dread as he humiliated and punished the weak. The inhuman, cruel figure was the model they were taught to love and identify with. We may suppose that it was in these training situations that those with the capacity for "satisfactory" release of their murderousness, already activated by storm troopers' propaganda and practice, would soon stand out as "suitable" from those whose depressive or humane defences remained in operation. The latter, it will be remembered, Himmler did not want for his exterminators. That these "refusers" were none the less the objects of jeering derision and contempt by the extremist groups is also well authenticated. After all, every medical student has experienced a somewhat analogous initiation ordeal when he begins anatomical dissection and attendance at surgical operations. We may call this stage of medical training a "microbrutalization". He too may feel a great sense of failure and treason to his sponsors and his high endeavour if he decides to quit, if his defences against the death constellation are too sensitive.

I have purposely introduced this last thought in order to stress the widespread readiness to exploit the human need to fulfil the group's expectations—in fact to *obey*—and to evoke guilt or at least painful conflict in the members if they cannot meet its expectations. In order to investigate this phenomenon empirically, Stanley Milgram set up an experiment in the psychological laboratory at Yale University, which he has reported in several publications.[16] Milgram relates his purpose to the terrifying readiness with which "thousands of ordinary Germans . . . took part in the Devil's work (genocide—H. V. D.) and many did so out of a compelling sense of duty". He cites C. P. Snow as asserting that "more horrible crimes have been committed in the name of obedience than for any other cause or ideology".

Milgram's experiment consisted in making unsuspecting groups of university students and other "ordinary" American men participate in a "learning" experiment in which the student became the "teacher", whose task it was to administer steadily rising degrees of electric shocks to a strapped-in "learner" who had allegedly had to be conditioned by these shocks to avoid errors ("to learn better") in a word-pairing test. The "teachers" were, of course, the real test subjects. The point was to record how far a man would go in carrying out Milgram's (the experimenter's) orders despite the obvious mounting discomfort he was causing the poor "learner" (who, unknown to the subjects, was realistically acting the part—receiving no *real* shocks in this mock-up). The situation was made more tense or realistic by the elaborate switchboard also carrying markings that read from "slight-shock" to "danger—severe shock", as the voltage rose. While at one end there was a suffering victim evoking the humane urge to stop, at the other there was the "teacher's" own professor overcoming his hesitancy to continue ("in the interests of science" or whatever) by graduated "verbal prods": "Please continue"; "The experiment requires that you continue" (cf. "Your country expects. . ."—H. V. D.); "It is absolutely essential that you go on", or finally "You have no choice but to go on". The conflict arises in the subject as he hears the "learner" beginning to manifest distress as the voltage is stepped up, which escalates to piercing screams to release him and so on. How far would these "ordinary" nice young men go in obedience to what were, in effect, criminal orders of a "legitimate" academic authority figure, before "making the break with authority by defiance"?

Milgram's dismaying and astonishing findings were that even with this low degree of expected zeal or commitment and without prior conditioning, *not one* participant refused *ab initio* to go on the moment he knew he was beginning to cause discomfort to another human being. Two-thirds of the subjects obeyed the experimenter to the last and severest shocks—so to speak against all moral imperative. Milgram had to come to the horrifying conclusion that these subjects, who, like the SS, behaved as "sadistic monsters", were in fact just "obedient"—a conclusion he compares with Hannah Arendt's disturbing verdict on *Eichmann* as not a monster but a bureaucrat who "simply sat at his desk and did his job". Milgram repeats Hannah Arendt's phrase of the *banality of evil*: ordinary people doing their jobs, without any particular hostility on their part "can become agents in a terrible destructive process". He continues:

> Moreover, even when the destructive effects of their work becomes patently clear . . . incompatible with fundamental standards of morality, relatively few people have the resources needed to resist authority.

Milgram's subjects, "Like the armchair moralists who would have advocated disobedience in the name of moral principle", knew and felt just as keenly what they *ought* to have done, but could not implement these values in action and found themselves continuing with the experiment despite inner protest.

In the subsequent interviews to find the motivations that inhibited revolt and, so to speak, involved the subjects more deeply in wrongdoing, Milgram found that the influence of the "experimenter" (as it were the ordering authority) had the effect of locking the subject in his predicament. He had "promised" to aid the experimenter (Not as binding as an oath of loyalty unto death, but still!—H. V. D.); there was the awkwardness at being a quitter; there was the absorption in the narrow technical performance—the wish to put up a good show, not concerned with the broader human consequences. These could be left to the experimenter to worry about. This in effect amounted to the surrender of responsibility for the subject's actions to the experimenter. "I wouldn't have done it by myself. I was just doing what I was told." Once a person has entered an authority system, he no longer responds with his own moral sentiments to the ordered action. "His moral concern shifts to the plane of worrying how well or badly he manages to fulfil the expectations the authority has of him." From this arises the dehumanization of the attitude towards the job which assumes the tyranny of a system. "The human element behind agencies and institutions is denied." Instead of being able to say "Why should the designer of the experiment be served while the victims suffer?" the subject becomes identified with the "great design", losing sight of its human base. Milgram found one subject repeating to himself "It's *got* to go on", having evidently completely internalized the mind of the experimenter-authority as he fantasied it and drowning his guilt feelings with it. We can see that even scientific discovery, let alone "noble" political or military causes, can thus become a goal detached from compassion—thousands of animals, and even human "guinea pigs" can be sacrificed in such dehumanized actions, in which ordinarily valid ethical norms are liable to be abrogated before the "higher purpose".

This fragmentation of the total human act, already noted by me, was, of course, a feature of the "division of labour" in the organization of the Nazis' genocide design. One "only" drove the trucks, another "only "marshalled the trains, a third "only shoved them in" or "only" sat at a desk making dispositions—always there is a "buck-passing", a diffusion and loss of final responsibility, so typical of all bureaucracies and complex industrial systems that facilitate this mentality of regression from full and integrated individual moral choices.

Milgram was also able to identify the nascence of a need to devalue the victim: many of his subjects did so *as a consequence* (or I would say as a guilt projection) of acting against the suffering person. Common comments in the post-experimental interviews were "He was so stupid and stubborn he deserved to get shocked". We recognize the same tendency as, e.g. in BS, BT and GM, to justify one's own action by pointing to the disobedience or viciousness of the victims who are felt as "only to have themselves to blame".* Equally impressive for an

---

* Norman Cohn relates that when the British marched German civilians round Belsen KZ, some of the Germans reacted by saying: "What terrible criminals these prisoners must have been to get such punishment"!

evaluation of the "helpless cog" attitude as a moral defence was Milgram's recording of subjects who could afterwards declare that "they were convinced of the wrongness of what they were asked to do", and thereby feel themselves virtuous. Their virtue was ineffective since they could not bring themselves to defy the authority. This finding reminds us of the complete split of a man like PF who afterwards managed to feel a lot of indignation against what he had to do. The ineffective "intellectual resistance" of all those who, whether in Hitler's Germany or anywhere in face of a wrong perpetrated by a tyranny, remained inactive, casts a dark shadow on all of us who are daily "passing by on the other side" (to quote the parable of the good Samaritan). There was even some poignant truth in those of my SS men who charged their "timid" bourgeoisie or the Wehrmacht with just this attitude and using the SS killer squads as scapegoats for their own ambivalence.

Milgram's experiment has neatly exposed the "all too human" propensity to conformity and obedience to group authority, and even managed to measure it in graduated voltage terms. His work has also pointed towards some of the same ego defences subsequently used as justifications by his "ordinary" subjects as my SS men, following their group ethos, employed in their legal defences and as enduring rationalizations. I refer to Leites's schedule. Milgram's own need to make his scientific point, by lowering his "off-the-street" unsuspecting subjects' defences against at least "passing" activation of their latent inhuman internal enclaves, may or may not have had deleterious or therapeutic after-effects. Our discovery of, and ability to conceptualize, the universal existence of the schizoid-paranoid phase in human development has given at least the beginnings of a psychological foundation to the understanding of "How could it happen?"

CHAPTER ELEVEN

POSTSCRIPT

In conclusion I should ask myself what I can claim to have contributed towards a greater understanding of the psychological and social forces which could issue in Germany in a vast official policy of organized terrorism and mass murder. My readers and critics may find differently. To have made a new generation aware of this most important and macabre sector of recent European history, and to have, hopefully, stimulated students of human behaviour to more rigorous methodology on all that my subject-matter portends, would be a sufficient reward. So far there has been no other such project as the Columbus Centre's.

I have gained from this study a clearer perception of the two-way interaction between the inner world of individuals and their culture patterns, and of the way this dynamism creates not only social institutions but also the climate in which they are worked. While focused on the "German case", I have been constantly aware of the pervasiveness of the paranoid element in other spheres of personal and group life. We have seen how rapidly the paranoid dynamic can spiral into displacing more humane—maturer—forms of power relations. The exercise of power as such is not necessarily paranoid-authoritarian. Gradients of power are a reality in nature and society, as in children and parents. Parental power and protectiveness, at whatever echelon of group life, has the function of creating conditions under which the weak and young can develop into self-respecting autonomy and equality under its reassuring shelter.

(1) The curse of authoritarianism is not that it exercises power in a "patriarchal" manner. Rather is it the way in which it makes both rulers and ruled perceive the disparity of power. It forces men into a collusive pattern of living out role models derived from the most hate- and fear-laden archaic levels of object-relations. I hope to have provided a picture of what a paranoid culture feels like to its members. As individuals even extreme representatives of the system could not be called clinically insane. Like the disease that the adjective recalls, this system rested on the collusive readiness to polarize the power poles in accordance with the omnipotence↔abject submission pattern, always projected where possible.

POSTSCRIPT

Like many of their fellow Nazis, and like all "zealots", from Tertullian* onwards, the men I interviewed illustrated above all the *tragedy of obedience*, as one side of the polarized social role expressing the coupled sadomasochistic object relation. If bullies are cowards, then killers are indeed terrified of their victims—the projected parts of themselves. This may be where the madness lies, and where the hunter and the hunted are interchangeable in fantasy. Backhaus[1] illustrates this point by a quotation from the Swiss writer Urs Schwartz concerning the association of anxiety (Angst) with cruelty observed in the Germans in Poland. Schwartz describes the gruesome squeamishness manifested in the cold and "refined" cruelty in exercising terror on the sick and old, the women and children—and especially when these were Jews. If one has an inner authority image of ruthless contempt for weakness and dependence, then these become terrifying parts of oneself that the inner tyrant-weakling cannot confront but must eliminate. One has to wear the iron mask of the aggressor while quaking with scarcely concealed terror—as a badge of obedience and conformity. The counterpart could be seen when the paranoid dynamic fell apart at the end of the Nazi regime. The murderousness implied in the "faithfulness unto death" and manifested in the compulsion to murder scapegoat victims abated when the hitherto self-protectively idealized omnipotent authorites were seen to fail. Then the direction of the hate and resentment in the subordinate terrorists often very quickly turned to execration of the very figures who were deified during their success. These leaders could only turn hate against themselves with their cyanide capsules (Hitler, Goering, Himmler, Goebbels and many others)—or else change back to "poor little cogs", as they claimed at their trials.

It would seem that the spiralling into ever deeper and more widespread paranoiac terrorism of so many great tyrants of history is due to this same object-relation. The dread and sense of persecution rests on the projection shared with their subjects of the omnipotence and pitilessness of the object. Since it is primarily inside, the enemy is everywhere and never sleeps, even in the most loyal subordinate's inner soul. He has to be unmasked, hunted down and destroyed before he can get you. They believe it is true that nobody loves them and that they are utterly lost if they let down the mask.

* An early Church Father (*c.* AD 200) to whom is attributed the statement "*credo quia absurdum*".

(2) In parallel with the omnipotence-weakness coupling of the paranoid social dynamic there runs the dichotomy of scapegoat categories into whom the to be feared and rejected "otherness" of the object is projected. Dehumanization and/or demonization—essential preliminaries to murder—are hall-marks of paranoid thinking and feeling, even if they do not result in murder. The repertoire of the persecuting figures or categories is, as already pointed out, remarkably stereotyped, with scarcely a change from what as a young resident at Bethlem Royal Hospital* I noted 45 years ago among its inmates suffering from persecutory delusions. Only the weak and the old, as Dahrendorf[2] had also pointed out about German public attitudes, were unexpected. Among the demonized, devilish-powerful conspiratorial group we meet those for whom Himmler had established special sections in his Chief Security Office: the Jews, the Freemasons, the Catholics (with Jesuits stressed), international financiers, communists, anarchists. This powerful "elders" and secret conspiracy element argues in favour of these being Father symbols, as Norman Cohn[3] has shown in detailed evidence. Others among the sufferers from persecution felt perpetually menaced by unseen enemies such as germs, especially of venereal origin, or by vermin, insects, dirt and excrement.

Erikson,[4] dealing with Hitler's imagery reflecting his hates and anxieties showed that some projection symbols, such as "Jews", could stand for both elements, e.g. sexual debauchery and "vermin". Hitler as much as anyone was responsible for evoking in predisposed followers the rich hotch-potch of scapegoat making, in which greed, lust, contamination, infection, degeneracy, senility and weakness are blended with demonic power and destructiveness, according to whether he talks of Jews, Frenchmen, Slavs, Western capitalists or the old German "establishment" and its timidity. Anti-paternal fear elements emerge in the series that can be schematized as: Jewish elders→circumcision →emasculation→tender, effeminate Christian humility and conscience. In fact, the rebellious son element as an aspect of the "romantic revolt" of the German young must not be underrated—nor its infectious power in comparable circumstances. Like the other "outlaw" gang leaders, Hitler's appeal was initially that of the elder brother, persecuted by his old man, who replaces the Father with a new "fresh" uncontaminated hero image to defy the foreign intruding devils, cleanse the defiled motherland and build the mystic thousand-year realm. Friedlaender[5]

* Shakespeare's historic "Bedlam".

brings textual evidence of how Messianic a figure Hitler felt, often weaving New Testament phrases into his Party speeches.

In its earlier phases then, the Nazi movement canalized a good deal of "Left" or directly parricidal emotion. Norman Cohn[6] has vividly portrayed a number of mediaeval precursor forms of millennialist uprisings of the hungry and oppressed. In their "ranting" zeal for cleansing the world of false and corrupt rulers and priests in the name of a charismatic leader, the anointed scourge of God, they aimed also at total renewal and an everlasting kingdom in which they alone would be the elect. Cohn pointed out some striking similarities of these millennialist "crusades" to the two great totalitarian upheavals of the "underdogs" in our time, aimed at establishing the rule of righteousness. Both, as we now know, ended in paranoid bureaucratic murderous police regimes much more complete and destructive of human liberty and justice than the (relatively) tolerant old regimes they superseded. In line with the foregoing we see the two sides of the bad object-relation. Edward Shils[7] has analysed the common features of the Russian and the Nazi systems, of which I list the major headings:—

(a) In-group exclusiveness and hostility to almost all out-groups sharply delimited from the former.

(b) Demands for complete submissiveness to the in-group as the only true source of beneficent change.

(c) The tendency to categorize persons with respect to selected characteristics and to make "all or none" judgements on strength of these. (Here belong such things as "Capitalist hyaena", "Red scum", "imperialist spy", "terrorist circles", etc.).

(d) The vision of the world as a scene of unceasing conflict (e.g. "class war", "survival of the fittest" as Darwinian sociology, "constant watchfulness", etc.).

(e) Disdain for sentiments of tenderness, for family bonds, for toleration of "enemies" as weaknesses in the in-group's struggle that demands total commitment and hardness ("a good Bolshevik"; a "real soldier").

(f) Belief in the existence of ubiquitous hostile conspiratorial influences and their masked control, even over quite remote spheres of life. Hence the complementary belief in the necessity to uncover and penetrate these and to achieve complete control, since one's in-group is the object of these conspiratorial designs and can only survive by manipulating and checkmating them, if necessary by violence, logically justifiable.

(g) The ideal of a conflictless, wholly harmonious society to be achieved only in the final triumph of one's in-group which holds the key to it.

These classical features of almost any totalitarian "orthodoxy", religious or secular, also fit the self-centred fantasy world of a paranoiac individual. It is obvious that, in respect of the Russian and the Nazi systems, the chief differences are in respect of choice of persecuting symbols or scapegoat enemies. But even in this area there has been considerable overlap: e.g. the elimination of the Churches; of "international finance" or "war mongers", and as has become clear since the Second War, of a shared belief in the conspiracy of world Jewry! In 1939-40 both regimes shared the objective of exterminating the Polish élite, of which the still equivocal authorship of the mass graves of murdered Polish officers at Katyn is a macabre reminder. Manifestly there are surface differences in doctrinal rationalizations and "metaphysical" justifications between the two totalitarianisms. I here refer to the underlying dynamisms and the paranoid degeneration into terrified ruthless dehumanization of the projection figures, the fear of "anarchy", weakness, democratic open-endedness and free thought and debate.

It was one of the more notable blind-spots of the Adorno team's theoretical assumptions in the study of authoritarianism that they equated it (High F) with the "Right" and democracy with "the Left", a claim still vainly made by Stalinism and its successors. This was doubtless due to good liberal identification of a "socialist" revolution with the American quest for curbing paternal arbitrariness of the rulers and enlarging the area of voluntary consent of the governed, diversity and pluralism. My own work in the Russian area taught me differently[8]. Hitler's more patent inhumanity provided an almost ideal diversion, drawing the limelight, which allowed the Soviet mass purges and MVD concentration camps to go on almost unnoticed by the world at large. The figures will one day make Hitler's look quite insignificant!

(3) Thomas Mann, once a proud German nationalist until cured by the Nazi enormities, spoke over the wartime B.B.C. radio on the

worst evil of totalitarianism. This, he said, was its power to awaken answering reactions in the humaner democracies who in self-defence had to abrogate much of their concern for freedom and respect of the person. The brutalization and paranoid regression, always a potentiality in mankind, has gone on as a continuing process, differently manifested, in many parts of the world, finding new foci of infection. Some of these bear the marks of Left millennialist revolt with its own violent dehumanization and paranoid categorization; others are more "straightforward" authoritarian "backlash". Milgram's experiment demonstrated the ready availability of the mechanism even in the absence of stress and mass excitement.

We need not doubt that rising bewilderment over economic complexities and insecurities, the disruption of families by war and commotion can enormously intensify the regressive pull. When rational self-help and capacity to control events seem powerless we revert to magical and omnipotent fantasy remedies. Here the most ruthless, who have gone the furthest along the "outlaw" road, are apt to gain power which is what the anxious, oppressed, vainly protesting seek against their oppressors. The hated Father's shoes are the prize.

In the last analysis, this book is a mental health man's cautionary tale. It is a psychiatrist's concern over the quality and maturity of society and its cultural climate as the nutrient matrix for the growing of whole and self-reliant human beings. I have only hinted at some phenomena that worry our own societies in a time of breathtaking technological and social change. We too have our high Fs, our Z fractions, our leaders that have failed and our stresses of adaptation. The less secure and therefore potentially more paranoid are hankering after new collective myths, and the heady anonymity of millennialist "total" solutions in the name of universal love and plenty, to replace the bad depriving parents. A recent volume, *Sanctions for Evil*,[9] takes up a searching analysis of some of these things where I leave off.

It is not a waste of time to hold inquests into epidemic social disasters. We hardly realize how fortunate we are in having the freedom to do this. As in medicine, so in the younger sciences of human behaviour we may, by retrospective enquiry, hope to fashion rational instruments for early recognition, prediction and eventual remedy of the many urges of destructiveness in our species.

REFERENCES

CHAPTER ONE

1. STORR, ANTHONY (1972). *Human Destructiveness.* London: Sussex University Press and Heinemann Educational Books; New York: Basic Books.

2. DICKS, H. V. (1950). "Personality traits and National Socialist Ideology". *Human Relations,* III, 2, pp. 111-154. Reprinted in Lerner, D. (ed.), *Propaganda in War and Crisis.* New York: George Stewart, 1951, pp. 100-161.

3. BENEDICT, RUTH (1935). *Patterns of Culture.* London: Routledge; Boston: Houghton Mifflin.

4. COHN, NORMAN (1966). *Warrant for Genocide,* p. 169 ff. London: Eyre & Spottiswoode; New York: Harper & Row.

5. BOWLBY, JOHN (1969). *Attachment and Loss,* Vol. I, "Attachment". London: Hogarth; New York: Basic Books.

6. PARSONS, ANNE (1969). "Is the Oedipus complex universal?" in her *Belief, Magic and Anomie.* London: Collier-Macmillan; Glencoe, Illinois: The Free Press.

7. WINNICOTT, D. W. (1950). "Some thoughts on the meaning of the word democracy". *Human Relations,* III, 2, p. 175 ff.

8. MONEY-KYRLE, R. E. (1951). *Psychoanalysis and Politics.* London: Duckworth.

CHAPTER TWO

1. DICKS, LT. COL. H. V. (1944). "The psychological foundations of the Wehrmacht". London: War Office Research Memorandum. D.A.P. 11/02. Restricted.

2. DICKS, LT. COL. H. V. (1944). "The German deserter". Ibid. Restricted.

3. DICKS, LT. COL. H. V. (1945). "The ten categories". Internal Memorandum. German Personnel Research Branch, Control Commission for Germany (British Element). Restricted.

4. DICKS, H. V. (1950). "Some Psychological Studies of the German character", in Pear, T. H. (ed.), *Psychological Factors in Peace and War.* London: Hutchinson (a U.N.A. publication).

5. BRICKNER, RICHARD M. (1943). *Is Germany Incurable?* New York: Lippincott.

6. SCHAFFNER, BERTRAM (1948). *Fatherland.* New York: Columbia University Press.

7. FROMM, ERICH (1942). *The Fear of Freedom.* London: Kegan Paul.

REFERENCES

8. DAHRENDORF, R. (1969). *Society and Democracy in Germany*. London: Weidenfeld & Nicolson; New York: Doubleday.

9. MITSCHERLICH, A. and M. (1968). *Die Unfähigkeit zu Trauern*. Munich: Piper.

10. BACKHAUS, W. (1968). *Sind die Deutschen Verrückt?* Bergisch Gladbach: Lübbe.

11. DAHRENDORF (op. cit.), p. 57.

12. FROMM (op. cit.), pp. 121-122.

13. SALOMON, E. VON (1931). *The Outlaws*. London: Jonathan Cape.

14. BACKHAUS (op. cit.).

15. GUMBEL, E. J. (1929). *Verräter verfallen der Feme*. Berlin: Malik.

16. BACKHAUS (op. cit.), p. 146.

17. WANGH, M. (1964). "National Socialism and the genocide of the Jews", *Internat. J. of Psycho-Analysis*, 45, p. 386 ff.

18. DICKS, H. V. (1950). "Personality traits and National Socialist ideology". *Human Relations*, III, 2, pp. 111-154.

CHAPTER THREE

1. BUCHHEIM, H., *et al.* (1965). *Anatomie des SS-Staates:* Vol I. Olten & Freiburg i/B: Walter.

2. HÖHNE, H. (1967). *Der Orden unter dem Totenkopf*. Gütersloh: Sigbert Mohn. (Serialized in "Der Spiegel" some time previously).

3. MANVELL, R. AND FRAENKEL, H. (1965) *Heinrich Himmler*. London: Heinemann; New York: Putnam.

4. SCHEFFLER, W. (1970). Article "Himmler" in *Neue Deutsche Biographie*.

5. ARONSON, SCHLOMO (1967). *Heydrich und die Anfänge des SD & der Gestapo*. Berlin.

6. LERNER, DANIEL (1951). *The Nazi Elite*. Stanford University Press.

7. GOERING, HERMANN (1934). *Germany Reborn* (English translation). London: Matthews & Marrot, cited by Lerner (op. cit., p. 75).

8. See "Einsatzgruppen in Polen". Mimeographed. Zentrale Stelle für Justizverwaltungen. Ludwigsburg. Vol. I, 1962; Vol. II, 1963.

9. BUCHHEIM (op. cit.), p. 57.

10. BUCHHEIM (op. cit.), p. 320.

11. SOLZHENITSYN, A. (1967). *A Day in the Life of Ivan Denisovitch*. Penguin.

12. COHN, N. (1966). *Warrant for Genocide*. London: Eyre & Spottiswoode; New York: Harper & Row. *See* especially Ch. VI (Rathenau's murder), Ch. VIII & IX (pp. 213-215).

13. REES, J. R. (ed.) (1947). *The Case of Rudolf Hess*. London: Heinemann; New York: Norton, 1948.

14. *See* "Einsatzgruppen in Polen" (op. cit.), quoting U.S. documents, Film 4, 328-332.
15. *See* MITSCHERLICH, A. AND MIELE, F. (1949). *Wissenschaft Ohne Menschlichkeit.* Heidelberg: Lambert Schneider. This is a report based on evidence at the Nuremberg trial of 20 German physicians and three high civil servants (1946-47) and also includes documentation on KZ inmates.
16. HÖHNE (op. cit.), in "Der Spiegel" No. 53 of 26.12.66.
17. BUCHHEIM (op. cit.), p. 338.

CHAPTER FOUR

1. Microfilms. Reel 27 of captured Folder 528/531 and Reel 28, Folder 532/533, taken from Hauptarchiv d. NSDAP, Munich. Filed 1938.
2. DICKS, H. V. (1950). "Personality traits and National Socialist ideology". *Human Relations:* 3, 2, pp. 111-154.
3. DICKS, H. V. (1950). Chapter: "Some psychological studies of the German character", in Pear, T. H. (ed.), *Psychological Factors in Peace & War.* London: Hutchinson (a U.N.A. publication).
4. DICKS, H. V. (1966). Chapter: "Intra-personal conflict and the authoritarian character", in *Conflict in Society* (ed. A. V. S. de Reuck and J. Knight). CIBA Foundation Symposium. London: J. & A. Churchill.
5. ADORNO, T. W., *et al.* (1950). *The Authoritarian Personality.* New York: Harper & Row.
6. ADORNO, *et al.* (op. cit.), pp. 234-235.
7. MURRAY, H. A., (ed.) (1938). *Explorations in Personality.* New York: Oxford University Press.

CHAPTER FIVE

1. HOESS, R. (1959). *The Commandant of Auschwitz* (English translation). London: Weidenfeld & Nicolson.
2. HOESS (op. cit.), p. 46.
3. HOESS (op. cit.), p. 87.
4. GILBERT, G. M. (1947). *Nuremberg Diary.* New York: Farrar, Strauss. In a later article dealing with "The mentality of SS murderous robots" (Jerusalem: Yad Vashem Studies, Vol. V, 1963, p. 36 ff), Gilbert stresses the schizoid personality, shown as inability to feel other persons as real, as part of the unconcerned killer's equipment.

CHAPTER SIX

1. *See* GILBERT, G. M. (op. cit.).
2. ADORNO, *et al.* (op. cit.), pp. 823-4.

REFERENCES

CHAPTER SEVEN

1. FREUD, S. (1930). In Vol. XXI of *The Standard Edition of the Complete Psychological Works of Sigmund Freud*. London: Hogarth, 1961.
2. V. BAEYER-KATTE, W. (1958). *Das Zerstörende in der Politik*. Heidelberg: Quelle & Meyer.
3. COHN, N. (1957). *The Pursuit of the Millennium*. Enlarged edition. London: Temple-Smith, and Paladin, 1970.
4. WANGH, M. (op. cit.), p. 392.
5. FENICHEL, O. (1945), *The Psychoanalytic Theory of Neurosis*: pp. 66 ff. New York: Norton.
6. WANGH, M. (op. cit.), p. 393.

CHAPTER EIGHT

1. WANGH, M. (op. cit.).
2. REES, J. R. (ed.) (op. cit.).
3. PIOTROVSKY, S. *Odilo Globocnik*, Polish State Publishing Office, 1950.
4. HÖHNE, H. (op. cit.).
5. Baseler Nationalzeitung, 5 Aug. 1938.

CHAPTER TEN

1. STORR, ANTHONY (op. cit.).
2. CORMIER, B. M. (1965) "On the history of men and genocide", Trans. 5, International Criminological Congress, Montreal.
3. WILLIAMS, A. HYATT (1960). "A psychoanalytic approach to the treatment of the murderer". *Internat. J. of. Psycho-Analysis*, 41, pp 532–539.
4. WILLIAMS, A. HYATT (1969). "Guilt and atonement. A Post-Freudian view". *Church Quarterly*, 1, No. 4.
5. STORR, ANTHONY (op. cit.).
6. BLACKBURN, R. (1969). "Personality types among abnormal homicides". Special Hospitals Research Report No. 1. (Privately cyclostyled.)
7. BLACK, D. A. (1970). *Psychological Research into Homicide*. (? in press).
8. DICKS, H. V. (1939). *Clinical Studies in Psychopathology*. London: Arnold.
9. WANGH, M. (op. cit.).
10. BROMBERG, W. (1951). "A psychological study of murder". *Internat. J. of Psycho-Analysis*, 32, pp. 117–127.
11. V. BAEYER-KATTE, W. (op. cit.).
12. FREUD, S. (1921). *Group Psychology & Analysis of the Ego*, in Standard Edition: Vol. XVIII. London: Hogarth, 1955.
13. COHN, N. *The Pursuit of the Millennium* (op. cit.).

14. FAIRBAIRN, W. R. D. (1952). *Psychoanalytic Studies of the Personality*. London: Tavistock Publications.

15. SCHAFFNER, B. (op. cit.).

16. I draw on MILGRAM, S. (1967). "The compulsion to do evil", in *Patterns of Prejudice*, I, 6, pp. 3-7.

CHAPTER ELEVEN

1. BACKHAUS, W. (1968). *Sind die Deutschen verrückt?* (op. cit.).

2. DAHRENDORF, R. (1969). *Society and Democracy in Germany* (op. cit.).

3. COHN, N. *Warrant for Genocide* (op. cit.), especially pp. 255-266.

4. ERIKSON, ERIK H. (1948). "Hitler's imagery and German youth", in Kluckhohn, C., and Murray, H. A. (edrs.) *Personality*. Cambridge, Mass.: Harvard University Press, pp. 485 ff.

5. FRIEDLAENDER, SAUL (1971). *L'Antisémitisme Nazi*. Paris: Seuil.

6. COHN, N. (1957). *The Pursuit of the Millennium* (op. cit.).

7. SHILS, E. A. (1954). "Authoritarianism: 'Right' and 'Left'", in *Studies in the Scope and Method of the Authoritarian Personality*. Glencoe, Ill.: The Free Press.

8. DICKS, H. V. (1952). "Observations on contemporary Russian behaviour". *Human Relations*, V, No. 2, pp. 111-75.

9. SANFORD, NEVITT, AND COMSTOCK, CRAIG (edrs.) (1971). *Sanctions for Evil*. San Francisco: Jossey-Bass.

INDEX

The names of authors referred to in the text are set in capitals. Page numbers in **bold** figures indicate the chief discussion of the references.

INDEX